35.00

Management Disasters

To

Dorothy

Sudershan, Vivek, Madhu and Sunil

For their unflinching understanding

THE AUTHORS

After three decades in teaching and industry in the USA, the UK and India **Dr O P Kharbanda** now runs his own consultancy advising clients in many parts of the world and across a wide range of industries. He is a Fellow of the Institution of Chemical Engineers, a Visiting Professor, and regular leader of seminars on corporate planning, cost estimating, project management and communication skills. Dr Kharbanda has published or contributed to eight books and more than 150 papers in scientific and technical journals.

Ernest A Stallworthy has for many years been a management consultant with his own company, Dolphin Project Management Services. He was previously a manager responsible for the cost control of large-scale projects in the petrochemical industry. He is a Fellow of the Association of Cost Engineers and a member of the American Association of Cost Engineers. Mr Stallworthy is co-author (with O P Kharbanda and L F Williams) of *Project Cost Control in Action* and (with Dr Kharbanda) of *How to learn from Project Disasters*, *Total Project Management* and *International Construction* – all published by Gower.

Management Disasters

and how to prevent them

O. P. Kharbanda
E. A. Stallworthy

Gower

© O. P. Kharbanda and E. A. Stallworthy 1986

Published by Gower Publishing Company Limited,
Gower House, Croft Road, Aldershot,
Hants GU11 3HR, England

and

Gower Publishing Company,
Old Post Road, Brookfield,
Vermont 05036,
U.S.A.

British Library Cataloguing in Publication Data

Kharbanda, O. P.
Management disasters and how to prevent them
1. Industrial project management
I. Title   II. Stallworthy, E. A.
658.4'04   HD69.P75

ISBN 0-566-02582-5

Po 01630
20.5.98

Coventry University

Printed in Great Britain at the
University Press, Cambridge

Contents

Illustrations

Preface

We have no doubt that most of our readers could produce their own stories of disasters encountered during their working careers. These disasters may have been technical, or perhaps financial, but more often than not they may be both, since the two are usually related. The reasons for such disasters are many but we would suggest that on analysis they will almost invariably be found to be man-made or man-caused and therefore preventable. At first sight they may well appear otherwise: an unavoidable accident or an unfortunate fire, but we are sure that *on analysis* the cause, when established, will be found to have been something that could have been prevented had the appropriate steps been taken. Of course we must first analyse what happened, for that is how we learn. If that analysis shows the cause to be human error or negligence, then most certainly we can almost invariably conclude: 'This *could* have been avoided, if ...'.

Our previous book on the subject of disaster – *How to Learn from Project Disasters* – carried on the jacket a drawing of a vicious vulture, poised menacingly on the deserted scaffold of a failed project. That set the scene. It is true that some of the case histories presented there were melancholy reading, so we and our publishers are all the more pleased with the reception that has been given to that book. Having exhorted for many years any who would listen to learn from the experience – and especially the mistakes – of others, it gives us great pleasure to know that our words are at last being heeded in some quarters.

Then, we laid emphasis on individual projects, all late in completion and costing many times their original budget, but very few of the projects were real disasters – they were all completed successfully in the end. What *was* disastrous was the way they were managed and what they cost. Whilst we saw that failure on a single project could well result in the collapse of a company, we did not develop that theme to any extent. This time, however, we are looking at companies and industries rather than at individual projects, with the objective of analysing what happened, so that we may see how such disasters can be prevented. How, in other words, to prevent others making the same disastrous mistakes.

This book is divided into six parts:

1   Setting the scene
2   The chemical killers
3   The cost of energy
4   The emerging technologies
5   The end – disaster!
6   Management is the key

Each part has three or four chapters and it is through Parts 2 to 5 that we take up a wide range of illustrative case histories from both the developed and the developing countries and analyse them to find out what went wrong. Each time we found that disaster could have been prevented. The key to prevention is undoubtedly good management so we bring our study to a close in Part 6 by highlighting those aspects of management that are crucial if disaster is to be avoided.

Needless to say, as we review our case histories we have the advantage of hindsight. We would not suggest for a moment that had we been there things would have turned out any differently. The point we wish to make is that disaster is *always* 'lurking round the corner' and management on the spot has to be vigilant, watchful and observant if potential disaster is to be anticipated and averted. It is for this reason that our concluding chapter, 'Prevention is possible', not only details the signs of impending disaster but the steps that have to be taken if it is to be prevented. To be effective such steps *must* be taken in good time: that is why what we call the 'early warning signals' are so crucial. The road to disaster is steep and downhill and once on that slippery slope it is most difficult to change course.

What are the lessons to be learnt from the dozen or so case histories that we have now brought to you? Each case is of course unique, but there are some common factors and general lessons to be drawn. These include:

Costs must always be assessed realistically.
Where experience is lacking it must be recruited.
Healthy human relations and good communications are vital ingredients of good management. In their absence disaster may well be at the door.
Politics often distort the picture and their impact can never be ignored.
There is a continuing need to battle against over-regulation, bureaucracy and indecision.
It is a common feature of most inventions that they can be used both for good or for evil. The choice is ours.
When something goes wrong, one must be prepared to reassess the situation and even to abandon the idea, rather than let things gradually disintegrate into disaster.

But above all, let us never forget that it is man himself who is behind any and every disaster, once we exclude natural disasters such as earthquakes and floods. The disaster may be caused by poor judgement, sheer neglect or a failure in human relations amongst those involved, but man remains responsible. The prevention of disaster therefore lies with man and his management. Man has made such disasters as we have reviewed possible and it is man, and man alone, that can prevent similar disasters happening in the future.

It is unfortunately true that man is so obsessed with his need for success that disasters have in the past been filed away, to be forgotten. A serious study of corporate failure and collapse only began in the seventies, but now quite a volume of literature is building up on the subject, largely with the objective of developing techniques that will allow investors to discern vulnerable companies and avoid them. We, however, believe that a more positive approach is desirable. Whilst 'failed', 'bankrupt' and 'bust' are not pleasant words, we should not merely seek to avoid their financial consequences. Surely, having developed a technique that sounds a warning, the next move must be to use it positively: that means taking such steps as are necessary to *prevent* disaster. Better still, why not manage your affairs so efficiently that you never start down the slippery slope that may well lead to disaster. The case studies show us quite clearly how one gets on that particular road – and it is largely mismanagement.

Most, if not all, of the books on management tell you 'How to do it'. Now we are telling you 'How *not* to do it!' We normally hear how things ought to be done and very seldom do we hear how they ought not to be done. If however, despite all you find yourself in trouble, then act with decision: take hold of the lessons in our concluding chapter and apply them with courage and resolution. Good luck!

O.P. Kharbanda, Bombay.
E.A. Stallworthy, Coventry.

Acknowledgements

Most of the data for our case studies has been culled from information widely scattered in the technical press and sometimes what might be called the popular press. Precise acknowledgement of our sources has not always been possible, although the list of references given at the end of each chapter is an attempt at this. In addition, we would like to make special mention of the coverage of the *Wall Street Journal* and the *New York Times,* which we have utilised to the full via the indexes which are published by them. Other indexes which we have used include the British Technology index, the Humanities index, General Science index and the Public Affairs Information Services Bulletin. We must still count librarians amongst our best friends, particularly those looking after the libraries of the American Library, the British Council, the Industrial Credit and Investment Corporation of India, the Indian Institute of Technology, the National Institute of Bank Management, the Tata Energy Research Institute and the University of Bombay, all in Bombay, together with the librarians at The British Institute of Management, the Institute of Bankers, the London Business Library, the Science Reference Library, the Aston University (Birmingham) in the UK and last, but not least, the New York Public Library and the Fairleigh Dickinson University Library at Rutherford, NJ, in the USA. Our grateful thanks go to them and their staff for their labour of love in tracing the almost untraceable books and journals we wished to use.

It will be seen that at times the listing of references is quite extensive. This is deliberate on our part and we would recommend the reader to scan the references, even if he has no desire to pursue the subject further by this route, since we believe the titles and headlines to be found there give a further insight into the subject dealt with.

Our thanks must also go to Michael and June Lawlor of The Forge House, Kemble (Glos.) for the use of their facilities – a "home away from home" for one of us and a beautiful countryside setting for our meetings together. Many of our ideas have been forged at The Forge House.

Lastly, and as always, our special thanks to our families for their patience, understanding and loving support whilst this book was in preparation.

OPK
EAS

Part One

SETTING THE SCENE

1 The road to disaster

There is always a road to disaster, so that in order to prevent disaster we must be able to discern that road and make a detour before we reach the point of no return. Our basic theme is that disaster is the consequence of mismanagement. That means that if the areas of mismanagement can be identified and corrected, disaster will be avoided. But there will sometimes be circumstances, although not so often as many would have us believe, when the faults *cannot* be corrected. There may well be external pressures, cultural forces, economic circumstances, that are too powerful to resist.

What then? The course of wisdom is then, we believe, to recognise the inevitable and 'cut your losses'. Too many, in such a situation, hang on to the bitter end, increasing the misery and spreading the disaster. It is human nature, of course. Pride is a very powerful emotion, almost as powerful as greed and there are very few people who are prepared to admit that they were wrong and had made a mistake. Even when they get as far as to admit a mistake in private, they are still most reluctant to make a public admission, as one has to do to change a policy decision, for instance, and set a different course.

It's a rocky path

The first disaster that we shall study in any detail brought the death of some 3,000 people and will result in many, many thousands more suffering the effects all their lives, and perhaps many in generations to come will also suffer. This is the disaster at Bhopal in India, with which we deal in Chapter 4. But whilst it is true that plant supervisors may well have to take some of the blame, and the state government may well incur censure for allowing a shanty town to spring up round the chemical plant, we believe that this is by no means all the story. We should also look at the faulty design, the nominal inspection and the poor plant operation that contributed so much to that disaster.

It has been alleged, of course, that a US company foisted a poisonous plant on a bewildered, innocent Third World country, but that is by no means the case. Of course the US company was looking for profits, but India expected and wished to benefit as well. It could well be, therefore, that the disaster at Bhopal is but part of the price that India has to pay as it strives to move from penury to prosperity. It could well be argued that what happened is by no means a proof of backwardness and incompetence, but just the inevitable consequence of a great industrial, agricultural and social revolution. It is now nearly forty years since India secured its independence and the country is seeing a spectacular boom in almost every product from steel to electronics. To quote an English journalist comparing India with the UK:(1)

> It is a startling success story. Her gross domestic product is the 14th highest in the world. Exports have grown fivefold in ten years. While Britain's manufacturing workforce is contracting daily, India's has leapt from five million to seven million in a decade.

As a result of this continuing industrial development, hundreds of thousands have swarmed into the cities, not just to get away from the countryside and its privations, as in Africa, but in search of work. And they find work. Thus Bhopal, a city no one outside India had ever heard of until disaster struck, has grown rapidly and is now a very average industrial city about the size of Birmingham.

This growth in prosperity in India is by no means limited to the cities. Many Indian states have enjoyed what is these days called a 'green revolution'. The enormous growth in agriculture means that fewer Indians starve, even though the population has doubled to some 700 million since independence.

Continuing the comparison

Whilst there is much social injustice in India, much the same can be said of most countries. Indeed if we go back in history in Britain, we can find many parallels between the India of today and industrial Britain some hundred years ago. Then in Britain children worked and sweated in the mills and the mines. Much of India may still work in conditions that are associated in Britain with the Industrial Revolution there, but the political and social climate is very different. In contrast to most of the world India has a jealousy guarded freedom of speech, with a press that revels in uncovering stories that those involved in them would rather have not seen published. The many excellent Indian magazines vie with each other in well-researched revelations of business and political scandal: we shall actually quote from one such investigative journalist as we review the circumstances that led up to the Bhopal disaster.

It is also true that the Indian Press seems to take a mischievous relish in the misfortunes of what was its former imperial ruler, Britain, laying much emphasis on the collapse of its old industries, such as textiles, shipbuilding and the coal mines. It is true that many in India still work in conditions reminiscent of industrial conditions in Britain: miners in faulty pits with poisonous dust; textile workers in humid, hot mills: asbestos factories careless of disease and foundries that splash molten metal. But there is also much confidence. To quote once again:(1)

> This is primitive capitalism, cruel and dangerous. But at least it brings hope and rising prosperity. The horrors of industry that affect Bhopal and the rest of India have almost vanished from Britain. But so has much of our industry.

The aspect that we wish to emphasise is that what is happening now in India has happened earlier, not only in Britain but in all the industrialised countries of the West. It seems to be an inevitable consequence of the pressures that exist in a developing, expanding society. It is under those pressures that companies and sometimes whole industries are brought to disaster. India, of course, is not the only developing, expanding society in the world. Much of the Near and Far East could be said to be in a similar state of flux and growth. Some countries, such as South Korea and Japan, have gone a long way along the road. Others, such as Indonesia, are in a position comparable to that of India, whilst the Republic of China seems to be just stirring from sleep. This means that wherever we look we have both the seeds of disaster *and* disaster. No one is immune.

So, disasters are all around us. We therefore need to develop ways and means, not merely of coping with disaster, but of preventing it. But before we come to consider prevention, we have to see how and why disaster comes. In other words, to take up the title of this chapter once again, first let us see clearly the road, before we turn to consider how to stop walking down that road.

The signs

When we look for signposts along the road to disaster, we look first at the end of the road. One obvious indicator that a company, for instance, has met with disaster is that it goes bankrupt. But not all companies that are in distress go bankrupt. Many of the smaller companies, particularly when family-owned, just cease to exist. Thus bankruptcy is only *one* indicator that disaster has come and to count bankruptcies is to get but a partial assessment of such disasters. However, in most countries bankruptcy is the only official indicator available, and hence the only yardstick when we wish to assess what is happening.

It is certainly true that the number of bankruptcies has been increasing almost everywhere. Whilst a growth in bankruptcies is often attributed to depression, the statistics do not support this view. There seems to be no direct connection between the state of the economy and the rate at which bankruptcy occurs. However, if bankruptcy is one end of that road to disaster, then a study of the history of bankrupt companies can lead to the development of techniques to forecast impending disaster. This has led to much research into the causes of bankruptcy and management experts are now busy developing ever more refined ways and means of reviving or rehabilitating failing companies and industries. Another group use similar techniques to detect companies on the road to disaster, as a guide to potential investors. In a world where more and more companies are going bankrupt every year, the subject becomes ever more important.

When we come to look at company collapse worldwide over the past few years we see no common factor. One writer (2) listing ten major business disasters over the past hundred years or so found them in businesses as diverse as newspapers, banking, transport, retailing and insurance as well as general manufacturing, thus demonstrating that failure can occur in any type of business, anywhere.

What do we expect to see when a company is on the road to disaster? One of the first problems is almost invariably a shortage of cash, so that as a consequence the visible sequence of events thereafter is likely to be:

    Unpaid suppliers, shut off supplies
    Bank calls in the loans

Employees leave (especially the good ones)
Rumours spread (quite often much exaggerated)
Competitors laugh
Unpleasant telephone calls
Telephone disconnected (unpaid accounts)
Landlord shows the premises to new tenants

But by the time such symptoms are visible for all to see, the company will be well down that rocky road to disaster and at a point of no return.

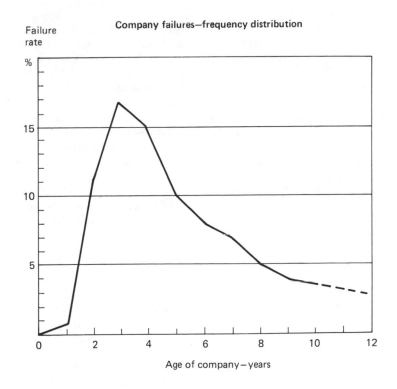

Figure 1.1 Company failures
This graph, relating the frequency of company failure to the 'age' of a company, demonstrates that most failures occur in the early years. (Derived from data presented by Altman.)

Casualties by the way

Whilst it is true that the number of bankruptcies is steadily increasing, this is not necessarily a sign that things are going sadly wrong. If a lot of people set out to walk a certain road, there are more that are likely to fall by the wayside. One study has established, for instance, that nearly half of all failures occur within the first two to five years of operation.(3) This is illustrated graphically in Figure 1.1. But once we appreciate that fact, we realise that the growing failure rate is not necessarily an indicator of increasing economic hardship, but perhaps an indicator of increasing prosperity. For instance, a large number of new businesses were formed between 1977 and 1979. Hence we must expect failures to peak over the years 1980 to 1984, irrespective of economic conditions. Failure thus becomes related to the frequency of formation of new companies! When we come to consider the emerging technologies, as we do in Part Four, we should therefore appreciate that a number of disasters, whilst not all necessarily inevitable, are nevertheless to be expected. This means that failure is not something to be ashamed of. You cannot have success without failure: they are two sides of the same coin. The decisions one takes can be right or wrong and that will not be known till much later. Those who are best at decision-making still make mistakes, but when they know that they have made a mistake they have both the courage to admit it and the resolution to do something about it. General Johnson, the founder of Johnson and Johnson, confessed: 'If I wasn't making mistakes, I wasn't making decisions.' Is it any wonder that one of the tenets of the company he founded is: you've got to be willing to fail. If you still doubt the value of this concept, listen to Emerson:

> You *need* the ability to fail. You *cannot* innovate unless you are *willing* to make mistakes.

The emphasis is, of course, ours. Toleration of failure is an essential part of any successful company's growth and that concept should come right from the top, as we have just illustrated above. Successful business executives have to choose between alternatives, and can sometimes make a decision that leads to disaster. But one should learn from disaster. If, by studying the way in which such disasters occur, we can learn how to prevent them, then we have indeed made a great step forward.

   Once the role of failure is recognised, there should be greater readiness to admit failure when it occurs. Failure can never be hidden, so surely it is better to first admit it and then take positive action to deal with it. Concealment only prolongs the agony. Rumours proliferate, the situation is likely to be dramatised and distorted. No, our advice to the chief executive faced with such a situation is: make a frank, honest, factual statement of the situation and set about resolving it.

The causes of disaster

There seem to be as many reasons as symptoms that bring a company or an industry to disaster – the reasons bringing us the 'why' and the symptoms being the 'how'. Perhaps as many as there are disasters, since at first sight each disaster seems unique. When one looks for a common thread, it is most difficult to find. For instance, construction companies all have one thing in common: their capital base is small in relation to their annual turnover. With all such companies, the turnover/capital ratio lies between 10 and 20, whereas with manufacturing companies the ratio is a tenth that: perhaps between 1 and 2 or even less. Such companies could therefore be considered to be more vulnerable. One major contract that goes sour can then bring about the failure of companies long established in this field. We consider such a case in Chapter 14, where we chronicle the history of an American construction company, Chemico, who passed off the scene in the middle of a major project in Algeria. But manufacturing companies come to disaster as well, and with even greater frequency, so the financial structure of a company can have little to do with its prospects, in terms of success or disaster.

Will experience save you?

Two leaders in the chemical and pharmaceutical industries world-wide, Ciba-Geigy of Switzerland and Bayer of West Germany, set up a joint venture in West Germany, Schelde Chemie Bruns-beuttel, to manufacture anthraquinone. The joint venture was started up in 1973 and the total investment by the two partners was some DM1 billion (US$330 million), of which DM260 million was the investment in the anthraquinone plant itself. The management have now decided to cease operations, their reasons being:

Technology now obsolete
Changed market prospects

In anticipation of this decision Bayer had already absorbed a loss of DM20 million in 1983 and the balance will be written off in 1984. At least they had the wisdom and the courage to 'cut their losses', but what a surprising result with two such well-known companies, leaders in the field. It appears, then, that even a long history and a wealth of experience will not necessarily ensure that disaster never strikes.

Have the experts the answer?

With such a confusing picture, let us see whether the experts can clarify the matter for us. The question to which we are seeking an answer is: Why do companies fail? Two management experts, Ross and Kami, conclude that it is bad management.(4) Bad management, for them, is to break one or more of the 'ten commandments' below:

> There must be a stategy
> There must be controls, including cost control
> The Board must participate actively
> No one-man rule
> Management must have depth
> Must know of and respond to change
> The customer is king
> Avoid the misuse of computers
> Do not manipulate the accounts
> The organisation structure must meet people's needs

The above list is commendable and very good advice, but their arguments are not convincing. No proof is presented that bad management is at the root of failure and collapse. They maintain, for instance, that IBM has not collapsed because it has a strategy, whereas Rolls Royce, who did collapse, had no strategy. But Lockheed, who also failed, were said to have a *faulty strategy*, which is very different to *no strategy*. We concur with their conclusions, believing that mismanagement is a fundamental cause of disaster, but we shall hope to demonstrate that from an analysis of the case histories we have selected for study.

Another writer (5) considers a total of 15 case histories in the business world and then concludes:

the basic cause of the business disaster is greed, human greed, simple and unadulterated. In most cases, the greed crossed over the line into corruption.

There seems to be no limit to this greed! Even people in high office are not immune. But is it at the root of company failure? We doubt it. We would rather suggest that greed leads to mismanagement and it is *that* that brings disaster.

Next we can take the views of a journalist.(6) Having analysed several failures he comes up with these reasons for failure:

The autocrat *
Resistance to change *
Overdiversification
Bad luck
Lack of control *
Decentralisation

At least three of the above reasons, those we have starred, echo the Ross and Kami commandments, but this writer expresses the view it is not these factors as such which lead to failure, but either too much or too little of each of the factors he has listed. So what do we make of that? What is too much? Or too little?

Some good advice

One excellent summary and analysis of this aspect of our subject is to be found in John Argenti's book titled *Corporate Collapse* (7) and it discloses a wide variety of causes. For instance, he quotes one writer who has found four symptoms to be dominant in companies which are in trouble. These are:

Lack of good leadership
An obsolete product
No sense of urgency
No understanding of cash flow

John Argenti, whilst analysing the findings of his various sources, tries to pick out factors that recur and gives what he calls an 'interim list' of causes which, when put together, might solve the jigsaw puzzle epitomised by business failure. The six major factors so identified are:

Top management
Accounting information
Change
The manipulation of accounts
Rapid expansion
The economic cycle

The manipulation of accounts, referred to above, is not necessarily illegal, but it can be and is often designed to be misleading.

There are a number of other factors, but these are mentioned less frequently and sometimes only once. They include planning, gearing, morale, shortage of capital, bad luck and a host of others. But, once again, surely all these are but aspects of management and are the responsibility of management. Surveying the whole spectrum of reasons given for failure, we come back time and again to various aspects of management. This leads us to the conviction that the nature and quality of the management is the crux of the matter. Disaster comes as a result of mismanagement!

Conclusion

The road to disaster is steep and downhill. Can companies be prevented from going down that road? Yes, we think so, but prevention requires prediction, the subject we come to in Chapter 3. Our review of the literature on the subject of prediction reinforces our conviction that the basic cause of disaster is mismanagement.

References

1 West, R., 'Pain and the power', *The Mail on Sunday* (UK), 9 December, 1984. (The article appeared under a banner headline: '2000 deaths – just the price of progress?')
2 Deeson, A.F.L., *Great Company Crashes*, W. Goulsham & Co., Bucks., UK, 1972.
3 Altman, E.I., *Corporate Financial Distress: a Complete Guide to Predicting, Avoiding and Dealing with Bankruptcy*, Wiley, 1983.

4   Ross, J.E. and Kami, M.J., *Corporate Management in Crisis*, Prentice Hall, 1973.
5   Barmash, I., *Great Business Disasters*, Ballantine Books, 1973.
6   Smith, R.A., *Corporations in Crisis*, Doubleday, 1966.
7   Argenti, J., *Corporate Collapse: the Causes and Symptoms*, McGraw-Hill, 1976.

2 How it happens

Having begun by looking at the road to disaster, we should already be getting an idea as to how disaster comes about. We believe that all disasters of the type that we are considering – the disasters that could have been prevented – are man-made. Man made them and man could have prevented them. As we shall see when we come to our case studies, each disaster is unique. No two are identical, just as no two men are identical. But at the same time we believe and will demonstrate that there are some characteristics shared by almost every disaster. We propose to look at some of these common characteristics before we outline the potential for prediction of such disasters. Prediction is, of course, a most valuable preliminary. If disaster can be predicted then the possibility is opened up for prevention, the theme we take up in Part 6.

Disaster is never pleasant for those involved, but the onlooker seems at times to get what we might call 'vicarious pleasure' out of disaster. It is always the disasters that make news, and the worse the disaster the more coverage it will get in the media. The terrible calamity at Bhopal in India, which we deal with in Chapter 4, is an outstanding example of this. The tragedy was a 'feast' for the media, occupying the front pages and prime news time on the radio and television worldwide for several days on end. The incident was in fact declared to be one of the ten most important news events of 1984, a distinction that Bhopal could well have done without. The media highlighted the terror and the pitiable plight of those who suffered: serious study of the incident, however, brings valuable lessons which, if learnt, will ensure that such an incident never happens again. It seems as though disaster has an almost hypnotic fascination for people. We are told that whilst it often brings out the best in people, it also brings out the worst.(1)

Why things go wrong

This is actually the title of a new book by Dr. Laurence J. Peter.(2) Many of our readers may well have heard of what has been called the *Peter Principle*, taken from the title of an earlier book he wrote. The rule in business that he said he had discovered was that people tend to be promoted till they reach a level beyond their competence. This, if it is true, is an obvious recipe for disaster. In his latest book he offers us a caustic sequence to his earlier work: the foolish things people do when they are put into a position where they become ineffective. Having stated that 'all useful work is done by those who have not yet reached their level of incompetence', he warns us that 'what happens is not only stranger than we imagine, it is stranger than we *can* imagine'. The examples he produces are often whimsical, and some of the most foolish come from the statutes and by-laws designed to regulate such things as fire protection. As an instance we have quoted to us the fire regulation in one state of the US that declares that 'fire hydrants must be checked one hour before all fires'.

But what is here a jest can happen in dread earnest. Safety regulations can easily incorporate equally foolish anomalies. If we return once again to the Bhopal disaster, you will see when you come to it that there were in all five separate causes of the accident. Whilst it appears that safety regulations were ignored, we can also wonder to what extent crisply written, clear and precise instructions would have contributed to avoidance of the disaster.

Signs along the road

When we come to look at a company and try to assess whether or not disaster is in prospect, there are certain 'indicators' that we can watch. There are actually a great many 'indicators' and the real problem is to determine which of the many are significant. Some, and perhaps the most important, are to be found in the management structure and the way a company is run. Others are to be found in the financial figures that a company publishes from time to time, as in the annual accounts. It is very difficult to assess the management of a company from the outside, but it *is* possible to study and analyse financial data. But of the information available from sources such as the company accounts, what is relevant when we are considering whether or not the company is heading for disaster? This is a real problem, and the experts in the field are in continuous debate, whilst the search for reliable indicators goes on unabated. We will revert to this subject once again when we come to Part 6, and turn finally, in Chapter 19, to an assessment of the means that are available for the prevention of disaster. Suffice it for the moment to say that there are indicators that can be developed from published company accounts that can be quantified at least to the extent of telling us whether the company we are looking at is 'poor', 'good' or 'excellent'. If the company is worse than 'poor' let us be realistic and speak of the real possibility of disaster ahead: if our company is better than excellent, it must be fantastic. Just to show how these indicators can work in practice, we present in Figure 2.1 a typical curve for a company in no danger of failure, using the nomenclature just outlined. Its status is plotted over time, since it is not only its present position, but its present position in relation to its past, that counts. Of course, the precise trajectory will vary from company to company. The vertical parameter on our graph is not quantified, but that can be done, as we shall see when we come to consider the techniques of prediction in the next chapter.

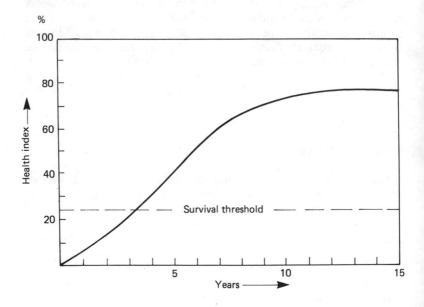

Figure 2.1 The health index
A typical 'healthy' company. The scale is uniform.

Disaster may lead to bankruptcy

Not all companies that have to cope with a disaster go bankrupt, but many do. Bankruptcy is a legal term denoting insolvency. The

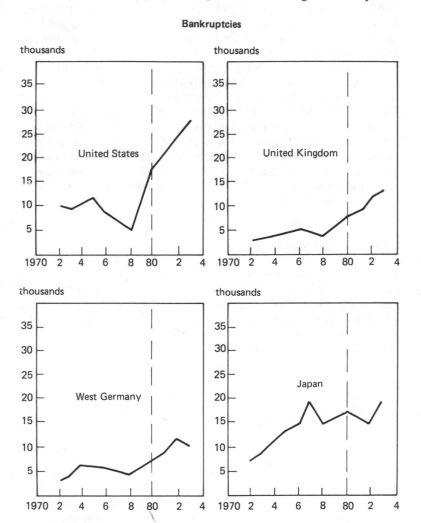

Figure 2.2 Company bankruptcies
Number of bankruptcies over a ten-year period for four major developed countries. (Sources: Tokyo Shoko, Dun and Bradstreet, Dept of Trade, Federal Statistics Office.)

individual or company declared bankrupt is unable to pay its debts. A representative (called the Receiver) is appointed by the Bankruptcy Court and distributes the remaining assets of the company for the benefit of its creditors. There are many good, instructive texts on the subject of bankruptcy (3, 4, 5) and we do not propose to deal with that subject at all, even though it is so closely associated with disaster and is, indeed, the ultimate disaster for many companies.

If, however, we see bankruptcy as a 'disaster indicator', the statistics tell us that the number of bankruptcies has been increasing almost everywhere. Figure 2.2 shows the number of bankruptcies since 1972 for four of the major developed countries. We are looking in this chapter to see 'how it happens'. Studying the graphs, we cannot blame the state of the economy for this increase, although perhaps many would like to. For instance the economy in the US began to pick up in 1983 yet the increase in bankruptcies was maintained, whereas in West Germany, still in recession, it declined.

Disaster is multiplying

We have already seen that disaster can come to any type of business, anywhere. It is also clear that if we take bankruptcy as a marker for company disaster, then the number of bankruptcies is growing steadily, not merely in total but also as a percentage of the companies in existence. Taking the US as an example, we see the failure rate has gone as follows:

Year:	1950	1960	1970	1980	1982
Failure rate: (per 10,000 firms)	.34	57	44	42	88

Research also shows that the context of failure is changing, although the reasons have yet to be determined. Before 1970 business with assets greater than US$125 million hardly ever failed, but since then at least 35 non-financial companies with assets greater than US$125 million have collapsed. Whilst in a free economy, such as the US and the UK, the law of the 'survival of the fittest' usually prevails, yet this is not *always* the case. The Chrysler Corporation in the US was 'bailed out' by the government to the tune of some US$12 billion, whilst the UK government did much the same for British Leyland, for a mixture of political, social and economic reasons. This type of action is much more prevalent in controlled economies, such as those of Israel and India and is also a predominant factor in Japan. In Chapter 1 we saw, as was demonstrated graphically by Figure 1.1, that failure was most likely in the early years of a company's life. If we now compare this factor for several different countries, we get the following result:(6)

Country	UK	USA	Israel	Japan
Average age at failure:	5-7	5-7	9-13	31
Failure rate: (per year, as %)	1-2	0.5-0.7	0.2-0.7	0.5

Tamari, whom we have just quoted above, finds that the pattern of corporate disaster is independent of the social, political and cultural factors prevailing in the four very different economies illustrated above. So then, these factors do not directly contribute to disaster. There is no law about it. Obviously they have an influence, but competent management should cope and we shall come eventually to the conclusion that the continuing and all-important factor is the ability of management to cope with a developing situation.

Better 'dead' than 'alive'

One method of combating the consequences of disaster is to segregate the disaster and its results and see whether what is left can be salvaged. Those companies confronted with disaster in one section of their business have survived because they had diversified and we have several such examples in our case studies. Others have had to sell some of their assets in order to stay in business. We think that a company in real trouble should contemplate selling its assets piecemeal and then distributing the cash to its shareholders. Admission of failure is hard and unpleasant, nevertheless acceptance of the fact that a company would be 'better dead than alive' could well be the best for all concerned.

A number of companies have been pursuing this course with a

measure of success. Voluntary liquidation (for that is what it is) seems to be easier for the smaller company, especially if they have 'hard' assets, such as land, or diverse operations which can be sold off as a 'package' without disturbing the rest of the business. For major companies, however, the operation can be both complex and time-consuming. For example, the liquidation of the giant Kaiser Industries Corporation, with interests in aluminium, steel, cement, broadcasting, the aerospace industry and engineering has already taken some four to five years.

Disaster is not inevitable

This is not the first time that we have studied disaster. What we learnt from our previous study (7) was, first and foremost, that disaster, when threatened, was by no means inevitable and that proper management could avoid disaster ever threatening. This time, we wish to go at least one step further than that. We propose to demonstrate the way in which disaster can be prevented. Once we start considering prevention, we have inevitably also to consider prediction. If we are to prevent something happening, we have to know that it is impending – that it is likely to happen. That calls for prediction. Hence, in setting the scene, as we are now doing, we shall take a long, hard look at the possibilities for prediction, and having taken the lessons to be learnt from our series of case studies, will apply them by setting out the course to be adopted for prevention.

Communications the link

Communications are the key to successful management. Hence, when things go wrong and disaster threatens, communications must always be suspect. To get things done, the efficient manager has to ensure a constant and prompt flow of information and instructions through his project team to the entire workforce – a workforce that can range from a few hundred to several thousand on a large-scale project – or up to a hundred thousand in a major company. Effective communication therefore, whether written or verbal, is absolutely essential.

In spite of the research that has gone into the subject of communications, the skills of most people in this respect are poor indeed. Peter Drucker, in a foreword to a book on the subject,(8) states quite bluntly that poor communication is the direct result of ignorance. He says that we do not know:

1 What to say
2 When to say it
3 How to say it
4 To whom to say it

Need we say more?

The chief executive

The effective implementation of everything that we have reviewed till now rests above all on the chief executive of a company. There has been great debate over the years about the appropriate managerial qualities that should be seen in the chief executive, a debate to which we have contributed.(9) The most interesting conclusion to which we came was that the management style called for actually changed, as the conditions in which a company operated changed. The early years, when a company is growing, often from a small base, demand a managerial approach very different from that necessary with a sizeable, mature organisation. Then again, if a company runs into trouble, turnaround can rarely be achieved by the management and the chief executive that brought it there. Once again, a very different style of management is called for than is either appropriate or possible in normal times.

It seems to be accepted that autocratic one-man rule is not the proper way in which to run a company. Indeed, when it comes to assessing a company, one-man rule is considered to be a significant factor in a qualitative assessment, contributing much to potential failure.(10) Argenti, who has attached numerical values to such an assessment, gives 8 negative points if the chief executive is an autocrat and a further 4 if he is also the chairman: and according to his assessment you only need 10 to be on the road to failure and collapse. This shows that in his judgment the chief executive plays a most significant role. In certain circumstances, of course, the autocratic style is very necessary: in particular, when a company is on the road to disaster and its course needs to be changed. But once potential disaster has been averted he should leave. Successful companies, it seems, are run with a subtle blend of autocracy and individual autonomy. There has to be a firm disciplinary framework of company policy, within which innovation and initiative will then flourish.

Conclusion

Good management is at the heart of any and every successful company. It is as essential as breathing! Whilst the literature on the subject is vast, it remains true that there are a few simple truths that have to be recognised and applied if disaster is to be avoided. In general, good results are best achieved by well coordinated and structured management teams, not by individuals, so that a key role in management is to ensure that such teams are there. Yet all this will be largely ineffective unless everyone can *communicate* with one another. Good communication is therefore fundamental to good management.

Looking to see how disasters occur, we see that whilst each disaster is unique, nevertheless there are some common strands to be found. Incompetence, the inability of someone to handle the job they have been given may well be behind many a disaster. Individual incompetence is the result of bad management. Good managers will not give people tasks that they are unable to perform. When we consider how disasters come, we are told that disaster is the result of bad management. Looking for signs of bad management and impending disaster, we see that the accounts of a company can sound a warning, if we take the right figures and compare them over time.

References

1   Ferrara, G.M. (ed.), *The Disaster File: the 1970s,* Macmillan, 1981.
2   Peter, L.J., *Why Things Go Wrong,* Morrow, 1984.
3   Bank of England, *Company Reorganisation: a Comparison of Practices in the United States and the United Kingdom,* London, 1983.
4   Chivers, D. and Shewell, P., *Receivership Manual,* Tolley, 2nd edn., 1983.
5   Kosel, P., *Bankruptcy: Do It Yourself,* Addison-Wesley, 1981.
6   Tamari, Meir, *Some International Comparisons of Industrial Financing,* Technicopy, UK, 1977.
7   Kharbanda, O.P. and Stallworthy, E.A., *How to Learn from Project Disasters: True-Life Stories with a Moral for Management,* Gower, 1983.
8   Parkinson, C.N. and Rowe, N., *Communicate: Parkinson's Formula for Business Survival,* Prentice-Hall, 1977. (Peter

Drucker wrote the Foreword to this book.)
9 Kharbanda, O.P. and Stallworthy, E.A., *Corporate Failure: Its Prediction, Panacea and Prevention,* McGraw-Hill, 1985.
10 Argenti, John, *Corporate Collapse: the Causes and the Symptoms,* McGraw-Hill, 1976.

3 Predicting disaster

The whole purpose of prediction, so far as we are concerned, is to be able to take preventive action, and so avert disaster. Preventive action needs forewarning and the earlier that warning the better. So not only do we seek a method for predicting potential failure, but require of 'that method that it gives us as much notice as possible. In our review of company and industry disasters, we have encountered projects that have failed and companies that have failed. Some of those companies, in particular, have sprung to life only to fail within two to three years at the most, so that in those cases there is very little time. The method of assessment must be such that the potential for failure can be seen at the outset so that the project may be cancelled and the losses curtailed.

When it comes to company failure, this has been a very fertile area for financial analysts. The approach has been to develop a series of financial ratios using the figures abstracted from company accounts. The attraction is that one appears to be dealing with precise numbers drawn from published, public documents. The mind of the accountant is such that a figure is a figure: whereas to the estimator, for instance, a figure can well be just an indication of order of magnitude. It is however unfortunately true that many of the figures that the accountant may abstract from the accounts to calculate a financial ratio are worse than unreliable: they are downright misleading.

Nevertheless, a very large number of prediction models have been developed. Some are claimed to be general, applicable to all industries: others are specific to a certain industry or country. Yet others are said to apply, for instance, only to the smaller business.

A formula for failure

Whilst there are a wide variety of formulae available in the

24

literature, we do not propose to discuss these or assess their merits, having done this elsewhere (1). There are also a number of companies who offer predictive services and their approach is based on formulae. But of course their formulae are *not* published and their use is restricted to subscribers who have paid for the privilege of an answer. On what data are these formulae based? The seven variables found to be the most important are:

1   Return on total assets, measured by the earnings before interest and taxes.
2   Stability of earnings, measured over time.
3   Debt service, a logarithmic relationship between interest coverage, working capital and total debt.
4   Cumulative profitability, measured by relating retained earnings to total assets.
5   Liquidity, the current ratio.
6   Capitalisation, which relates the common equity to total capital, both averaged over a five-year term.
7   Size of firm, its total tangible assets, adjusted for any recent reporting changes.

Let us now see how it all works in practice by considering a specific example.

The commercial approach

Performance Analysis Services Limited are but one firm offering predictive services in relation to the financial status of companies, and they offer the PAS Score as part of their advisory service, from their London offices. From the brochures advertising this approach to prediction we learn that it starts from research and development work done by a certain Dr. Taffler, who is also a director of the company. (2, 3, 4) The system has been programmed for a micro-computer and serves as a confidential customer information system. The customer can either approach PAS Limited with specific requests or purchase the program and derive his own answers by feeding in the relevant data from the published accounts of the company he is interested in. It is claimed that by using PAS a credit manager can 'monitor his credit risk exposure, focus attention on the high risk debtors and highlight opportunities to promote products and services to the healthiest companies'.(5) We are further told that 'the PAS Microcomputer System is designed by users for users and provides the credit manager with an invaluable tool for assessing credit risk ... to maximise trade, minimise bad debt exposure and optimise credit limits'.

Management appraisal

All the foregoing approaches to prediction we might well describe as part of a 'numbers game'. However, if we listen to Argenti, another researcher in the field, we do not need the financial indicators, except to a very minor extent. What we must have, however, is an intimate knowledge of the company and especially its top management. The concept was first described in 1977.(6) With Argenti, failure is seen as the culmination of a sequence starting with management defects that bring mistakes, which in turn produce symptoms. These symptoms, and their scores, are presented in Figure 3.1. These scores (called the A-score) are all bad marks, so that the ideal company would score zero. There is a probability of failure once the score gets above 25, and a company is at risk once the figure goes above 35. Companies not at risk usually score less than 18, so the 'grey area' with Argenti is between 18 and 35. If a company is in the grey area then caution is necessary. We have a warning signal and steps should be taken that would reduce the A-score below 18.

However, whilst a pass mark is 25, if the total in the 'Defects' section is more than 10, then there is cause for anxiety even if the total score is still less than 25. It will be seen that this approach assesses the management capability of a company and gives substantial weighting to the chief executive and his board of directors. Management defects lead to mistakes, and thence to failure. A company that had scored 15 for 'Mistakes', but still had a score of less than 10 for 'Defects' might well be at risk, but the lower score for 'Defects' would tend to indicate that the management were competent to deal with the situation.

The various scores presented in Figure 3.1 must be used in full or not at all. Intermediate or partial scores are not permitted. The philosophy behind the use of the A-score is that if a company is in trouble, then that is due to management defects and the consequent mistakes, which will have been there for a number of years and should be noticed by a careful observer long before the signs of financial distress are there. The A-score thus attempts to quantify a qualitative judgment. It is therefore highly subjective and the observer needs to visit the company and its factories, meet its directors and get to know them well, in order to make objective

The Argenti score board

DEFECTS: In Management —

8	The chief executive is an autocrat
4	He is also the chairman
2	Passive Board—an autocrat will see to that
2	Unbalanced Board—too many engineers or too many finance types
2	Weak Finance Director
1	Poor management depth

In Accountancy —

3	No budgets or budgetary controls (to assess variances, etc.)
3	No cash flow plans, or ones that are not updated
3	No costing system. Cost and contribution of each product unknown
15	Poor response to change, old- fashioned product, obsolete factory, old directors, out-of-date marketing

TOTAL DEFECTS. 43   PASS: 10

MISTAKES:

15	High leverage, firm could get into trouble by a stroke of bad luck
15	Overtrading. Company expanding faster than its funding. Capital base too small or unbalanced for the size and type of business
15	Big project, gone wrong. Or any obligation which they cannot meet if something goes wrong

TOTAL MISTAKES: 45   PASS: 15

SYMPTOMS:

4	Financial signs, such as Z-score. Appears near failure time
4	Creative accounting. Chief executive is the first to see signs of failure, and in an attempt to hide it from creditors and the banks, accounts are 'glossed over' by, for instance, overvaluing stocks, using lower depreciation, etc. Skilled observers can spot these things
3	Non-financial signs, such as untidy offices, frozen salaries, chief executive 'ill', high staff turnover, low morale, rumours
1	Terminal signs

TOTAL SYMPTOMS: 12

TOTAL POSSIBLE SCORE: 100   PASS: 25

Figure 3.1 The Argenti sequence
This table presents the weighting given by Argenti to the various aspects of management performance in order to assess a company's viability. Note that the higher the score, the worse the company.

assessments. That is normally not easy and takes time, but a knowledgeable banker is in a position to do so. The A-score is clearly based on the premise that failure starts at the top, and we believe that to be a valid premise. So the approach suggested by Argenti is sound enough; the problem lies in its day-to-day application. Perhaps it is better to learn the lesson that has come via the A-score, that the chief executive determines the health of his company. Hence, if a company is failing, then its chief executive is failing and the road to health may lie through replacing him. That is a familiar story, is it not? We shall examine the role of the chief executive and the sort of person he ought to be in Chapter 18. Here we have a method of evaluating his abilities and the prospects of the company he leads.

Assessing the smaller company

The two major approaches we have outlined have been demonstrated to work quite effectively in relation to companies of substance and especially companies that have been in existence for a number of years. But what of the smaller company? The smaller company presents a real problem, because apart from the problems in assessment associated with their size as such, many have not been in existence all that long. That is one reason why they are small: they have not had time to grow. Alternatively they may not wish to grow, and hence do not avail themselves of the various incentives that are available. Despite the problems, however, it is said to be possible to make a sensible assessment of the status and prospects of a small business. For instance, the firm offering the PAS Score (Performance Analysis Services Ltd., London) already referred to above also offers a 'Smaller Company Service', catering specifically for this sector. Because of the commercial implications, details of the technique being used are not published, but the company claims:

> When granting credit it is implied that risk is measured and accepted. A reliable source of up to date and accurate solvency reports is therefore essential for the credit manager who relies upon external agencies for his risk assessment.
> The PAS Smaller Company Service is designed specifically to ensure that the credit manager knows the solvency position of his key customers as given by their latest information available and thereby makes his decision making easier.

The service offered claims to supply a financial analysis of named companies, a summary of the last five years of profit and loss and balance sheet information in a standard format and conventional ratio analysis. A typical PAS Solvency Report presents amongst other data a Financial Profile as set out in Figure 3.2. This shows the company's relative strengths and weaknesses on a scale of 1 to 10. The PAS Score is presented on a lineal scale, from 1 to 100, whilst when the Z-Score, also shown in Figure 3.2, is negative the company is said to be 'at risk' of failure. Perhaps we should explain that the 'Z-score' is one of those financial models to be found in the literature on the subject to which we referred earlier.(1)

What we find remarkable is that the use of the service is limited, in practice, to those seeking to protect themselves from loss. The concept of prediction analysis with a view to prevention is just not there. Whilst there is no doubt that the most effective and perhaps the quickest method of assessing the health of the small business is that proposed by Argenti, which we discussed above, Argenti makes no mention of the small business in his analysis and discussion of results, but there is no reason why the approach should not be completely effective. Insofar as the approach

	PAS financial profile				
	1978	1979	1980	1981	1982
Profitability:	3	3	2	4	4
Working capital:	4	4	5	3	3
Financial risk:	2	5	5	5	2
Short-term liquidity:	1	2	2	1	1
PAS-SCORE:	9	25	22	19	10
Z-SCORE:	−0.38	1.35	0.06	−0.63	−2.49

Figure 3.2 The smaller company service
Here we have an extract from a PAS solvency report. Such reports, commissioned by the client, are updated regularly as new accounts become available. (With thanks to Performance Analysis Services Ltd., London, for permission to publish.)

outlined by Argenti, as detailed in Figure 3.1, lays a great deal of emphasis on the 'chief executive' and the vast majority of small businesses are managed by one man, usually the owner, the approach amounts to an assessment of his personal and particularly entrepreneurial qualities. Whilst certain countries, such as the US and the UK, have specific schemes and programmes designed to encourage and assist the smaller business, wherever we go in the world it is finally the local bank manager who has to face up to this problem of assessment. If he could be encouraged to use the A-score approach, which translates a subjective assessment into a quantitative evaluation, he could well perform a most valuable service not only to his bank, but to his customers.

Encouraging the small business

Most countries seek to encourage the formation and growth of the small business through the use of various incentives and their fiscal policy. Of course, the definition of the 'small business', in terms of either the capital employed or the number of employees, varies from country to country, but such businesses are contributing an ever-growing proportion of the GNP in a great many countries. Whilst this is generally true in relation to manufacturing industries, it is especially true of the service industries. The contribution of the 'small scale' sector is about a third in the UK and India, and rising steadily, whilst in the US it is some 40 per cent and nearly 70 per cent in Japan. These figures are developed by measuring the employment offered and the output of such firms by value. Overall there seems to be steady decline in the large manufacturing units producing items like cars, trucks and ships, but the small firm, even when working in the same industry, seems to prosper. And in the service industries the small business undoubtedly both prospers and predominates.

In Britain the encouragement of the small business is seen as a solution to its serious unemployment problem. The idea has been to build up the self-employed sector through the use of a variety of incentives and the various incentives on offer have been growing steadily. For instance, during the period from 1979 to 1983 the Conservative government passed over 760 measures designed to support the small firm.(7) They enjoy generous loan guarantee schemes and by 1983 the government had provided an 80 per cent guarantee on loans to small firms totalling US$500 million (£329 million). Since 1981 the individual has been given tax relief for investment in new or expanding businesses. Not all such incentives are used for the purpose intended and a letter to the editor (8) in this context declared:

> Junk all subsidies and tax incentives for small businesses. There is no shortage of money available if you know where to look and if you don't know (or can't find out) then you shouldn't be in business in the first place.

So one wonders whether the various incentives serve the purpose in view. Perhaps the small business that they are designed to encourage would succeed anyway, and the less efficient, who ultimately fail, just have a 'happy holiday' while the money lasts. We could even pose the question: Don't incentives just increase the number of failures?

When we turn to India, where the small business is everywhere, we see quite clearly that some of the policies have failed. Apart from numerous incentives, including low-interest loans, tax holidays, sales tax and excise tax exemption and a host of others, there are special facilities and attractions offered to those prepared to set up industries in the so-called backward areas. The idea, of course, is to disperse industry more widely and provide employment in areas where it is sadly lacking. Various state and central government bodies offer assistance and in some cases, where for instance high technology is involved, the entrepreneur needs only to put some 10 per cent of his own money into the total cost of a project. On this background, the way in which the system is taken advantage of is of interest.

It appears – and of course this happens not only in India, but everywhere – the easy availability of finance attracts the incompetent, encouraging the unemployed to become self-employed and then style themselves 'businessmen'. There is virtually no assessment of the capabilities or the credentials of the budding entrepreneur. Whilst much good advice is on offer, no one is there to see that it is taken. As a result, more than 50 per cent of such new businesses fail and the finance, largely public money, has been spent to no purpose. There is even evidence that many such firms have been set up specifically to 'siphon out' such funds.

Thus the policy to encourage and support the small business has turned into a farce in some countries. But what is the answer? Probably the best solution is to kill the whole idea completely, since it is more than likely, as we said earlier, that those who succeed would succeed in any case, whilst those who fall by the wayside should never have started anyway.

The government and the small business

In Chapter 17 we shall be very critical of government bureaucracy and its use of regulation. For the moment let us see how governments fare when they seek to encourage the small business. We have already seen that the systems set up to encourage the small business are quickly abused, but we would not blame governments for that. That only illustrates an abiding problem of government: responsible for multitudes of avaricious, greedy people.

The Economist Intelligence Unit carried out an in-depth comparison of government policy in a number of European countries, to find that the different countries used widely different tools.(9) West Germany concentrated on capital credit, the UK used taxation relief, whilst Belgium assisted in relation to business premises. In the USA, on the other hand, the SBA (Small Business Administration), set up in 1953 to cater for the needs of this sector, sought to ensure that the small business had access to the market, adequate financial support and access to government contracts, irrespective of the economic advantage there might be in using the big contractors.(10)

Another review of government policy towards the small and medium-sized company in various countries has appeared in a book with the title *Innovation and the Small and Medium Sized Firm* (11) whilst a series of five articles in *Management Accounting* provides a very comprehensive survey of what is happening in the UK. It is said that tax incentives, the UK approach, do much to stimulate growth and prosperity of this most important sector of the economy. However, there are a number of areas where a lot can still be done. Life should be made simpler for the small business, a factor that is probably more significant in the US even than it is in the UK. Over-regulation can easily strangle a new business at birth – we cited a fascinating example in our earlier work on project disasters, under the caption: 'The snail *vs.* the US government'.(12)

Yet, despite all the encouragement and the incentives, the failure rate in the small business sector of the economy in every country is much higher than the average for industry as a whole. We are sure that the reason is the one common to all business failure – bad management. In the small business management has fewer checks and controls: there are fewer people around to provide them. Nevertheless the small business has a vital and continuing role to play. It can be innovative: xerography, insulin, the zipper, the ball point pen and the jet engine, to name but a few well-known items now seen worldwide, were all contributed by an individual inventor working in a small organisation.(9) In addition, the productivity appears to be much higher.(13) If the small businessman can be encouraged to look at himself and his company objectively and learn from the mistakes of others like him, using the techniques we are now bringing forward, then we believe this book will have made a significant contribution to the economic well-being not only of the small businessman himself, but to the economy at large.

Having now seen the limits in the application of prediction models to the small business, where the failure rate is much higher than in the rest of the economy, we can but encourage further application in this sector of the economy. We have found one proprietary model, the PAS score, which has been specifically adapted for the small business, but those who need it most fail to use it. It is the credit manager who benefits, by learning whom to avoid! The small business sector is seen as vital to prosperity, encouraged to grow, and growing in almost every country in the world. The devices used by various governments to encourage such growth vary widely but tax incentives, as offered in the UK, and capital credit, the major inducement in West Germany, are seen to be effective tools.

The two alternatives

We have made only a brief survey of the various methods that can be used to predict the financial future of a company, but nevertheless we have seen that there are two main tools: the A-score put forward by Argenti, that assesses management capability and a 'numbers game', that makes a quantitative assessment of company status. Before we recommend a specific course of action – for that is our intention – let us weigh these two basic alternatives in the balance. In dealing with numbers, the final score is but a finite number. The reports issued also give an assessment, but these are not intended to replace the number, only to support it. The decision taken still rests primarily on a number. Once the appropriate cut-off point has been decided, there is no judgment involved. The classification is purely mechanical and the answer is either 'yes' or 'no'. This is the case with the Taffler model and its proprietary derivative, the PAS score, discussed above, together with the many others on the market which we do not have the space to discuss. Both the PAS score and the so-called Z-score much publicised by Altman are based on financial ratios derived from published data in the annual report of a company. However, the approach is purely empirical and some assert that the approach is 'statistically unsound and lacks theoretical underpinning'.(14) A critical abstract of the paper by Barnes just referred to (15) significantly concludes: 'Altman *et al* take note'. At the other extreme is the purely subjective model, as proposed by Argenti, where the data in the published accounts are considered to be of little value. How then does one score? Let us quote:(16)

> It relies upon the observer actually visiting the suspect company, meeting its directors, seeing its products and forming his own views. In this instance the A-score reflects the opinion of many financial experts that balance sheets alone are not enough. *You need to go there.*

Another subjective model used a point-weighted assessment of management and organisational attitudes.(17) It is a performance system of appraisal and it presumes close access to the management. Well, which would you choose, the subjective or the objective approach?

There is no infallible answer

Having reviewed some of the approaches open to us if we wish to avoid failure, we see quite clearly that no single procedure, method or model is infallible. It therefore must be best to use two or perhaps more methods at the same time and if that approach is to have value, the separate methods chosen must be independent of one another. But what if we use two separate approaches and they give two different answers? This is a very good question and we are afraid that there is only one good answer: use your own judgement!

Since we are writing, above all, for those who are involved in management, and are concerned with the management of a particular company, then we would expect them to know that company well. They are therefore in a position to begin by using the A-score approach described in some detail above. One must remember that the lower their *respective* proprietary A-score, the better the health of a company and that the 'pass mark' is reckoned to be 25. A score less than 25 and, better, less than 18 indicates that a company is not at risk. Whilst the score is still below 35, the company is at risk, and the weighting in the scoring will indicate the road to recovery. This is one most valuable aspect of the A-score approach. It shows you very clearly what is at fault and therefore what needs to be remedied if failure is to be averted. Assessment of the imminence of danger is dependent to some extent upon the size of company with which we are involved. With the smaller company, a score between say 20 and 25, whilst seeming to indicate that the company is not at risk, will nevertheless demand further examination and the application of additional tools. Notice that we are warning, when we say this, that there is no magic associated with that number 25.

Conclusion

There is obvious benefit, in our view, in using a tool that will enable failure and the consequent disaster to be predicted. Advance warning can give management enough time to change course, if only it will take heed, and thus the ultimate disaster will be prevented.

The present available methods for prediction are both subjective and objective. Neither of these two approaches is perfect, but their combination can be quite useful. But prediction, by itself, is of no consequence unless it is followed by preventive action.

References

1   Kharbanda, O.P. and Stallworthy, E.A., *Corporate Failure: Its Prediction, Panacea and Prevention*, McGraw-Hill, London, 1985.

2   Taffler, R.J., 'Forecasting company failure in the UK using discriminant analysis and financial ratio data', *Jnl. of the Royal Statistical Society, Series A (General)*, Vol.145, Part 3 (1982), pp.342-358.

3   Taffler, R.J., 'The assessment of company solvency and performance using a statistical model: A comparative UK-based study', *Accounting and Business Research*, Autumn 1983.

4   Taffler, R.J., 'Empirical models for the monitoring of UK corporations', *Jnl. Banking & Finance*, 8, 1984.

5   Brochure: *The PAS Microcomputer System: a Confidential Customer Information System*, published by Performance Analysis Services Ltd., London.

6   Argenti, J., 'Company failure: long range prediction is not enough', *Accountancy*, August 1977, pp.46-52.

7 Article: 'British Small Business: reports of its birth are much exaggerated', *Economist*, 288, 23 July 1983, pp.66-73.
8 Letter to the Editor in *Economist*, 288, 23 August 1983, p.6.
9 Fairley, A., 'UK is Europe's Small Business Laggard', *Economist Intelligence Unit*, 24 November 1983.
10 Dyson, K. and Wilks, S., (eds), *Industrial Crisis: a Comparative Study of the State and Industry*, Martin Robertson, 1983.
11 Rothwell, R. and Zegueld, W., *Innovation and the Small and Medium Sized Firm*, Francis Pinter, London, 1983.
12 Stallworthy, E.A. and Kharbanda, O.P., *Total Project Management: from Concept to Completion*, Gower, 1983.
13 Article: 'How mini-factories boost production', *Financial Times* (London), 7 September 1984, p.20.
14 Barnes, P., 'The prediction of company failure', *Managerial Finance*, (UK), 10, No. 1 1984, p. 11.
15 ANBAR 1984, published by the British Institute of Management.
16 Argenti, John. 'Predicting Corporate Failure', London: ICAEW, Summer 1983. (Accountants Digest No. 138, available from the Institute of Chartered Accountants, London.)
17 Boocock, K. and Drozd, F.A., 'Forecasting Corporate Collapse', *Chartered Accountants Magazine*, (Canada), November 1982, p. 54.

Part Two

THE CHEMICAL
KILLERS

4 The Bhopal nightmare

Whilst we call the terrible accident at Bhopal in India a nightmare, in truth it was no nightmare: it was real, very real, although it happened in the night. The world had never heard of Bhopal, a town with a population of some 800,000 in Central India and the capital city of the State of Madhya Pradesh, until the morning of 3 December 1984. From that day onwards for at least a week, Bhopal dominated the front pages of the popular press worldwide, and also received worldwide TV and radio coverage. It became one of the ten major events in the year 1984, a distinction it could well have done without. This terrible accident, which happened in the Indian company's Golden Jubilee year (the company was established in 1934) brought a tragic end to a year of celebrations.

How it happened

Union Carbide had a plant manufacturing Sevin and other pesticides at Bhopal. Sevin is manufactured by taking methyl isocyanate (MIC), itself manufactured by reacting methylamine with phosgene, and reacting it with alpha-naphthol. Let us now go back to 10.15 p.m. on the night of Sunday, 2 December 1984.

Just before the end of the shift the shift supervisor asked an operator to wash the piping around one of the three MIC storage tanks (No. 610). Since the valves on the tank leak at times, a slip blind is inserted near a valve to seal off the tank and so prevent the ingress of water. It was first thought that water had entered via this line. Water in the tank would initiate a polymerisation reaction which is highly exothermic (produces a lot of heat). However, the results of the inquiry later initiated by Union Carbide suggest that water actually entered via the nitrogen pressure line (see Figure 4.1.).

What happened next?
11.00 p.m.
The new shift operator noticed that there was a pressure rise in Tank 610, but assumed that this was due to it being pressurised with nitrogen by the last shift in order to transfer its contents to the pesticide unit.
11.30 p.m.
The operators sensed a little irritation to their eyes because of a small MIC leak. That was not an unusual phenomenon, so it was ignored.
12.00 midnight
Temperature and pressure continued to build up in Tank 610 and water sprayed over the tank proved ineffective. Pressure built up to several times the permissible limit and then burst a rupture disc, blew the safety valve and MIC gas rushed straight through a 33 metre high atmospheric vent line out into Bhopal's cool night air.(1)

It is not clear whether the operators and their supervisors took any preventive or remedial action, but since none of the Union Carbide personnel were seriously affected, the assumption is that they abandoned the plant and fled to safety, presumably because the situation was quite hopeless and beyond redemption. A siren was sounded, but this made confusion worse confounded and in fact brought people to their death, for those living in the neighbourhood rushed into the streets and to the plant to help put out what they thought to be a fire in the plant. It appears that no practice drills were ever held. The various safety devices were never checked to see whether they were working, whilst the community living near the plant had never been warned about the serious dangers, or trained so that they knew what to do in the event of an emergency.

The scale of the disaster

This worst ever industrial tragedy has left over 3000 dead and some 250,000 perhaps with permanent disabilities. For the dead the nightmare was brief but for the unfortunate survivors the nightmare had just begun. In this context figures have no meaning as the bodies were hurriedly claimed by surviving members of the family for the last rites. All the members of some households were completely wiped out, in many cases without any record and no death certificates. A partial count some two months later showed 159 orphaned children, 169 widows, some 1000 cases of blindness and 2300 pregnant women in need of care and continuous monitoring. Of the 1400 confirmed and recorded deaths, no claim was registered for compensation on behalf of some 300, whilst in 275 cases there was no clue other than snapshots taken at the time of post mortem. Typical of the survivors is Suresh, a boy of 13 who says: 'I can't play for long like the others. I turn breathless very quickly.' Shravan Singh, a lathe operator, can operate the lathe no more. 'I find myself breathless', he says, 'if I exert myself for just five minutes.' His four-year old son coughs incessantly at night, whilst his wife, Kamla, cannot cook for she gets breathless just carrying a pail of water. Their other two children, Rajni, who is eight, and Durga, just six years old, simply stare at nothing.(1)

The entire town was turned into a gas chamber and many died in their sleep. Others woke to intense irritation in their eyes or a choking sensation in their lungs. Gasping for fresh air, they rushed out into the street, only to make matters worse for themselves. To quote an eyewitness:(2)

> There was total confusion. People were running helter skelter. No one knew what had attacked them.

What was even worse was that no one, not even the Union Carbide managers, appreciated the seriousness of the incident. Some eight hours after the event, and even after seeing dead bodies piled in heaps, Union Carbide's chief Medical Officer, L.D. Loya and the plant works manager, J. Mukund, were maintaining that 'MIC is an acute irritant, but certainly not lethal'. Across the world at their Headquarters in Danbury, Connecticut in the US, Jackson B. Browning, director of health, safety and environmental affairs for Union Carbide dismissed MIC as 'nothing more than a potent tear gas'.(3) The managing director of the Indian company, V.D. Gokhale, was quoted as saying: 'It was a freak and inexplicable accident ... in the event of a pressure build-up the gas would normally be automatically diverted through a vent scrubber. Within minutes of detecting the abnormal pressure level ... the gas release was stopped and the plant shut down.' More about that scrubber later, but these ill-informed declarations certainly qualify as the under-statements of the century. In the face of this callous and unhelpful attitude by the officers of the company, the local doctors had to rush to the library, seeking for clues and possible antidotes.

It is a fact that MIC is extremely poisonous, both in its liquid and its gaseous form. Symptoms of exposure, as found in the literature (it *was* there to be read) and confirmed by the actual cases in Bhopal, are irritation in the eyes, on the skin and in the lungs. In the lungs the gas forces out the intra-cellular water (technically called 'oedema'), causing breathing trouble and ultimately death. Dr. N.R. Bhandari, dean of Hamidia Hospital in Bhopal and his colleagues learnt all this the hard way: learnt that 'there is no antidote to MIC'.(2)

The only possible treatment appeared to be the administering of oxygen and giving antibiotic shots to control any secondary infection of the damaged lungs. There was found to be no precedent, this being the first time that so many people had been exposed to the gas at one time, and with such a high degree of exposure. All leaks till then had been 'minor'. The chemistry and toxicology books were found to contain little information of help in the emergency that faced the whole town of Bhopal.

Safety systems – the silent witnesses

The Union Carbide plant had, in all, five safety systems, but not one of them came to the rescue. Let us examine them one by one.

Vent gas scrubber

Following release, as when a safety valve vents, and as happened, the vented gas goes through a scrubber, which is supposed to neutralise or detoxify the MIC gas by means of a caustic soda solution. But, at the time of the accident, the scrubber unit was under repair, and there was no caustic soda scrubbing system in operation. The gas went straight on through.

Flare stack

At the top of the flare tower there is an automatic ignition system, which is supposed to ignite and burn toxic gases high in the air. The flare tower serves the entire plant, and is connected via vent lines to a number of vulnerable plant items, including the MIC storage tanks. But, at the time of the accident, the connecting pipeline was under repair, although that would not have helped much, since the pilot light at the tip of the flare stack was not lit. This was an economy measure, since the factory was largely shut down at the time.

Water curtain

This is a device which shoots a jet of water some 12 to 15 metres into the air, thus creating a 'water curtain' around sensitive areas of the plant. The water would knock down the MIC vapour and convert it to harmless products – either dimethylurea or trimethylbiuret. The water jets were turned on, but they could not reach an MIC emission pouring out of the top of the scrubber at a height of some 30 metres.

Refrigeration system

A 30-tonne Freon refrigeration system is designed to circulate coolant brine at between −10°C. and −15°C. through cooling coils

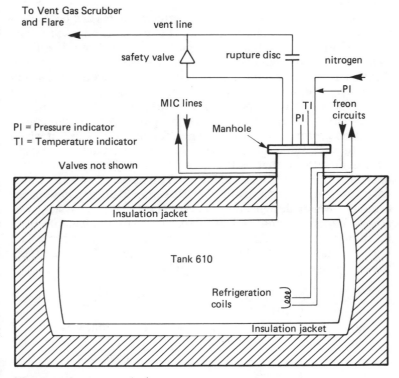

(diagrammatic representation)

Figure 4.1 Tank 610
This diagram gives an outline of the facilities associated with Tank 610. There were three such storage tanks for the deadly methyl isocyanate.

in the MIC tanks, to prevent vaporisation of the MIC. However, at the time of the accident the system was out of commission, the refrigerant, Freon 22, having been removed for use elsewhere.

Spare storage tank

The MIC storage system consisted of three tanks, each holding some 60 tonnes. Of these, one is should always be kept empty, for just the type of emergency that arose that night, but it appears that it was *not* empty. When the pressure in Tank 610 rose, the simple opening of the valves connecting it to the empty tank would have relieved the pressure and perhaps have prevented the disaster. It would certainly have minimised it. But in the confusion no one thought to do that.

Perhaps the impact of the various safety systems can be made a little clearer by an outline diagram, Figure 4.1. You will notice that whilst the tank is buried in concrete and insulated, it still has to have vents and piping connections. It was through the rupture disc that all the gas escaped. In any event, it appears that the safety devices were designed to take care of a minor gas leakage, and they could not have coped with a sudden gush of gas, some 30 tonnes within half an hour, as in fact happened. The total quantity permitted in storage is only 40 tonnes, for safety reasons, of which some 10 tonnes may have polymerised and so stayed in the tank. The final truth on that will only be established when tank 610 is opened and its contents examined and analysed. But some truths have now come to light, truths that are summed up by a newspaper headline: 'Plant design badly flawed'.(1) The safety system was grossly underdesigned and even had its various elements been functioning, they could never have coped with the uncontrolled release of gas that actually occurred. For instance, J. Mukund, the works manager, is quoted as saying:(1)

> The flare tower is not designed to handle anything but a small quantity of MIC such as perhaps a few hundred litres per hour. It could not have taken the 40 tonnes that was released during the accident. That would have created a massive explosion – and the flare tower would have collapsed. The proposition is altogether absurd.

It almost looks as if they were better off with this particular safety precaution out of action, as it was.

Safety considerations dictate that a hazardous plant should be equipped with a whole series of indicators, gauges and recorders with a range of inbuilt alarms that warn the operators of an abnormal condition or impending danger. It is also advisable to have interlocks which automatically shut down critical parts of the plant before conditions get out of control. But the plant at Bhopal had antiquated indicators and gauges with none of this sophistication, and far too few of them. For instance, each of the three stainless steel MIC storage tanks (see Figure 4.1) had just one pressure gauge, a liquid level indicator and a temperature gauge on the tank itself. The ranges of these gauges were purely arbitrary: presumably they were standard stock items. The temperature gauge had a range of -25 to $+25°C$., irrelevant in summer if the refrigeration was not working. The pressure gauge did not read up to the setting of the relief valve. There was just one temperature alarm setting, with no controller, and by the time it was activated it was already far too late. It seems that the Bhopal plant did not measure up to the standards found in many chemical plants in India built *without* any foreign collaboration, so far as its instrumentation was concerned.

The danger signals were ignored

Now that the history of the plant has been reviewed, we are told that there were many warnings as to its inherent dangers from the day it was first commissioned back in 1980. Several accidents had occurred and leakages of MIC gas were fairly common. But not so common around the site were safety gas masks.

As a result of a serious accident in 1982 an elaborate Safety Manual had been prepared, highlighting the various departures that had taken place from recommended safe practices. The operation manual prepared for use in the Bhopal plant, for example, spells out what can happen (1):

> ... the pressure in the tank will rise rapidly if MIC is contaminated. This reaction may begin slowly, especially if there is no agitation, but it will become violent ... bulk systems must be maintained at low temperatures ... the low temperature will not eliminate the possibility of a violent reaction. It will, however, increase the time available for detection of the reaction and safe disposal of the material before reaction reaches a dangerous speed ...

It seems that such operation and safety manuals were just filed away. Certainly they were not put into practice, for then the cooling system for the MIC storage would have been seen as a safety precaution and never put out of action.

In retrospect, it seems that they had been sitting on a time bomb there in Bhopal, and it is a wonder that it did not explode much earlier. What is worse, the earlier warnings given by way of the accidents that had already happened, some of them fatal, had been completely ignored. Whilst the US plant was fitted with automatic alarms, the only leak detector at Bhopal was the human ear and eye!

One wonders to what extent the losses being made played a role. The plant had been set up at a cost of some US$25 million, but it had always made a loss, largely due to a gross under-utilisation of the available capacity. This may well have arisen due to poor marketing effort, which failed to bring home to potential users the benefits of the product. However that may be, the continuing losses led to an indiscriminate economy drive. Both operating and maintenance staff were reduced in numbers and the quality of staff employed also fell. That always happens in such situations. Several personnel specially trained on the plant both in India and the US were either transferred to other Union Carbide plants in India, or left in frustration following the introduction of a voluntary retirement scheme. The economy drive resulted in such neglect of routine maintenance that leaky valves, for instance, were just left to leak.

The influence of poor communications

An integral part of good management is good communications. But, once the accident had happened, the Union Carbide management, both in India and the US, were very slow in producing the facts and what was said seemed to be self-contradictory. The chairman of the company, Warren M. Anderson, did take the initiative to the extent of travelling from the US to visit the site within a week of the accident, but on arrival in Bhopal he, along with other company officials, was arrested and charged with 'negligence and criminal corporate liability and criminal conspiracy'. This was a token arrest only, since after six hours detention in the Union Carbide guest house at Bhopal he was released and flown to New Delhi. After his release, Anderson is quoted as saying:(4)

> Somebody had to say that our safety standards in the US are identical to those in India or Brazil or someplace else ... same

equipment, same design, same everything.

But it wasn't so. Later it was admitted that the design and detailed engineering of the plant had been left entirely to the Indian subsidiary and the Head Office in Danbury did not even have copies of the drawings of the Bhopal plant. Also, in sharp contrast to the manual controls at Bhopal, the similar plant in the US at Institute, West Virginia had several computerised and automatic fail-safe devices. Technically, whilst the parent US company holds a majority shareholding (50.5 per cent) in the Indian company, yet because of the Indian regulations, the Indian company is managed and run by Indians with such assistance from the parent company as may be required. It is also interesting to note that whilst plant operating experience at Bhopal was transferred to the US parent, the reverse never took place.

So far as the liability aspects are concerned, suffice it to say that the dust in Bhopal had hardly settled before senior lawyers had descended on the city: the media described them as 'ambulance chasers'. Some 30 cases have already been filed in the American courts on behalf of numerous clients in Bhopal, claiming compensation and punitive damages on account of the alleged negligence by Union Carbide. Whether or not these cases can be pursued in the American courts remains to be seen, but the impact on Union Carbide business worldwide is likely to be severe. The claims already total some US$300 billion, and even if they were settled at but three per cent of that total, that would still exceed the total assets of the company. There is indeed talk of Union Carbide taking shelter under Chapter 11 of the Bankruptcy Act in the US, as was done by John Manville when that company was faced with claims from thousands of people affected by asbestosis and related diseases due to long exposure to asbestos fibres (see Chapter 5).

The warnings that went unheeded

It has now become apparent that the local legislation on the subject of pollution and the environmental aspects of chemical plant operation is rather loose and lacks precision. The implementation of the regulations is thereby left to local inspectors and others who do not really appreciate the grave dangers that could arise. It is a bureaucratic jungle and corruption is so rampant that there is no difficulty in evading the legal requirements. Nevertheless there are those who take these matters very seriously. One

such was a local journalist in Bhopal, Rajkumar Keswani, who in a
series of articles warned of the 'time bomb' that had been built in
the city of Bhopal, but his message went unheeded. In September
1982 he wrote in the Hindi weekly *Rapat* about 'a possible
explosion that could reduce all Bhopal to a city of the dead'. A few
weeks later another Hindi weekly, *Prachand*, detailed the possible
harm from the 'killer Carbide plant'. Some six months before the
accident, Keswani wrote in *Jansatta*, a Hindi daily, citing some of
the accidents that had already occurred and concluding that not a
year had passed since the plant came into operation, without there
being accidents.

When the plant was first set up in 1969 it was located outside the
Bhopal Municipal Corporation limits, but over the next five years
a dozen residential colonies grew up around the plant and the
immediate area became densely populated. In 1975 the then
administrator of the Municipal Corporation, M.N. Buch, issued a
notice asking the company to shift the plant. The result, according
to Keswani: 'The plant stayed and Buch was transferred.' The
company donated US$2000 to the Corporation for the building of
a park and the notice was withdrawn.(5)

The subject was also raised in the State Assembly on 21
December 1982 and the then labour minister, Tara Singh Viyogi,
replying on behalf of the government, claimed that the plant had
foolproof safety arrangements. In answer to the call to move the
plant away from the thickly populated area of Bhopal, he replied:
'There has been an investment of Rs.250 million (about US$20
million). It is not a small stone which can be removed just like
that. There is no danger to Bhopal.' Famous last words!

A Union Carbide inspector, C.S. Tyson, was quoted by the *New
York Times* as saying that the safety systems at Bhopal were 'not
up to American standards'. He had been deputed to Bhopal in
1982 in this connection and noted that the safety system there was
indeed manual, whereas in the States it was automated. This visit
of his led to a comprehensive report pointing out the various
deficiencies in respect to both operation and maintenance at the
Bhopal plant. Shortly after this the Indian company got the
permission of the government to an extension of foreign collaboration on the clear understanding that it would acquire from the
parent company the necessary technology and know-how for
'handling emergency situations like toxic gas releases, sometimes
accompanied by fire, endangering the safety of the community'.
But alas, it all remained on paper. No positive action was ever
taken.

The lessons to be learnt

Unfortunately, the story of the disaster at Bhopal has been surrounded by much sensationalism in the media. It is refreshing, therefore, to meet some sober appraisals of the event and its consequences.(6,7) Mike Hyde, writing in *Chemical Insight*, is concerned not so much with who is at fault as to seek to draw helpful conclusions for those companies using advanced technology in the developing countries. The hope is also expressed that in the future politicians, environmental agencies, governments and the chemical companies themselves will pay closer attention to the hazards associated with such chemicals. Indeed, this has already started to happen. Within a week of his return from India, the chairman of Union Carbide, testifying at hearings in Washington, recommended stricter regulations. This is quite a change in attitude, since till now the chemical industry has strenuously protested against what they have described as 'over-regulation' in the industry. Bhopal has changed all that. Mike Hyde goes on to make the following additional points:

1 The Bhopal tragedy should serve as a useful lesson to the third world.
2 Standards of operation and maintenance may well be improved as a result.
3 There may be a reluctance to license advanced technology without assurance as to management control.
4 Multinationals may in the future opt for a minority interest, to safeguard their long-term future.
5 Companies will tend to go further down the road towards 'zero risk' and recognise the need to be frank and honest with the media.

Conclusion

Bhopal has alerted other chemical manufacturers everywhere to review their own safety procedures. These include such major companies as Dow, DuPont, Monsanto and W.R. Grace.(8) Whilst stricter regulations were already on the way in the US John Page, Director of Safety and Occupational Health for DuPont, points out that 'there is no way they can possibly enforce regulations if management is not committed'. This is equally true for Bhopal. Meanwhile, the disaster at Bhopal will continue to be featured in the press from time to time. The after-effects of the tragedy will continue to occupy the attention of both doctors and scientists, seeking to improve their knowledge. No doubt efforts will be made to keep track of the various complications that will ensue over the years as a result of exposure to that lethal gas, MIC.

There seems to be no doubt that the Bhopal disaster was a man-made tragedy. It occurred as a result of faulty design, poor maintenance and faulty plant operation. It could and should have been prevented. The International Organisation of Consumers Union, at their World Congress, meeting in Bangkok in December 1984, declared: 'Bhopal – never again'. We shall see.

And more recently, a two-day International Symposium in London in November 1985, attended by more than 200 delegates, drew a number of practical conclusions, the world having learnt meanwhile of another 'mini-Bhopal' at Union Carbide's West Virginia plant in the USA in August 1985.(9) These, taken together, made it very, very clear that Bhopal *was* a man-made disaster. That is, man could have prevented it ever happening, had the appropriate steps been taken. The least we can do, then, is to listen – and learn!

References

1   Series of articles by Praful Bidwai in *India Today* and news items in *Times of India* between December 1984 and March 1985.
2   Article: 'The lessons of the Bhopal disaster', *Update*, 12, 25 December 1984, pp.18-25.
3   Article: *Business India*, 17/30 December 1984, pp.67-77.
4   Article: 'All the world gasped', *Time*, (US Edn.), 17 December 1984, pp.20-31.
5   Article: 'The Bhopal disaster: UCIL's criminal negligence', *Business World*, 31 December/13 January 1985, pp.16-7.
6   Article: *Chemical Insight*, issue early January 1985, pp.3-8. *Chemical Insight* presents Mike Hyde's view of the chemical industry.
7   Article: *PetroChem News*, 17 December 1984.
8   Article: 'Bhopal leading to stricter legislation: bigger impact on chemical companies safety procedures', *Economist*, 293, 22 December 1984, p.70. Further references have been made in many subsequent issues of the *Economist* up to September 1985.
9   Symposium: 'The Chemical Industry after Bhopal', held 7/8 November, 1985, in London. In all, 14 papers were presented.

5 The killer fibre

Asbestos and its related products have been used in homes, schools, offices and factories for decades, mainly as insulation but also as a structural building material in the form of sheeting. The material is strong, stable, cheap and fire resistant. But it has now been realised that it can kill. Asbestos fibres, when inhaled, cause lung cancer (mesothelioma) and other respiratory diseases. This hidden danger has received worldwide publicity over the past ten years or so, largely due to the powerful and expanding lobbying of environmentalists everywhere, but especially in the US.

So powerful has this lobbying been that the dangers and risks associated with asbestos have been much exaggerated. Multi-million dollar lawsuits have been taken out against manufacturing companies, thus adding to public concern. The nature of the campaign can be seen from the headlines that cap articles and news items on the subject. Typical of the many:

Asbestos hysteria
Asbestos – Strip Tease
New debate over asbestos
A recurring hazard
Asbestos litigation – fatal fibre
Future shrouded in asbestos dust
Asbestos in schools – government action
The urgent search for asbestos substitutes
Asbestos fallout – Claims

Notice the way in which some of these headlines echo words used in the context of atomic explosion, thus implying that the risks and dangers are comparable. But of course they are not.

There have already been some drastic commercial consequences associated with the campaign. For instance, the world's largest manufacturer of asbestos products, Manville, has over 50 000 claims pending against it from its employees, product users and others in relation to asbestos-related injuries and their after-effects. That company has estimated that the cost of the claims now pending or likely to be raised could make the company liable for some US$2 billion by the year 2000.(1) This far exceeds its assets and it has therefore taken the precaution of filing an application under Chapter 11 of the Bankruptcy Act in the US. But we will enter into more detail concerning Manville later. Canada has been a large producer of asbestos in the past and blames the decline of the industry there on the environmental lobby in the US! Canadian production has indeed halved since 1979, with exports to the US also being halved over the same period.

What are the risks?

The health risks associated with asbestos fibre have been known for some fifty years, but are very difficult to quantify. What effect asbestos products have on those living with them, such as house-holders or workers in buildings where asbestos products are present, is not really known. Deaths from mesothelioma amongst asbestos workers and in their families in Britain and the US have been assessed at around 2 000 a year.(2) But when we turn to those living and working where asbestos products are used, the risk of disease is estimated to be some 9 per million, an insignificant figure and considerably lower than the risk of accident in the home.

But what steps can be taken to minimise the risk that there is? Firstly, the use of asbestos products can be abandoned and suitable substitutes used in their place. Such substitutes have been developed, so that is an eminently practical approach. The second step would be to remove asbestos products from existing buildings. But this is not only expensive and time-consuming, but it can be quite dangerous. Stripping out asbestos can result in the 'strippers' (those who strip the material) being exposed to asbestos dust and the resultant risks unless very elaborate precautions are taken. The end result could well be that many more people are killed in *that* process than were at risk whilst the asbestos was in place. It could kill many more than it saved.

The regulatory process

It is extremely difficult to determine what exposure to asbestos for humans is really 'safe'. Because of this, the regulations tend to be extremely conservative, insisting on very low levels of exposure that of course minimise such risk as there is. Taken to the extreme it is true to say that *all* chemicals are dangerous and in large enough doses would be carcinogenic. Since just about everything is a chemical of one sort or another, the implication is that we are all at risk, always. In a sense this is true, but we also realise that to live a normal life we have to accept a degree of risk and we are prepared to take what we consider to be calculated risks. People are always prepared to take risks to earn their daily bread, whether it be as a miner or a stuntman.

The chemical industry has been subject to a sharply increasing degree of regulation over recent years (3) and 'regulation drafting' has become a growth industry for the bureaucrats in a number of countries. The implementation of regulations always costs money, so the manufacturers were continually complaining that over-regulation was so increasing their costs that business was becoming impossible. But the Bhopal incident, with which we dealt in detail in Chapter 4, may well change all this.

The maximum asbestos dust level to which a British worker can legally be exposed is 0.5 million fibres per cubic metre of air. Across the Atlantic in the US it is 2.0, over an average 8-hour working day, although as a temporary measure that figure has been reduced to 0.5 since late 1983. However, this limitation was struck down when challenged in court by the industry. The government agency concerned with fixing such limits, the Occupational Safety and Health Administration (OSHA) is now seeking, after a series of public hearings, to reduce the figure to 0.2 or 0.5.(4) The building trade and the unions would like to see the standard fixed at 0.1.(5) But an agreement on this could take a long time.

The manner in which this lower level would be reached would be left to the manufacturers, who have two major options: engineering control (stopping the fibres getting into the air) or respiratory protection (stopping them getting into the lungs). Part of the problem is that accurate and reliable measurement of the dust content in the air in working areas is not easy. The usual method of testing is by using what is called 'phase-contrast microscopy', where an air sample is passed through a filter and the fibres counted. This is reliable at low levels, with well trained technicians, but is obviously liable to human error. Electron microscopy is more sophisticated, but much more expensive and perhaps not practical for field use.

Then again, there is continuing controversy as to what dust level is really dangerous. The industry's trade group, the Asbestos Information Association, declares:

> Asbestos is a carcinogen. There's no question about it. In the same breath I would say, however, that there is no scientific evidence that demonstrates that a two-fibre standard represents a significant risk to workers.

On the other hand, unions are pressing for the figure to be lower still: perhaps 0.1. The most dangerous work areas appear to be, for example, boiler rooms where asbestos used as a wrapping material. is dry, soft and fragile and tends to fly off into the air.(6) No matter what standards are set, it is really impossible to quantify the risk to human life that exposure will bring. Nevertheless, attempts have been made and it has been said that lifetime exposure of workers in the industry results in 64 more cancer deaths per 1 000, as compared to those not engaged in the industry. Since there are at least 375 000 such workers in the US alone, we are talking about something like 100 000 extra 'early deaths' worldwide from this one cause in this generation, with all the related misery and suffering that comes as the disease takes hold.

The road to disaster

The Manville Corporation, as we have already mentioned, is having to deal with thousands of claims for compensation and punitive damages. As a consequence the company filed a suit for bankruptcy in 1982, having found that it could not reach any settlements with claimants despite 15 months of negotiation. The company filed under Chapter 11. This is a precautionary step that can be taken, enabling the company to reorganise and restructure whilst the courts determine the total liability of the company, not only in respect of claims already filed but also claims likely to be made in the future. All these claims arise, of course, from the sufferings of those with asbestos-related diseases.

The intention is to split the company into two companies, one carrying the entire liability but few assets, whilst the other would continue to carry on the rest of the business. After meeting operating expenses, that company would transfer all residual cash to the company carrying the liability for claims, to assist it in meeting those claims. Meanwhile, of course, all payment of dividends to shareholders would be suspended.(7) The company is so involved in the litigation relating to the large number of claims it has to deal with that its chief executive officer, John A. McKinney observes 'You must be under the mistaken impression that we're a manufacturing company.' His commercial vice-president Curtis Links is even more explicit, saying 'We're a law firm.' They even joke about it, asserting that the company's name should really be 'Manville, Manville and Manville, Attorneys at-law'.(8) It certainly appears that virtually the whole of the time and energies of the officers of the company, together with some US$25 million in money is being spent on the problems relating to claims, including putting together a complicated financial package to free the manufacturing side from some US$2 billion of potential claims. Meanwhile, of course, the price of the shares on the stock market has plummetted. In addition the financial credibility of the company has been seriously eroded due to no fault of its own. As one executive said, 'We didn't get into this business to cheat anybody.'

When we cross the Atlantic to Britain, it is much the same story. There the firm of Turner and Newall are in deep trouble because of their involvement in the manufacture of asbestos products. The trend can be seen from the following figures:(9)

Year:	1977	1978	1979	1980	1981	1982
Profit after tax, £m.:	29	21	10	-7	-4	-10

This company has to some extent forestalled disaster by diversification. They began that process some twenty years ago and since then have gradually switched over from mature low growth products to specialised high growth products. They also undertook work on asbestos substitutes, such as polypropylene, glass fibre and rock wool. In the continuing attempt to restructure and so survive the company sold its BIP Vinyls group for some £25 million and planned to sell its American chemical company, Philip A. Hunt for some US$90 million.(10) Unfortunately for Turner and Newall the option to file for protection, as is done in the US under Chapter 11 of their Bankruptcy Act, is not available in Britain. This means that there is no escape for them from all the legal costs and potential claims, except by going bankrupt. That would mean, of course, the closing down of the company. At the moment, the risk of collapse is such that the company is valued on the stock market at some 10 per cent of the book value of its assets, whilst the lawyers make hay ...

The fastest growth industry

The fastest growing industry in the world today is very evidently not the manufacture of asbestos products, nor indeed any other manufacturing industry. It is a service industry that seems to deserve this title – the legal profession. This is certainly true in the US and we would expect it to be true elsewhere as well. In the US the lawyers (attorneys) are willing to fight your case for a share of the spoils. Of course they do not win every case they take up on this basis, but it seems to be a highly profitable and very attractive business. The impact of lawsuits has played havoc not only with the asbestos industry, but many others. The Bhopal tragedy (Chapter 4) seems very likely to fall into the same pit, with wide and very serious repercussions throughout the entire chemical industry. The share which the lawyers take can apparently vary considerably from case to case, but a study by the Rand Corporation in the US (11) showed that typically it could be one third, or more. The original claims are of course exaggerated but the final award can still be for very considerable sums. For example, awards in relation to claims against the asbestos industry in the US have ranged from US$25 000 to US$1 million, the average being US$40 000. In Britain, in one case, Turner and Newall settled for £650 000, against an initial claim of £1.6 million.

Who pays? Certainly the company pays in the first instance, but to some extent they can insure against the risk. Manville, for instance, took such insurance with 21 companies. Three of its main insurers have agreed to pay a total of US$315 million. If the total eventually paid reaches US$2 billion, as seems to be expected, most of the balance will have to be found by the issue of new common stock, if the company is not to collapse. An interesting development in this area is the fact that Manville are now suing the federal government, claiming that since 1964 their officials knowingly exposed tens of thousands of shipyard workers to dangerous levels of asbestos. If successful, this would mean that the government would have to accept at least part of the costs. Once again of course the lawyers are kept busy and it is we the consumers, who will ultimately pay all, in the increased taxes and cost of the products on the market.

Where will it all end?

What the end of this story will be can only be a matter for conjecture. The Rand Corporation study to which we referred earlier estimates that the number of asbestos-related diseases in the US by the year 2020 will total some 75 000, but a New York doctor puts the figure some five times higher. The total of claims by the end of the century may well be of the order of US$200 *billion*, perhaps even US$400 billion, with more than half a million claimants.(12) The basis for such claims has now been accepted by the courts, together with the fact that even if the company is unable to pay the victim should still receive compensation. But difficult questions remain. Who is liable? What is a fair payment? And above all – how can such incidents be avoided in future? Some progress has been made in dealing with the first two points by setting up a claims facility.(13)

Companies faced with such issues are advised to be completely open and honest, sharing whatever they know with the public via the media.(14) They must not speculate and they must respond to the requests made by the media. Handling disaster is an art, but it can be learnt and *must* be learnt for survival. Unfortunately the profit motive will always play a dominant role. For example, whilst every attempt is being made in the developed world to phase out asbestos products and replace them with substitutes, Turner and Newall's subsidiary in Zimbabwe is being prevented by the government there from reducing its output of asbestos.

Asbestos removal – the problems

Whilst the manufacture of asbestos products is a dying industry, the business of asbestos removal is flourishing, despite the risks involved.(15) So widespread has been the use of asbestos in the past that it is estimated that some 700 000 public, commercial and apartment buildings throughout the US contain asbestos material, together with some 40 000 secondary, public and private schools. In Orange County in California alone it is estimated that some 200 000 homes contain the objectionable material in some form or other. The 'asbestos removers' see a great future and there are now training courses offered by trade associations, such as the Association of Wall and Ceiling Industries and educational institutions such as the Georgia Institute of Technology. We doubt, despite this, whether many of those rushing into this business know what they are getting into and in most cases it is probably wiser to leave the material where it is unless it has started to disintegrate and there are loose fibres in the air.

Another recent survey (16) indicates that 20 per cent of the public buildings and apartment complexes have asbestos present in an easily crumbled form. This represents a very high risk and its removal would cost a great deal. Because of the wide use of asbestos products in the past many, and particularly school children, are said to be at risk for years to come. The presence of asbestos in schools is seen as a major health hazard and the issue has become so important, attracting so much public attention that in the US specific legislation has now been enacted – the Asbestos School Hazard Detection and Control Act of 1980. Whilst the existence of asbestos materials in schools, with the possible long exposure of the children over a period of years is seen as a serious health hazard, its removal could be even more hazardous. Yet the law continues to pursue its asinine course, with the Environmental Protection Agency fining the New York Educational Board US$240 000 for failure to comply with its regulations on the use of asbestos in schools.

The removal of asbestos is an expensive business, costing up to US$10 per square foot. Whilst this is seen as the final, permanent solution, temporary solutions have also been proposed, as being cheaper in the short term, such as encapsulating the asbestos with a sprayed-on coating, or encasing it by building a structure round it. Despite the controversy surrounding such alternatives (17) it is a rapidly growing business. Whilst some 90 per cent of pre-1974 school buildings contain asbestos products, hardly any of them have been dealt with as yet. The encapsulators have found that schools, till now, have provided them with half their market, but they are now predicting an explosion of business in the private sector. Of course, litigation is not far away. School Boards across the US are now filing lawsuits against the asbestos products manufacturers and suppliers in an attempt to get *them* to pay for its removal.

One problem is that asbestos is used in boiler rooms and the like because of its heat resisting properties, which means that the substitute or the encapsulating material must also be heat resistant. We cannot enter into a discussion as to the merits of the wide range of alternative materials and encapsulating processes that are becoming available, but we can mention one as illustrative. That protective process uses a sodium silicate spray, which is said to penetrate the asbestos up to a depth of three inches. The individual fibres are thus coated. This suppresses dust, the hazard is much minimised and the life of the asbestos material in service extended. That sounds fine, but the application costs money and requires some skill if it is to be effective.

Conclusion

There are some very valuable lessons to be learned from this case study. First and foremost, those companies working with asbestos should never have concentrated all their efforts within one industry: they should have diversified from the very beginning. When we turn to consider the regulatory bodies who have a responsibility for the welfare of both the workers and the public, there is a need not to succumb to the mass hysteria that seems to be so readily aroused through the media. The benefit/cost ratios should always be kept well in mind, although safety must remain the primary consideration. A more reasonable approach to such problems is achieved if the public really understand what is involved and this brings us back once again to the policies to be pursued by companies handling dangerous materials. Such companies must be frank and honest, taking care to educate the public as to the risks they can run.

We seek, of course, to learn lessons that are of general application. In this particular industry, whilst there is undoubtedly a real risk and threat to health to those engaged in manufacturing, processing and handling asbestos products, the risks to those living and working where the products have been installed may well be much exaggerated.

References

1   Article: *Business Week*, 24 December 1984, p.56.
2   Article: 'Asbestos: strip tease', *Economist*, 292, 15 September 1984, p.85.
3   Kharbanda, O.P. and Stallworthy, E.A. *How to learn from Project Disasters*, Gower, 1983. See Chapter 2, 'Killed by kindness'.
4   Cahan, V., 'New debate over asbestos', *Chem. Eng.*, 91, 23 July 1984, p.20.
5   Article: 'OSHA begins asbestos talks', *Eng. News Record*, 213, 5 July 1984, p.87.
6   Article: *Eng. News Record*, 12 August 1984, p.11.
7   Article: 'Manville reorganisation plan resolves nothing', *Business Week*, 5 December 1983, pp.24-5.

8   Keefe, P.W., 'Manville: what price Ch.11', *Duns Business Monthly*, August 1984, p.50.
9   Article: 'Turner and Newall's future is shrouded in asbestos dust', *Economist*, 284, 18 September 1982, pp.86-7.
10 Article: 'Turner and Newall – mummy holds baby's hand', *Economist*, 286, 12 February 1983, p.85.
11 Kakalisk, J.S. *et al*, 'Costs of a litigation', Study by *Rand Corporation*, US, 1983. Also a series of 4 very exhaustive articles by Paul Brodeur in *The New Yorker*: 'A failure to warn', 10 June 1983, pp.49-101; 'Discovery', 17 June 1985, pp.45-111; 'Judgment', 24 June 1985, pp.37-80; and 'Bankruptcy', 1 July 1985, pp.36-80.
12 Article: 'Mounting claims', *Economist*, 284, 25 September 1982, pp.19-20.
13 Jackson, R., 'When the wrangling must end?', *Reinsurance (Gt. Britain)*, 16, August 1984, p.147.
14 Stevens, A., 'And now for the bad news', *Chem. Eng.*, 91, 26 November 1984, p.99.
15 Article: 'Asbestos removers flourish despite risks involved', *Eng. News Record*, 212, 16 August 1984, p.11. Also a study titled 'Asbestos' in the UK magazine *Which?* mentioning the Asbestos Removal Contractors' Association, London.
16 Article: 'Asbestos: the problem grows', *Science Digest*, 93, January 1985, p. 32.
17 Article: 'Asbestos controversy: a controversial alternative', *Chemical Week*, 20 June 1984, pp.33-4.

6   The unlovable Love Canal

The Love Canal is to be found near Niagara Falls, the honeymooner's paradise, so when we first saw the name we thought it had something to do with lovers. Who knows – perhaps you could take an idyllic stroll along its banks and gaze together into its clear waters. But no: the canal is named after a certain William T. Love who came to Niagara Falls in 1892 and planned to build a canal to provide inexpensive transport for goods being manufactured in the locality because of the cheap power available via the electricity generators harnessed to the Falls. Excavation work started some two years later but the canal was never completed. William Love's dream was finally abandoned in 1910, the canal – or perhaps we should call it a ditch – being taken over by a firm later called Hooker Electrochemical.

The canal then lay fallow for some thirty years until 1941, when Hooker thought that it would be a suitable site for the disposal of industrial wastes from its Niagara Falls manufacturing operations. These arose from caustic and chlorine manufacturing and the canal was thought to be eminently suitable for the purpose because the bottom and sides had been lined with impermeable clay as a prelude to its use as a canal carrying water. Hence the wastes would not leak or leach into the ground and would be safe. This disposal of waste went on for some ten years and finally the canal was covered over with some 10 feet of impermeable clay. It is obvious that up to this point the chemical company had dealt with the disposal of their waste products efficiently and with due care and consideration.

The site is sold

This waste land attracted the attention of the Niagara Falls Board of Education, who proposed to build a school and a park on the site. The firm of Hooker sold the land to the Board 'in consideration of one dollar' and the deed of sale stated clearly:(1)

> The premises ... have been filled with waste products and the [Board] assumes all risk and liability ... no claim, suit, action or demand by the [Board] for injury or death ...

This was in 1953. It is clear that in purchasing the land and accepting the conditions of conveyance the Board also accepted the risk and possible liabilities. They proceeded with the grading of the site, which involved the removal in all of some 10 000 cubic yards of fill, taking the level down in parts by some three feet. Remember.that the final protective clay layer laid by Hooker was some 10 feet, so there is now a danger that in parts it is down to five or six feet: all these measurements would be subject to a substantial margin of error.

Some four years later, in 1957, the Board had the intention of transferring part of the property to private developers, whereupon Hooker ventured to remind them of the risks involved quite clearly, saying:

> ... the land was not suitable for construction where underground facilities would be necessary ... [Hooker] could not prevent the Board from selling the land, but the property should not be divided for the purpose of building homes and hoped that no one will be injured.

Later Hooker went so far as to oppose the sale of the property, explaining the background and the potential hazards. They said:

> We [Hooker] were still making use of the property and were reluctant to sell. It should not be used for the erection of any structures ... the Board felt that this was the only property available for a school and the [Hooker] management concluded that if the property was so important to the Board we should make a gift of the same ... to be used only for the construction of a new school and of a park ...

The Board in turn confirmed shortly afterwards that this was indeed so, confirming that:

> there was a mutual understanding that the property would be

used only for the construction of a new school and the maintenance of a park. [Hooker] feel very strongly that subsoil conditions make any excavation undesirable and possibly hazardous. There was also an inwritten understanding ... that the Board would not dispose of the land in any way that might lead to digging or construction work ...

Yet in that same year (1957) and again in 1960 the city constructed storm sewers across the landfill site, cutting both the clay covering and the walls of the disposal area. This exposed some of the chemical waste, resulting in minor skin irritations to the children who played in the area.

It gets worse ... and worse

In 1974 part of the property went by way of deed to a certain L.C. Armstrong. However, the original relevant provisions of the original deed were incorporated in the new deeds. Meanwhile the construction in 1968 of an expressway through the southern portion of the Love Canal required the removal of some buried wastes and soil.

The first reports of chemicals seeping into the basements of some homes on the edge of the property appeared in October 1976 and a task force was set up jointly by the City of Niagara Falls, Hooker and the Niagara County Health Department, resulting in a report suggesting means whereby the situation could be overcome. A further study was commissioned in 1978 from the firm of Conestoga-Rovers of Waterloo, Ontario, in Canada, the objective being to prevent the further migration of waste from the canal. Meanwhile the situation locally got so bad that the nearby school was ordered to be closed temporarily and pregnant women and children living in the immediate vicinity were evacuated. Shortly afterwards some two hundred and fifty families were evacuated, their homes being purchased, whilst remedial work on the canal itself was begun.

The following year (1979) a very high rate of birth defects and miscarriages were observed amongst residents in the vicinity of the Love Canal. The American Institute of Chemical Engineers Task Force on RCRA (Federal Resource Conservation and Recovery Act) reported:

The design of the Love Canal site was well within the standards of RCRA. What went wrong with Love Canal can be attributed in large part to a lack of monitoring, invasion of the site itself, and lack of remedial work.

Despite this report the US Justice Department filed a lawsuit at the end of 1979 against the Hooker Chemical Company, relating to the company's earlier use of the Love Canal. In April 1980 the State of New York filed a US$635 million suit against Hooker and its parent company, Occidental Petroleum. However, studies prepared by the Research Triangle Institute and the Atmospheric Science Center for the EPA (Environmental Protection Agency) showed that the air inside homes adjacent to the Love Canal was even cleaner than the outside air. Yet the media, driving public opinion, built up a scare situation to such a degree that President Carter declared a State of Emergency in the Love Canal area, necessitating the evacuation of some seven hundred families. According to the governor of New York State, this was medically unnecessary but had to be carried out because of the panic that had been caused. The New York State Department of Health sought to clarify the situation by making the following statement:

> We have not yet been able to correlate the geographic distribution of adverse pregnancy outcomes with chemical evidence of exposure. At present there is no direct evidence of a cause-effect relationship with chemicals from the canal.

The EPA itself gave Hooker credit for doing what was appropriate in the circumstances. Although the waste was disposed of before the latest regulations were in force, they said that Hooker 'would have had no trouble complying with RCRA regulations. They may have had a little extra paperwork, but they wouldn't have had to change the way they disposed of the wastes'. Thus in the forties Hooker met the legal requirements of the seventies.

Another view

As we all know, every story has two sides to it, depending upon who tells the tale. Real truth, if there is such a thing in this context, must lie somewhere between. So far we have been presenting the story of the Love Canal as seen by Hooker, supported by various independent and official agencies. Let us now see the story as others saw it.

What is possibly an extreme view is presented in a famous book by Michael Brown called *Laying Waste: The Poisoning of America by Toxic Chemicals*. This book has become the popular authority on the situation and it claims to tell the truth, the whole truth and nothing but the truth. The book formed the basis of the struggle by the Love Canal Homeowners Association. The book has received a great deal of praise in certain quarters. It has been described as 'one of the best examples of tenacious, dedicated journalism'. Other tributes run:

> [it is] strong, readable and humane
> [it] takes the reader on a macabre journey
> [it is] a vitally important book

However the book has been subject to fairly detailed scrutiny and some obvious discrepancies have been highlighted.(2) For instance, the book declares that 'Hooker issued no detailed warning ... only a brief paragraph'. In fact that 'brief paragraph' is the longest in the entire deed. Again, the book asserted that there was 'no evidence that Hooker had verbally warned the Board'. Possibly not, but there was quite a volume of written evidence of warnings given on a number of occasions. Yet again, the book asserts that the 'Love Canal dump failed to meet RCRA standards'. As we have already seen, that is manifestly untrue.

Looking back, it would seem that Hooker did not meet the public relations challenge soon enough. Whilst the story was still local, they kept silent, and only seemed to stir to action when the story hit the headlines in the national press during 1978. Even then they were too slow and too late. Their first really concrete action came some two years later with a series of brochures called 'Hooker Factline'. The public accusations were met with facts and figures, but the critics had been much quicker off the mark and had already built up a strong anti-Hooker image in the public mind. Even at that stage, the company's response was somewhat meek and muted. Despite the strong evidence available to them to refute Brown's allegations, Hooker decided not to sue either author or publisher, not wishing, they said, to 'give the book free publicity'. But the publicity already given resulted in the parent company's stock falling in value by some US$500 million.

What are the lessons?

In retrospect, we must ask what are the lessons that can be learnt from the story of the Love Canal. Is it an isolated incident, or has it parallels elsewhere? It most certainly has parallels elsewhere, the wide publicity serving to highlight the fact that there are any number of similar dumps for chemical waste scattered across the US, all with hidden dangers and presenting a potential risk to the community at large. It has been estimated that some US$16 billion would have to be spent before existing dumps could be modified to meet the latest and much more stringent regulations now prevailing in the US. This cost will have to be met, either directly or indirectly, by the community. The repercussions are not of course confined to the US. The implications of the incident go far beyond national boundaries. What has happened over the years in the US has its counterpart in the other nations of the developed world and the developing countries are not far behind.

The US Congress has passed a bill that will create a 'Superfund' to pay for the cleaning up of chemical dumps, to be financed by a tax on chemical products. Once again, of course, the consumer has to pay in the end. However in our judgment such an exercise can be self-defeating, since it ignores the real issue. The problems at the Love Canal arose because of mismanagement – in that particular case, mismanagement by an Education Board. But in many other instances, no doubt, it will have been mismanagement by the chemical company who dumped their toxic wastes. The real answer, therefore, is to recognise the fact that chemical plants produce wastes of various kinds, some dangerous, and ensure that such wastes are properly managed within the community. Extremely severe legislation is no solution, since once regulations go beyond what is economically feasible, they are circumvented one way or another. The profit motive will always reign supreme.

The role of government agencies

As we follow the history of the events associated with the Love Canal we see that the first real 'scare' was created by a report issued by a government agency – EPA. Their study alleged damage to local residents despite the fact that another report which they themselves had commissioned said that there was no causal evidence. Merely because it was a government report, it was accepted as authoritative and much of what happened after that was a direct result of the conclusions published in that report. Yet a panel convened by the EPA later concluded that 'the report was not a study at all in scientific terms' and that there was no substantive evidence 'that the people of Love Canal are at increased risk from proximity to the waste dump'.

However, the EPA used the Love Canal case to justify further regulations, which the industry called 'over-regulation', alleging that there were some 50 000 similar dumps scattered around the country. Once again the agency had not approached the subject factually, since a House of Representatives subcommittee took the agency to task, saying:

> While this report has many methodological flaws, the inadequacy of its fundamental data base alone is enough to discredit the study ... the estimate of the number of sites and the degree of hazard they pose is little better than pure guesswork.

How did the agency prepare their estimate? It was based on extrapolation from 232 known dumps, of which only 24 were actually visited. Another critic pointed out that the EPA definition of a hazardous substance was so sweeping – any substance that is flammable, corrosive, reactive or toxic – that every home would have several samples in its cupboards.

It is bad news that makes news

It is unfortunately true that the only real news, so far as the media are concerned, is the 'bad news'. They report the air crashes, never the many thousands of flights that end safely. Because of this, industry in general keeps away from the media and as a result its viewpoint goes by default. Mike Hyde has some sound advice for management in this context:(3)

> Industry has to take the media as it finds it and should never wait for its critics to attack or allow attacks to go unanswered. It must adopt a much more positive, proactive stance, in its own defence. There is no one to put industry's case but the people who work in it.

What is more, the bad news is often quoted wrongly, but that can only be countered if you have the facts. This demands that companies should be open and frank, especially when talking to their neighbours, and ensure that public statements are carefully prepared, explicit and clear. For instance, a company opening a new factory in a new area, or even adding a new plant to an existing works, does well to maintain a consistent monitoring from the very beginning of the atmospheric conditions in the locality. Then later, if accused of bringing about change, it has at least factual data to refer to. Then a news sheet can be issued throughout the locality, letting people know what is going on and why. It helps a lot if it can be demonstrated not only that the processes used in manufacture are harmless, but that the products are beneficial.

There is an impression that manufacturing processes have wrought incredible harm on the environment over the years, but at long last a full length book has been published putting another view.(4) The author, a columnist, educator and commentator, takes an optimistic view. He asserts that contrary to popular belief, the 'standard of living' and the 'quality of life' are not declining. On the contrary, he avers that the trend is altogether in the opposite direction. In relation to our present subject he states:

> Environmentalism ... has become one of the great engines of popular thought and action in the world today. From the Clean Air Act to the Love Canal, from Three Mile Island to dioxin, from carcinogens to ozone depletion – the idea is omnipresent. In terms of specifics the environmental viewpoint is often valuable. As a comprehensive vision of our time, however, it is, in my judgment, typically both wrong and damaging ... the environmental movement has argued that the overall quality of our lives is poor and getting worse. Such a view is incorrect ...

Of course, healthy debate on the subject is to be encouraged if a balanced viewpoint is to be established and sound conclusions reached. Typical of such debates is an article 'Should pollution laws be loosened?' (5). The Chairman of the Council on Environment says 'no' whilst the Chairman of the Wilderness Society says 'yes'. Both views as there expressed may be extreme. Every regulation or standard laid down should be assessed in depth and its cost set against the benefits that are to be gained. Risk is always present and we are all prepared to take risks – we take them day in, day out. The problem is to determine what is the appropriate acceptable level of risk, recognising that it can never be completely eliminated, except at a completely unacceptable cost.

Conclusion

There does seem to be a conclusion to this story, in that after years of legal wrangling the former residents of the Love Canal area – those who have suffered miscarriages, had children with abnormalities and been forced to abandon their homes, are finally going to receive something. A court has approved a settlement in which Occidental, the present owners of the Hooker company, will settle for a sum somewhere in excess of US$5million.(6) Individual payments range up to US$700 000 but one mother, expressing the emotions of many, said that if she had received the whole sum that still 'wouldn't compensate me for the anguish I face every time I look at my daughter'.(7)

The story of the Love Canal demonstrates, above all, that whilst the proper steps can well be taken to ensure the safe disposal of dangerous waste products, subsequent action by others can defeat the objective in view – and those who first put the waste there *still* have to carry the blame.

Meanwhile, it appears that the incident at the Love Canal has become a benchmark, for reading of a chemical dump in Williamsburg, Ohio, we are told by the media that it is 'like Love Canal'. Certainly this particular subject has provided material for a vast number of articles and some books. Hazardous waste, as it is called, continues to receive a great deal of attention. The advice to companies involved in its disposal remains the same: be frank, honest and open and provide full information as early as possible.

References

1   Article: 'Love Canal: the facts 1892-1980', *Factline No. 11,* June 1980. *Factline* is a periodic publication issued by Hooker Chemical Corporation.
2   Zuesse, E., 'Love Canal: the truth seeps out', *Reason,* February 1981, pp.17-33.
3   Article in *Chemical Insight,* late December 1982, pp.7-8. (*Chemical Insight,* published twice monthly, presents Mike Hyde's perspective on the international chemical industry.)
4   Wattenberg, B.J., *The Good News is the Bad News is Wrong,* J.W. Inc., 1984. A condensation of this book was published in the US Readers Digest for May 1984, from p.101.
5   Article: 'Should pollution laws be loosened?', *US News,* 94, April 1983, pp.51-2.
6   The 1983 Annual Report of Occidental Petroleum Corporation. (The Hooker company is part of the group.)
7   Purgavie, D., 'Dermot Purgavie's America', *Daily Mail* (London), 21 February 1985, p. 10.

Part Three

THE COST OF ENERGY

7 The nuclear stalemate

Until 1973 oil was far too cheap for serious consideration to be given to the possible alternatives. It was most convenient in use and far cleaner than its major rival for energy production, coal. But the ten-fold increase that resulted from the so-called 'oil crisis' of 1973 brought about a drastic and qualitative change in the entire energy scenario. Nuclear fission had already appeared on the scene as an alternative source of power for electricity generation, but the sharp rise in the oil price gave increased incentive for its development. Many alternatives to oil were evaluated and of these nuclear energy seemed the most promising. So promising, in fact, that it was said that the eighties would be the decade of nuclear power. But almost as soon as a programme for the proliferation of power stations using nuclear power began doubts were being raised as to their safety. The so-called 'anti-nuke' lobbies sprang up all over the world (1), spreading from the US. The campaign received real impetus following upon the Three Mile Island accident on 28 March 1979. Only a few years earlier the French premier Jacques Chirac had expressed the hopes and aspirations of the Western world when opening the very first conference of the European Nuclear Society in Paris in April 1975:(2)

> For the immediate future, I mean for the coming ten years, nuclear energy is one of the main answers to our energy needs.

His words could be said to have come true with respect to France itself, but not elsewhere. This is demonstrated by Figure 7.1, where we compare the share which the several major fuels have in electricity generation in two other major industrialised countries with France. The Three Mile Island disaster has, we are sure, been

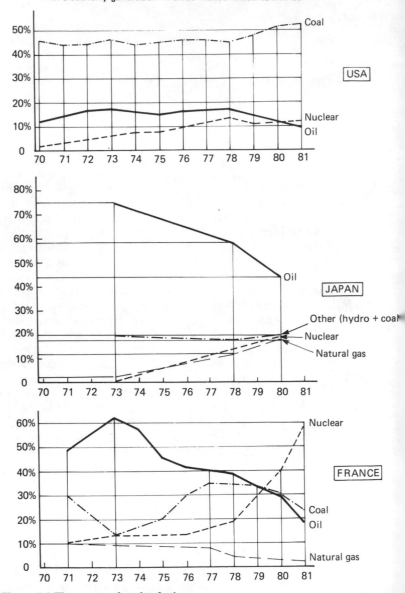

Figure 7.1 The usage of major fuels
These graphs illustrate the extent to which nuclear fuel has displaced other major fuels for the generation of electricity in three major industrialised countries, the USA, Japan and France. (Reproduced by courtesy of Compagnie Francaise des Petroles, Paris.)

a major factor in changing the nuclear promise into a nuclear stalemate for a great many countries and the US in particular, so let us have a brief look at that accident.

Three Mile Island

This nuclear power plant in Pennsylvania in the US was in all probability completed rather hastily. It was brought into operation just at the end of 1978 in order to qualify for substantial tax benefits.(3) Only a few weeks later it had to be shut down for two weeks because two safety valves had ruptured during a test and this was only one of a number of technical 'bugs' that had to be eliminated. It also appears that not enough time had been allowed for the training of the operators in the use of the emergency procedures.

Then, on 28 March 1979 at 4.00 a.m. a pump feeding water to the steam generators stopped because of a malfunction. The emergency pumps took over automatically but failed to function, since certain valves, which should have been open, were closed. This could only have been due to negligence. As a result the water backed to a secondary loop, resulting in a pressure rise inside the reactor. This caused a relief valve to open and then it became stuck in the open position, leading to a drop in pressure and the activation of the emergency core cooling system. Water poured into the reactor and then out through the open relief valve. A further malfunction in the instruments gave erroneous readings, causing the operators to believe that the reactor core was safely covered with water coolant when in fact it was not. The operators therefore shut down the emergency system, thinking it not necessary. As a result the reactor rods reached the dangerous temperature of 2 500°F., which could have led to a 'meltdown' – a dreaded word in the nuclear dictionary. This complicated chain of events led to some hundred flashing lights and a multitude of alarms sounding, completely confusing the plant operators. As a consequence it took them nearly two and a half hours to understand the real problem confronting them.(4)

Fortunately no one was killed or injured but there was considerable panic. Thousands fled their homes and many more thousands prepared for evacuation. What began as a series of seemingly small and in themselves insignificant incidents brought about a major catastrophe. For instance, a key signal went unnoticed because it was erroneously covered by a yellow maintenance tag whilst another useful visual display was, by mistake, located at the *back* of the control panel.

The loss? Some US$2 billion in money and – far more serious – a loss of public confidence. The lesson: with nuclear plants safety must come *first* and it must *stay* first.(3) Fortunately this sad incident is well documented (5,6,7,8,9), both officially, through reports by the US Department of Energy and the Pennsylvania Department of Health and unofficially through the many articles that have been written on the subject throughout the world.

How safe are nuclear reactors?

There is no doubt that the safety record of nuclear power plants is outstanding. Even the Three Mile Island incident in fact affected no one outside the plant and no one inside the plant was injured. Yet it seems that is not good enough. It is felt that ordinary standards are not adequate: it is believed that the stakes are far too high and the risks far too great. Whilst the Three Mile Island incident has been put down to human error, this only brings the problem back to the designer. He must design so as to take account of potential human error. In retrospect, the plant at Three Mile Island is considered to be rather complex, thus inviting human error.

The literature bearing upon the risks aspects is rather confusing. An American report (10) suggests that the experts may have underestimated the risks of a major nuclear accident by a factor of 40. Yet another study points out that the loss of life in nuclear accidents has been far less than was previously anticipated. Whilst there seems to be complete uncertainty amongst the technical experts, there is no doubt at all that the nature of the risk and what is at stake has been brought home most forcibly to the public mind by the horrors depicted in a film widely seen, *The Day After*. The subject of risk analysis is fairly new, having developed over the past fifteen years or so.

Before then, there was no attempt at all to estimate the probability of failure. The situation was met by the designer using a large 'factor of safety' in order to reduce the risk of failure.

With the introduction of the techniques of risk analysis, the probability of a meltdown, the worst that could happen in a nuclear reactor, during one year's operation was put by some at 1 in 20 000. A German study some four years later put the figure at 1 in 10 000, making a nuclear plant still safer than an ordinary house to work in. But an analysis of more than 19 000 malfunctions, of which 169 were serious, put the risk of meltdown at 1 in 500, which is quite alarming. However, all these calculations are so uncertain that extreme caution is necessary in their use. A series of five articles (11) dealt at length with two basic questions:

Can the potential risk be measured?
Can a new generation of safer reactors be built?

The answer to the first question appears to be 'maybe' and to the second: 'yes'. Yet, even though the risks are small, and can be still further reduced, it has only taken one major accident – Three Mile Island – to strike a near lethal blow at the already ailing nuclear industry in the US, with repercussions worldwide. The discovery, as published in the *New York Times*, that someone falsified tests for leaks in the reactor system just prior to the accident only made matters worse! A variety of disparaging comparisons have been made to emphasise the dangers said to be inherent in the nuclear power plant. For instance, it is pointed out that such a plant has some ten million parts, whereas there are a mere three hundred thousand in a jumbo jet. This comparison is made to emphasise the overwhelming complexity of such plants and hence the great risks that, by implication, are involved. However, when compared with coal, it is said that coal, with its mining and pollution hazards is a more dangerous source of energy than atomic fission.(12)

Nuclear power plants in the United States		
Year	Orders placed	Orders cancelled
1953 to 1971	131	–
1972	38	7
1973	41	–
1974	28	7
1975	4	13
1976	3	1
1977	4	10
1978	2	14
1979	–	8
1980	–	10
1981	–	6
1982	–	18
1983	–	1
(1984	–	10)

Figure 7.2 Status of orders for nuclear power plants
This table listing orders placed and cancelled for nuclear power plants in the US demonstrates the drastic change that has taken place since 1978. (Data from paper by M. Leepson in *Editorial Research Reports* 2, No 4, 1983.)

The hidden dangers

The danger in the background is of course that of radioactivity, a danger the more feared because there is nothing to see. Fears are expressed not only in relation to the operating plants, but also in relation to the radioactive wastes which are a by-product of their

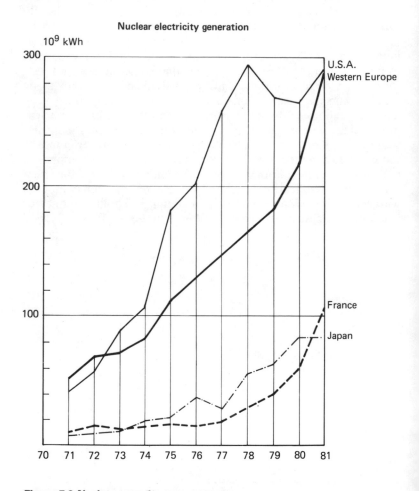

Figure 7.3 Nuclear capacity grows apace
This graph illustrates the rapid growth of nuclear electricity generation since the early seventies in the major industrialised areas of the world. (Reproduced by courtesy of Compagnie Francaise des Petroles, Paris.)

operation. The critics of nuclear power tend to exaggerate such risks, whilst the proponents assert that nuclear power plants are absolutely safe and certainly far safer than any other type of power plant. At the moment the critics seem to be having their way, because in the US at least more than one hundred nuclear power plants that had been planned have been abandoned since 1972, whilst since 1978 no new plants have been put on order.(13) In Figure 7.2 we present the history of orders for nuclear plants ordered and cancelled in the US since 1953. In part the lack of new orders has been due to the rapidly mounting costs of such plants, which we shall look at later, but the character of the criticism that has been levelled at such installations is well illustrated by the publication of a small booklet entitled:

The Official Government Nuclear Survivor's Manual – Everything there is known about effective procedures in case of nuclear attack.

One opens the booklet only to find that every page is absolutely blank! Of course, nuclear war has nothing to do with nuclear power plants, but the two have become closely associated in the public mind.

Seeking to dramatise the risks associated with nuclear war (14) on the basis of official and other reports, popular journalists present grim predictions, picturing a world of frozen darkness, the sun obscured and ground temperatures dropping by some 40°F. The citation of a precise temperature drop lends credibility to such dramatic assessments of the future in store, but the problem is that similar consequences are, by implication, attributed to accidents in a nuclear power plant – which is a nonsense.

Nuclear power plant developments worldwide

The highlighting of the 'hidden dangers' has had its repercussions not only in the US, but worldwide. For instance, we see that Egypt's ambition to have 40 per cent of its electricity derived from nuclear energy by the year 2000 is now unlikely to be achieved. South Korea is said to be re-assessing its programme.(15) In both these cases rising costs are said to be the motivating factor. However, the Austrian voters have banned the use of nuclear power, even though one plant is now complete whilst Sweden, at present getting 40 per cent of its electricity requirements via nuclear energy, has decided to phase it out.(16) Indeed, in Europe only France is going ahead steadily with a nuclear power plant building programme.

On the other side of the world Japan, despite its experience at Hiroshima, is developing steadily. With 25 nuclear reactors in operation and another 7 due to come into operation shortly, that country will then be getting 34 per cent of its electricity requirements from nuclear power plants and the aim is to more than double this by the year 2000. Japan has kept the plants well away from major cities and has one of the safest operating records in the world. The most serious accident to date occurred in 1981 at the Tauruga plant, located north of Osaka, when radioactive water flooded the plant and spilled into the scenic bay by which the plant had been built. This accident led to even more stringent regulations being enforced.

When we come to look at the US, we see that despite all the furore, it is still the largest user of nuclear power, with more than ninety plants in operation. The US is followed by the USSR and France, who have only half as many. Figure 7.3 sets out the status for the major countries using nuclear power. In the US, despite Three Mile Island, 17 operating permits for new reactors have been issued since that incident and three plants went on stream in 1983.(17) Indeed, at Three Mile Island itself, the No.1 Reactor, which was not damaged, may soon be starting up again. There is no doubt that necessity governs the situation: the power is needed, the investment has largely been made and the only sensible approach, economically, is to put that investment to work. But who pays for the faulty equipment that led to the accident with No.2 Reactor? Whilst the total loss was of the order of US$2 billion, the manufacturer ended up paying only some US$37 million. Even more awkward is the question that arises with respect to the cost of those plants that have been cancelled. The manufacturers have a very substantial stake and there are complex legal questions to be resolved.(18) One writer suggests that there has been a loss of up to US$15 billion in relation to plants cancelled or abandoned since the late seventies.(19)

In the UK the problem has taken on a different form. The Central Electricity Generating Board, the only producer there, is anxious to continue building nuclear power stations, but has to fight through a morass of argument occasioned by the need to gain planning approval. A second nuclear power station is projected at Sizewell, some eight miles from the coast in Suffolk (Sizewell B), but the enquiry for that has taken 26 months. There was a 15-member secretariat and some sixteen million words are said to have been spoken.(20) At the last meeting in the 800-seater concert hall that had been hired for the purpose, there were eight people on the stage and just three in the audience. The American-style pressurised water reactor is proposed and the plant would have a capacity of some 9 000mW, reducing the dependence on coal in the UK to below 50 per cent. Strong opposition was voiced by organisations such as *The Town & Country Planning Association, Campaign for the Countryside* and *Friends of the Earth* but it seems the project will eventually go ahead.

But investment cost is a problem

One problem that has to be faced, particularly in the US, is the way in which the cost of building nuclear power plants is skyrocketing. To take a typical example, let us review the cost of the 1100mW Fermi 2 unit being built for Detroit Edison.(21) Over the years, the estimates have gone as listed in Figure 7.4. Such a record makes a mockery of cost estimating and project management, yet we assert that a cost escalation some fourteen times the original estimate and completion running some ten years late is typical.

The end result of such escalating costs for nuclear power plants

---

The revised estimates

The 1100 MW Fermi 2 Unit for Detroit Edison:

Date of Estimate	Capital Cost US$ million	Startup Date
7–1968	230	2–1974
9–1972	511	4–1977
2–1977	894	9–1980
12–1979	1,300	3–1982
6–1981	2,000	11–1983
3–1984	3,100	12–1984

Figure 7.4 The mounting cost
The successive cost estimates for the 1100mW Fermi 2 nuclear power plant illustrates a very common trend.

is, of course, that the coal-fired plants begin to appear competitive once again, even allowing for the escalation in the price of coal that will inevitably occur over the lifetime of the plant.(22) Operating data for 1983 in the US indicates that the nuclear and coal electrical generation costs ended up roughly the same, at about 3.50 cents a kilowatt.(23) Indeed, there has even been talk of some nuclear plants, currently half-finished, being converted for coal firing. One such is the 800mW nuclear power plant being built at Moscow, Ohio. It is suggested it could be converted to a 1300mW. coal-fired unit over some six years, with about 45 per cent of the investment already made being reusable.

However, despite all the pessimism, it is refreshing to see that even in the US it is still possible to complete a nuclear power plant in some six years.(24) The basis for such a success is said to be:

Innovation
Speedy completion on site
Keep it simple
Real team effort

All these, except the first, are basic principles of project management which we are continually urging upon our readers.(25)

A look ahead

Whilst it is true that the nuclear power plant is now much more expensive that it was a few years ago, yet it still has a place for the production of electrical energy. Some countries do not, like the US, have a choice between nuclear energy and coal as a source of power. For instance, Japan has no significant sources of coal within her borders, whilst in France coal is scarce and expensive. In both these countries the nuclear programme is being pursued with vigour, and with success. It is also well to realise that there are only three sources of energy of real significance on a worldwide basis – coal, oil and nuclear fission. Each has both advantages and disadvantages, and the first two are finite: they will come to an end one day. Nuclear power is here, it works, the technology is well understood and it is already making a substantial contribution in a number of countries. This is illustrated in Figure 7.3 above. A substantial investment has been made in developing the technology to date, and that investment will not be lightly abandoned. Perhaps Sir Brian Flowers, one of the pioneers in the field expresses the realities of the situation best when he says:(3)

Nuclear power is the only energy source we can rely upon at present for *massive contribution to our energy needs up to the end of the century*, and if necessary beyond.

The emphasis is given by Sir Brian, not by us. In a very honest and candid review of the subject (3) the first chairman of the Atomic Energy Commission in the US says that he has become a severe critic of the industry and also sets out what, in his opinion, has gone wrong. He makes the point we have already made, that nuclear power *cannot* be abandoned, and discusses ways in which it can be made safer for the future. In assessing the value of his remarks, we remember that not only was he an early promoter of the use of nuclear power for the generation of electricity, but despite his enthusiasm for a development programme he did not fail to warn of the radiation hazards and recommend steps to be taken that could lead to their reduction or even elimination. He had a full knowledge of the risks involved and declared: 'The rash proliferation of atomic power plants is one of the ugliest clouds overhanging America.' The present situation is well summed up in the last chapter of his book, where he says:

Nuclear energy is by no means finished: it remains one of the great hopes of mankind ... but we need to back away from our present nuclear state in order to find a better way, a route less hazardous to human health ... The decade of the 1980s will be crucial ... never before have we been so gravely menaced by what our science and technology have created ...

and then concludes:

We *have to make a new start* in order to find a better, cleaner, safer way of producing electric energy from the atom ... the best way to achieve plenty of energy for all is through the creation of more energy ... safe energy.

The Third World is littered with the corpses of ill-considered nuclear ventures, from Mexico through Iran to the Philippines. In each case, one or more of the elements vital for success have been lacking. Either the technology was not there, or the necessary industrial base, whilst politics often played a dominant role. Yet, despite the stalemate that seems to have developed in the West, the East, including Japan, Taiwan, South Korea, to some extent India and soon China, have pinned their hopes to the continuing development of nuclear power. For them it is sheer necessity.

Their positive attitude may yet reverse the current trend in the West where, apart from massive objection and resistance amongst the general public, many of the plants now in operation are said to be 'managerial and financial disasters that have produced higher electric bills ... opponents and critics are ready to write its [nuclear power's] obituary'. But they are likely to be disappointed.(26) In 1984 alone, 34 new plants were brought on stream, increasing the world's nuclear capacity by some 17 per cent.

Conclusion

Whilst the major accident in the nuclear power plant at Three Mile Island brought much adverse publicity and the public campaign against the proliferation of such power stations is being maintained, it is evident that such plants will continue to be built and brought into operation worldwide. The prevention of disasters, such as did occur at Three Mile Island, come back to sound design, effective safety measures and proper regulation, all of which are currently possible and are being applied quite effectively in many countries with continuing programmes for the construction of nuclear power plants. There is no doubt that the nuclear power industry still has a future.

References

1 Kharbanda, O.P. and Stallworthy, E.A., *How to Learn from Project Disasters: True-life Stories with a Moral for Management,* Gower, 1984. See Chapter 2: 'Killed by kindness'.

2 Stobaugh, R. and Yergin, D., (eds), *Energy Future: Report of the Energy Project of the Harvard Business School,* Random House, 1979.

3 Lilienthal, D.E., *Atomic Energy: a New Start,* Harper & Row, 1980.

4 Lynch, D., *Your High-performance Business Brain: an Operator's Manual,* Prentice Hall, 1984.

5 Cantelon, P.L. and Williams, R.C., *Crisis Contained,* US Dept. of Energy, 1982.

6 TMI Advisory Panel on Health Research Studies, *Mobility of Population within 5 Miles of TMI,* Harrisburg, Pa., 1981.

7 Zeigler, D.J. *et al,* 'Evacuation from nuclear technological disaster: TMI Case Study', *Georg R,* 71, January 1981, pp. 1-16.

8 Ford, D.F., *Three Mile Island: Thirty Minutes to Meltdown*, Viking, 1982.

9 Hu, Tei-Wei and Slaysman, K.S., 'Health related economic costs of TMI accident', *Socio-Economic Planning Science*, 18, No.3 1984, pp.183-193.

10 Report: *Economist*, 284, 31 July 1982, pp.77-8.

11 Articles: 'R_x for nuclear power', *Technology Review*, 87, February/March 1984, pp.33-56.

12 McCracken, S., *The War Against the Atom*, Basic Books, 1982.

13 Stokes, H.S., 'Asia's nuclear power boom', *Fortune*, 109, 16 April 1984, pp.84-7.

14 Article: 'Debate over a frozen plant', *Time*, (US edn), 24 December 1984, p.124.

15 Article: 'Push for nuclear power recalibrated', *Business Korea*, 1, pp.12-14.

16 Fairlamb, D., 'Europe counts on nuclear energy', *Duns Business Monthly*, 122, December 1983, p.75.

17 Article: 'Premature Obituary for Nuclear Power', *Fortune*, 109, 20 February 1984, pp.123-4.

18 Article: 'Nuclear power: who carries the can?', *Economist*, 286, 29 January 1983, pp. 35-6.

19 Eppinger, J., 'Nuclear energy on the brink', *Science Digest*, 93, February 1985, pp. 56-9.

20 Hargreaves, Ian, 'A 16 million word fallout', *Financial Times*, (London), 8 March 1985.

21 Article: 'Where utilities and anti-nuclear activists agree', *Business Week*, 16 April 1984, p.185.

22 Guentcheva, D. and Vira, J. 'Economics of nuclear vs. coal: big is beautiful?', *Energy Policy*, December 1984, pp.439-451.

23 Article: 'Nuclear and coal equal in 1983 generating costs', *Energy*, 10, No.1, Winter 1985, p.27.

24 Article: 'Man of the year: Wm. B. Derrickson', *Eng. News Record*, 9 February 1984, p.48.

25 Stallworthy, E.A. and Kharbanda, O.P., *Total Project Management: from Concept to Completion*, Gower, 1983.

26 Cover story: 'Pulling the plug', *Time*, 13 February 1984.

8   Synthetic fuels – still a dream

Let us first define what a synthetic fuel is. It is a liquid fuel derived from a solid fuel, such as oil from coal or shale. There has been a lot of interest in synthetic fuels because oil, or more properly petroleum and gas are among the least abundant of fuels, particularly in comparison to coal. When petroleum and all its products first rose sharply in price, during the so-called 'oil crises' of 1973 and 1979, a lot of interest was displayed in coal and all its possible products, since coal began to be competitive in price as compared with petroleum, but the position is changing once again. The cost of winning coal rises steadily over the years, with inflation, since much of that cost is labour cost. However, in the case of petroleum products, prices have been falling since 1980, with supply exceeding demand. This trend is likely to continue, unless there is a major political upheaval in one or more of the producing countries.

There are more reasons than the direct economic advantage that synthetic fuels might have over petroleum products to create the substantial interest being displayed. For instance, even when coal is a bargain in terms of its fuel value, its use is limited. It can be used economically to generate power in thermal stations, but it is of no use at all in transport applications. Here liquid fuel dominates, so that the conversion of coal to liquid fuels can be very attractive once the price is right. Then again there are countries, such as South Africa, who have no other choice. With practically no local oil resources and constantly under the threat of an embargo on oil imports, that country has developed the production of synthetic fuels on a major scale. Their most recent plants, SASOL TWO and SASOL THREE, together represented an investment of some US$7 billion and use some 70 million tonnes of coal a year.

Is synthetic fuel a viable proposition?

We do not know whether the plants, even the more recent ones, that have been built in South Africa are viable and can make a profit, because the prime motivation for their construction was strategic, not economic. Because of their strategic importance, all details of their operation have been withheld. It is on record that the *South African Coal, Oil and Gas Company,* SASOL for short (the initial letters are derived from that same name, written in Afrikaans) insist that this new generation of plants are economically viable (1) but whether that is in fact so we do not know. That will only be known when this 'oil from coal' process is adopted elsewhere in the world.

Whilst there was considerable enthusiasm for such projects, especially in the US, immediately following the 'oil crisis' of 1973 and it was anticipated that such plants would be multiplying worldwide within a few years, that has never happened. The birth of this new industry, expected at that time to strain the available resources of engineering manpower and the plant fabrication facilities, was hailed thus:(2)

Synfuels are a-coming!
There's no business in sight.
Their plants will be bright.
Won't they hurry, hurry, hurry on?
Won't they hurry, hurry, hurry on?
Synfuels are a-coming -
But will they a-light?

The US construction company Fluor played a large part in the construction of the latest synfuel plants in South Africa and in 1979 they signed a marketing agreement with the South African company for the use of their coal conversion technology in the US.(3) Yet, despite the wide publicity that Fluor has given to the availability of the process in the US, nothing much seems to have happened. One obstacle, apart from the continuing recession, could be the low thermal efficiency of the process, which some observers allege will make the process obsolete within ten years. Another problem is the environmental impact of such plants. There is a very high usage of water, gaseous effluents need extensive treatment and there is a very large volume of ash to be disposed of. Another problem lies in the fact that areas rich in coal, tar sands and other raw materials for synfuels are usually deficient in water resources. But are these the real reasons for the fact that the production of synthetic fuels from coal remain but a dream, so far as the construction contractors who would like to get the work, are concerned?

What went wrong?

There seems to be no doubt at all now that plants are *not* going to be built for the manufacture of synthetic fuels: not even in the US, where the Government planned financial participation and was prepared to provide large subsidies in order to reduce the financial risk for private investors.(4) Despite the potential support the grand billion-dollar schemes still remain a dream. This comes out clearly in the titles given to the many articles that have appeared both in the technical and the popular press on the subject in the US. Typical of such headlines are:

Synfuel hopes burn out
Synfuels not in this century
A fading dream
Synfuel program dead
Synfuel – the fragile future

And so we could go on ... and on. The term 'synfuel' is of course, the americanisation of the phrase 'synthetic fuel' and the headlines speak for themselves. There is no doubt, as read these various articles, that the basic reason for the failure of the 'synfuel program' in the US is the fact that oil prices have been falling and even more importantly, no one knows what is going to happen next with oil prices. The future is completely unpredictable. Most certainly the steady rise in oil prices anticipated in the late seventies has not come about.

A number of major synfuel projects were conceived not only in the US but all round the world. There was great enthusiasm, detailed plans were being made and even finance was arranged. But one by one the schemes were dropped in the face of the changing assessments of the economic situation. Typical of these was a gasification plant (gasification is the first step in changing coal to oil) at Beulah, North Dakota in the US. This plant was conceived by the *Great Plains Gasification Association*. The project was completed at a cost of US$2 billion including US$1.5 billion of government aid, but it could have accumulated losses of some US$800 million in its first ten years of operation. This means that the project could only operate with government aid – and that

aid is continually under threat. Even Exxon, the largest corporation in the US, with revenue and capital exceeding US$100 billion,
abandoned its shale project after spending billions of dollars. The
commentary on the collapse of that company's schemes makes the
point that such massive projects, which have a profound effect on
the local environment, will only succeed if the government
regulations relating to safety, health and the protection of the
environment are both clear and practical, if the end products can
be competitive in the open market and land leases are available at
reasonable rates.(5)

The Synfuel Corporation

This corporation was set up in 1980 by an Act of Congress, with
the promise of funds totalling US$88 billion over twelve years. The
specific objective of the corporation was to reduce the nation's
dependence on oil. This hope has since largely faded away and the
company itself may have disappeared by the time this book is in
your hands, having spent – or perhaps misspent – some US$10
billion!(6) A certain Edward Noble at one time advocated abo-
lishing the corporation because it had become 'the pot for a lot of
mischief', but on becoming its chairman he changed his tune and
declared: ' ... [it] could be an insurance policy' in the case of
another energy crisis. He has elaborated on this theme saying:(7)

> We don't need synfuels today. But the lead time is absolutely
> too great to wait until you need them.

Perhaps we should explain that term 'lead time'. It is the time
taken from commencing the design of a plant to its successful
operation. Such plants had been planned on the grand scale,
would have cost billions of dollars and taken many years to
complete. It is alleged that only such major installations can be
operated economically, but that is a concept that is coming
increasingly under suspicion. Indeed, one successful instance we
quote a little later tends to indicate the opposite.

A Senate Committee investigating the activities of the Synfuel
Corporation found that it was being run like a 'family-owned'
business. That could be a good thing in this day and age, but that
was not all. They alleged numerous instances of mismanagement
and misconduct. With some two hundred employees, there were
just two project awards in three years, the administrative costs
being as high as US$35 million. No wonder the corporation was

termed 'the greatest pork barrel in US history'. Victor M. Thompson Jr., the president, resigned following criticism. It was said that he was also chairman and chief executive of the Utica Bankswares Corporation and did not inform the corporation of his personal involvement. Two part-time directors, Milton Mason Jr. and C. Howard Wilkins Jr. resigned when the Congress called on them to submit detailed financial reports of their non-governmental financial involvement. Another director, John Carter, resigned due to conflict of interest with his private business activities. All in all the corporation has been losing directors and managers almost as fast as projected synfuel projects have been falling out as contenders for federal aid through the corporation.

With this background it is no wonder that attempts are now being made to wind up the corporation, although the pretext is the objective of reducing the budget deficit. President Reagan has sought to cut as much as US$8 billion out of the US$14 billion currently available to the corporation to help it finance synfuel projects. As a compromise a cut of US$5.4 billion has now been agreed. Meanwhile the vacancies caused by the various resignations have not been filled, with the result that the corporation cannot assemble a quorum, should it wish to sanction aid. Applications continue to pour in but the majority of these remain incomplete and lapse by default. The corporation has been left totally ineffective, with its employees wondering not only about the future of the corporation but also their own future. Recent applications for aid include a wide range of projects in terms of size, from 300 to 40,000 barrels per day oil equivalent. Some are for oil conversion processes, some for the manufacture of methanol or ammonia, from raw materials such as high sulphur coal and tar sands. But whatever their merits they are not likely to receive support via the Synfuels Corporation, despite that being its only reason for existence, if it survives.

Have synfuels a future?

Coal was a major source not only of energy but also of gaseous fuels and industrial chemicals until the advent of cheap oil and natural gas. Whilst the sharp rise in the cost of petroleum products through the seventies revived interest in coal, particularly as a source of synthetic fuels, its economic advantage is by no means as great as had been thought. This has been largely due to the interplay of market factors. Synthetic fuel projects became attractive as oil prices rose, but the oil producers, seeing the danger, particularly in the context of reduced demand due to the recession, cut their prices. Their strategy has to some extent paid off, since numerous synfuel projects around the world have been cancelled. Had these projects been implemented oil prices would have dropped even further because of the continuing and increasing over-capacity.

The only commercial process operating today for the production of synfuels from coal is the Fischer-Tropsch process, first developed in Germany before the Second World War and further developed by Sasol in South Africa. This is an indirect gasification process. That is, gas is first produced and this gas changed to liquid fuels by a further catalytic process. The various process steps are indicated in Figure 8.1. The direct production of liquid fuels from coal is expected to be more economic, but such processes have yet to be proved commercially. But there is no simple solution and much will depend on local demand, since the range of products, both gaseous and liquid, from the two alternative processes is likely to be very different.

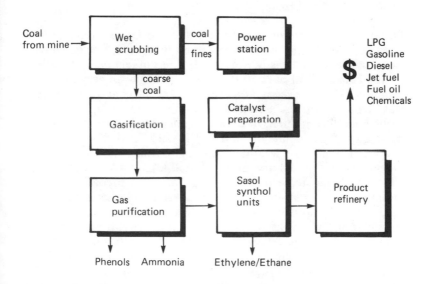

Figure 8.1 Simplified flowsheet for Sasol Two
Coal is sized and screened, with the sized coal going to a gasification unit. Purified synthesis gas passes to the synthol reactors, where exothermic Fischer-Tropsch reactions produce gases which are condensed and distilled, to produce a range of motor fuels and by-products as indicated.

World coal reserves are estimated to be far greater than those of petroleum and natural gas, with the result that forecasters tend to predict a future for coal, in the long term. For instance, one exhaustive study (8) made two basic assumptions:

A doubling of the world population between 1975 and 2030
Higher growth of energy usage in the developing countries

This leads to the conclusion that the liquefaction of coal could begin on a major scale around the year 2000 and rise to more than 30 million barrels per day (oil equivalent) by the year 2030. However, coal liquefaction is unlikely to start outside South Africa before the mid-nineties, but could be well established by the year 2020. All this assumes that neither nuclear nor solar energy will become major contributors over the same period. But that is very much in the long term. In the short term it seems fairly certain that the interest in synfuel production has collapsed.

Prospects for the US

Of all countries, there is no doubt that the US offered the best prospects for the production of synfuels from coal, since coal is so freely available and easily won there. It has in fact been described as 'the Persian Gulf of coal'.(9) Yet there has been very little real progress. After the second oil crisis in 1979 the coal industry there was characterised as 'a somewhat frumpy middle-aged ballerina rushed out of retirement to fill an unanticipated gap in a show that must go on. Suddenly the old girl is back in demand'. In this context it is no wonder that some of the major oil companies, including Continental and Shell, started taking a keen interest in what was being termed 'black gold', buying up coal fields and initiating process research. The interest in synthetic fuels was indeed so widespread that an exclusive Newsletter covering the subject worldwide was published by McGraw-Hill with the title *Synfuels*. An 8-page review was published weekly for a subscription of US$400 a year.

But the initial enthusiasm soon waned, as we have seen, due largely but not entirely to the falling price of oil, which made the production of synfuels from coal steadily less competitive. Synfuels are still believed to have a future in the US, but any immediate action has been stalled by the oil glut and the more realistic cost estimates that are now being made.(10, 11) Much of the initial inertia has been attributed to the alleged mismanagement and incompetence of the Synfuel Corporation. In a report issued late in 1983 (12) a US Senate Committee stressed this, giving concrete examples. Unless there are major changes the corporation is likely to collapse, and many prospective synfuels projects with it.(13) But another problem it appears, besides mismanagement, is the fact that the technology is still not there.(14) Whilst it is true that South Africa have made major strides in this area their technology is some fifty years old. Various alternative processes are being investigated and some show promise, but the very novelty of the processes coming forward means that cost estimates for major installations – and they have to be very big to be worthwhile – are highly suspect.

To illustrate this point, we would mention one study of the cost estimates and performance of 44 pioneer process plants built by the private sector in North America over the past 15 years.(15) This report found that very large cost estimating errors resulted from the unproven technology and the complexity of the plants. Such plants handle solid materials, demanding a very different approach to the liquids/gases type of installation with which those involved were actually familiar.

A case in point

However, we would not wish to create the impression that the programme was a complete disaster. To illustrate the type of development that can be successfully carried out, let us cite the case of the plant at Cool Water in the Southern Californian desert south of Los Angeles in the US.(16) Here we have a blend of new and old technology. This project was said to be the United States' first commercial-scale plant to produce a clean burning gas from coal, that is then used to generate electricity. The Bechtel Power Corporation's Los Angeles Power Division started construction in December 1981 and the plant was completed in the fall of 1984. To quote the project manager:

> The 100-megawatt Cool Water Project is a commercial-size module to establish a technological and economic basis for 500-megawatt or larger facilities – to demonstrate the ability to compete in cost with direct coal-fired plants but without their pollution problems. Cool Water's successful operation may launch a new breed of power plant, one that could be in commercial operation by the 1990's – which is much sooner than other alternative power-producing options.

The 100 megawatts of power will be produced from 1 000 tonnes of coal a day and will serve some 50 000 customers of Southern California Edison, the nation's fourth largest utility.

The process goes as follows: coal will be ground, mixed with water to form a slurry and then pumped to a gasifier, where it will be combined with oxygen. Under high pressure and temperature partial combustion takes place, producing a gas which is then cleaned and desulphurised, using proven processes. This clean gas is then burnt. The electricity is produced in two phases: first the gas, through combustion, drives a gas turbine generator: then, waste heat from the turbine is used to produce steam in a heat recovery boiler, which combines with steam from the gasifier to drive a *second* steam turbine generator. The advantages are said to be that, as compared with conventional coal-fired plants, where cleanup takes place *after* combustion, here it occurs *before* combustion. This means that much smaller volumes of gas have to be handled and it is possible to use a wide range of coal types whilst maintaining atmospheric emissions well below California standards. In addition, utilities with a heavy investment in oil- and gas-fired units will be able to convert to a coal-based synthetic fuel without making major modifications. Thus the final objective is the replacement of gas and oil firing by coal.

Whilst the project, costing some US$300 million, has been privately financed, when decreases in oil and natural gas prices put viable economic operation of the plant in jeopardy, application was made for price support guarantees to the Synthetic Fuels Corporation. This has been granted, with Cool Water receiving a commitment for up to US$120 million in price support during the first five years of operation, to compensate for the differences between actual production cost and the prevailing price of conventional energy supplies. The Southern California Edison project manager comments:

> After five years we expect the plant to be operationally viable. Costs for fossil fuels are likely to increase while those to produce synthetic fuels drop as technology improves.

But, in the context of the synthetic fuel programme, we see that the plant is *not* commercially viable as built, its profitability being threatened by falling oil and gas prices. As we have seen from our survey, it is this fundamental economic fact, generated by the decline in demand for energy, that is at the root of the failure to develop synfuels worldwide.

New Zealand has a go

Because of this sensitivity to the price of oil, the financial risks associated with the design and construction of a synfuel plant are quite high and those who finance them have to share those risks. This is well illustrated by a plant being built in New Zealand, concerning which one article carried the headline: 'Is it sinful for bankers to think big in New Zealand?'(17) This natural gas-based project is estimated to cost some US$1.7 billion and is being built at Motunvi on the west coast of North Island. Its basic products will be methanol and petrol, the New Zealand government taking a 75 per cent share, and Mobil 25 per cent. The first step, the production of methanol, involves a proven ICI process for which the construction company Davy McKee are licensees and have been engaged as contractors. The second step, however, the conversion of methanol to petrol, involves a newly developed Mobil process using zeolite catalyst proved to date on a 150 gallon per day pilot plant in their laboratories in New Jersey. The

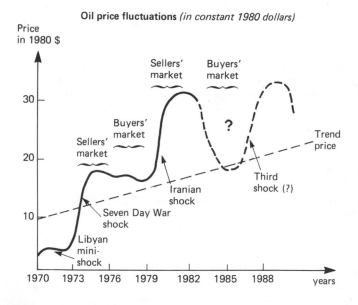

Figure 8.2 Fluctuations in the oil price
This graph gives an approximate indication as to the sharp rise in the price of oil on the world market since 1970. If the expected fall fails to materialise, the trend will of course be much steeper. (Reproduced by courtesy of Compagnie Francaise des Petroles, Paris.)

commercial plant now being built is some three thousand times bigger. We have demonstrated in the past that scale-up, though not necessarily of such a magnitude as this, is feasible (18) but we still await project operating results to demonstrate its success.

Probably the most important aspect of this unusual installation is that it shows that the production of synfuels is not completely dead. Despite all the pessimism a few projects have survived (19) but there is no doubt that no major steps will be taken until there is a clear economic advantage – and that will only come if oil prices harden once again, which appears unlikely until the end of the eighties, if the technical forecast presented in Figure 8.2 is any guide. Whilst it is always possible that there could be a major process technology 'break through', offering a competitive process even at the current prices of coal and liquid fuels, this could well take twenty years to bring to maturity, with major plants in full operation. Whilst there seems to be no doubt that synfuels will eventually be needed, the great question is: when? One commentator said:

> Even if the price of oil shot back up, you still wouldn't have industry flocking back to synfuels. That won't happen again in this century.

This may well be true, although we would expect a series of smaller projects to go forward. Here the financial risk would be less and such plants would establish the feasibility of the technology, ready for a time – perhaps – when such plants became a necessity.

Conclusion

We have seen, in our review of the efforts that have been made, worldwide, to inaugurate the production of synthetic fuels, that only urgent economic or strategic necessity gives the necessary spur. In South Africa major plants have been built, using long established, effective but probably expensive technology. The spur there was strategic. Elsewhere the economic climate has not remained favourable long enough for such plants to be designed and built. Whilst the 'oil crisis' of 1973 caused the US government to inaugurate a major project for the financing of such projects, this has never moved forward on any significant scale and is now likely to collapse. Whilst the causes of failure are said to be mismanagement and incompetence, we suspect that had realistic viable projects been to hand they would have been pursued with vigour and received the appropriate support. But the technology is not yet proven. The known processes are expensive and cheaper alternatives have yet to be successfully demonstrated. That may take many years.

References

1 Mosert, D.F. 'A client's view on project planning and cost control as applied to jumbo petrochemical projects'. An address given by Dr. Mosert, of SASOL Limited, at a symposium on project planning and cost control, organised by the South African Institute of Building, September 1979.
2 Wall, J.D., 'Synfuels: birth of an industry', *Hydrocarbon Processing*, 60, June 1981, pp. 119-123.
3 News article: 'Fluor and SASOL in Mktg. Pact', *International Roundup*, October 1979. (This is a monthly employee newspaper published by Fluor.)
4 Blakely, T., 'Financial assistance planned for synfuels plants', *Hydrocarbon Processing*, 60, June 1981, pp. 124-6.
5 Article: 'Synfuel hopes burnout', *Fortune*, 109, 23 January 1984, p.41.
6 Bunnell, R., 'The fragile future of synthetic fuels', *Nations Business*, 72, March 1984, pp.42-3.
7 Kharbanda, O.P. and Stratton, A., 'Energy feedstocks in the chemical industry', *Chem. Ind. News*, April 1984, pp.921-2.
8 Stobaugh, R. and Yergin, D., *Future Energy: Report of the Energy Project at the Harvard Business School*, Random House, 1979.
9 Sheets, K.R., 'Synfuels: Washington's $15b orphan', *US News*, 94, 17 January 1983, pp.58-9.
10 Folkerts-Landau, E., 'Synfuels: the $88b mistake', *Policy Report (Case Institute)*, 5, September 1983, pp.1+.
11 Subcommittee on oversight of government management: 'US synthetic fuel corporation: a report', Washington DC, September 1983.
12 Pasztor, A., 'Fading dream', *Wall St. Jnl.*, 204, 9 August 1984, pp.1+.
13 Merrow, E.W. *et al.*, 'Understanding cost growth and performance shortfalls in pioneer process plants'. Report prepared by the Rand Corporation for the US Department of Energy, September 1981.
14 Article: 'Is it sinful for bankers to think big in New Zealand?',

Economist, 283, 12 June 1982, pp.93-4.

15 Article: 'A synfuel alternative', *Bechtel Briefs,* January – February 1984, pp. 7-9. (*Bechtel Briefs* is published for the employees and friends of the Bechtel Group of companies by the Public Relations Department of Bechtel, from San Francisco.)

16 Kharbanda, O.P. and Stallworthy, E.A., *How to Learn from Project Disasters,* Gower, 1983. See Chapter 12, 'The pilot plant *can* be skipped'.

17 Article: 'The synfuel survivors – despite many obstacles, they are moving ahead', *Chem. Week*, 7 September 1983.

18 Editorial: *Fortune*, 23 January 1984, p.3.

9 The anatomy of a coal strike

The United Kingdom is often described as a favoured nation in an increasingly energy-hungry world, since it possesses a wealth of coal, North Sea oil and gas, together with an abundance of spent nuclear fuel from its nuclear power plants. The sharp increase in the cost of OPEC oil in 1973 brought a reassessment of the future of coal in the UK. The coal industry there is almost entirely the responsibility of the National Coal Board (NCB), who in 1974 brought out a *Plan for Coal*, involving the investment of some £1 400 million over the following decade. It was a programme for expansion and included the spending of some £8 million on an intensified programme of exploration to decide on the best sites for future development. However, despite this ambitious plan, coal production has stagnated at around 100 million tons per year as illustrated in Figure 9.1.(1) If we turn to consider the energy requirements for the UK, we find that the 1974 plan for coal, if it had been achieved, would have provided coal far in excess of actual requirements, as illustrated below:

Energy consumption:	Coal	Oil	Others	Total
1984 (consumption):	80	135	100	315
1985 (forecast as 1974 plan):	145	165	140	450

The figures are in million tonnes of coal (equivalent) and it will be seen that coal, if it could have been provided in accordance with the plan, would have been grossly over-produced. In fact, there had been over production for a number of years, allowing the Electricity Generating Board to build up very large stocks of coal at the power stations, whilst the Coal Board itself was also accumulating massive stocks at the pithead. Indeed, it was the

efforts of the Coal Board management to improve the economics
of coal production by proposing the closure of uneconomic pits
that brought on the Coal Strike that began in March 1984.

There is nothing particularly novel about a coal strike, particularly in the UK, but this particular coal strike deserves our
attention, in that it can most justly be termed a disaster – indeed,
a disaster for all concerned. First and foremost, it lasted for a
year and is most certainly the longest national strike that the
UK has ever known. Probably it is the longest national strike that

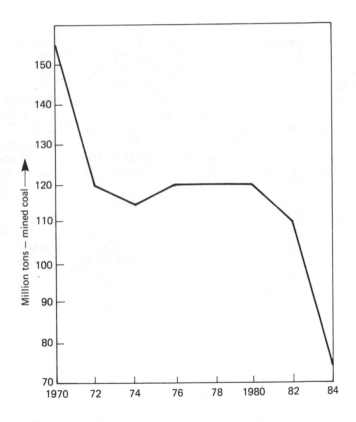

Figure 9.1 UK coal consumption
Here we have a graphic indication of the fall in coal consumption since 1970.
The collapse in 1984 was of course due to the coal strike.

the world has ever known, although we would not venture to be too positive about that. The strike began early in March 1984 – we will not venture to give a precise date, since it began in one area and then spread. It was ended 'officially' by the National Union of Mineworkers (NUM) at the beginning of March 1985, although at least one coalfield, the Kent coalfield, remained on strike for at least another week. When the strike started no one could have predicted that it would last as long as a year and further that the miners would finally return to work without a settlement. But let us not run ahead of our story.

Management reorganisation

As we have said, the coal industry in the UK is largely national-ised, being run by the National Coal Board (NCB). We trust you will remember the initials, since we propose to refer to the two major parties to the dispute, the NUM and the NCB by their initials only from now on. Mr. Ian MacGregor had been appointed Chairman of the Board and he began to institute a management reorganisation, involving rationalisation and the placing of much more responsibility with the management of the various areas into which the industry was divided across England, Scotland and Wales. There is no coal mined in Northern Ireland. The Head Office, located in Hobart House, London, was to be massively reduced. This approach met with much opposition within senior management, made up of those who had worked their way up inside the industry. They resented an appointment from outside the industry and feared he would prepare parts of the industry for privatisation. Further, the process of decentralisation threatened their prospects.

At the same time, production was to be further rationalised, with major new investment in new pits and pits that could be developed economically. This meant, of course, that uneconomic pits would be closed down. This type of rationalisation had been going on apace throughout industry in the UK for the last ten years. A great many unprofitable companies, overstaffed and with low productivity, had been pruned in a similar fashion to bring them into profitability in the face of a recession and stiff competi-tion from overseas. Indeed, Mr. MacGregor had just completed a very similar operation on another major nationalised industry, British Steel. There is no doubt that this countrywide exercise to improve productivity and increase efficiency, at a time of reces-sion, made a substantial contribution to the high level of unemployment in the UK, which was running at more than 3 million, or some 13 per cent of the working population. But till now, because of the continuing subsidy from the government and the protection afforded by a strong union, the coal industry had not been seriously affected. It was, however, grossly uncompetitive and this was affecting the efficiency of other industries dependent on coal: largely because of the high cost of electricity via the Electricity Generating Board.

A pit is to be closed

Over the years a great many worked out and uneconomic pits had been closed in various parts of the country. It is said that some three hundred had been closed over the past ten years or so. So a pit closure was no novelty. Since such pits as *were* closed had mostly been in existence for many years, communities had grown up around them and it was usually the case that the pit was the chief, if not the only source of work in the locality. This type of development had given rise to what is called the 'mining village'. Thus, when such pits closed, the village lost its work, and died. There had been no specific policy that would bring alternative employment to such villages. Insofar as such villages were in what had been styled 'depressed areas', it had been government policy over the years to provide grants, subsidies and the like to firms to encourage new industry to set up there, but such industry was rarely labour-intensive when it came, and so such policies had little impact. The NCB had a policy whereby they offered work to redundant miners at other pits in other localities, but not only were people reluctant to leave their local communities, but there were a lot of practical problems, created chiefly by the scarcity of property to rent.

Crisis came – or was created. We would not dare to take sides and can only tell you that both sides in the dispute allege that the other took occasion to create a crisis situation. Crisis came on 1 March 1984, when the Yorkshire Area Pit Review Board was first told that the NCB planned to close Cortonwood Colliery, located in South Yorkshire, because of its heavy losses. The following day, in London, the NCB announced a national strategic plan to cut production by four million tonnes in 1984-85 with the possible loss of 20 000 jobs. It is suggested that these announcements were made *as if* the decision had been taken and was going to be acted upon irrespective of the views of the NUM. This is suggested by the comments of Mr. Arthur Scargill, the union president, on the event. He wrote, as the strike was coming to its end:(2)

On 6 March last year, NCB Chairman Ian MacGregor announced a pit closure programme which the Board claimed was designed to bring coal supply into line with demand. That programme involved the removal of four million tonnes of capacity from annual output, and meant the closure of 20 pits and the loss of 20 000 jobs. The NUM was already facing NCB threats to close five valuable and viable pits, each with an important contribution to make to our industry.

The 6 March announcement was final proof that, under Government instructions and Mr MacGregor's management, the NCB was on course to sabotage the very future of Britain's nationalised coal industry.

As a consequence (it was said) of the decision to close their colliery, the Cortonwood men walked out straight away and so did those at nearby Bullcliffe Wood, which was also nominated for closure. Four days later, on 5 March 1984, all the South Yorkshire miners struck in support, thus turning a local dispute into something very much bigger. Following the further announcement from London, which Mr. Scargill called 'butchery', the Scottish miners walked out and four days after that, on 12 March, the whole of Yorkshire followed them.

The 'domino' effect

It would seem that this sequential strike action, with area following area, was part of a plan developed by the NUM executive. It was expected that one coalfield after another would respond to the militants' strike calls, thus circumventing the union rule book's requirement that a national strike can only be called after a national ballot showing more than 50 per cent in favour of the strike. At least three such ballots had been held in recent years. Each time the national executive of the NUM had recommended strike action and each time they had failed to get a majority vote, so it must be assumed that the executive believed that much the same thing would happen again. It therefore relied on the 'domino effect' to get all the miners out on strike.

But things did not work out quite as had been expected. By 5 April it was clear that the Nottinghamshire miners were going to work on and rebuff their union. They had held a local ballot which was against strike action and they maintained that all the while the NUM refused to organise a national ballot they would continue working. They were not alone, although the Nottinghamshire coalfield was the biggest that took this view. There was further significant support in the Midlands, and some support in Lancashire. As a result, some 50 000 miners stayed at work, out of a total of about 185 000 men said to be members of the NUM.

The flying pickets

It was of course an integral part of NUM policy to maximise the effect of the strike, in the expectation that the greater its effect on the national economy, the sooner their ends would be achieved. By the middle of March 1984 the pickets from the areas already on strike had succeeded in shutting the Scottish and Welsh coalfields, with more than 100 000 miners out on strike. This type of picketing had been made illegal: it was only lawful to picket outside your *own* place of work. On 14 March the NCB obtained a High Court injunction to stop 'flying picketing', but the union ignored the injunction and carried on, mobilising major pickets and paying the men who went on picket duty. They did *not* provide any strike pay as such. The NCB never enforced the injunction it had secured. It could have gone to court and secured heavy damages and fines could have been incurred for what is called 'contempt of court', but the NCB never initiated such action, despite having secured the injunction. One wonders why, having secured the injunction, they never pursued it.

The NUM asked other unions not to cross their picket lines. Whilst the Railway, Transport and Seaman's unions promised support, they were largely unable to give it, because the response of their membership was very patchy. As a result the intensity of picketing increased, both outside working pits and at places that were major users of coal, such as coke plants and coal-fired power stations. Picket violence escalated, particularly in Derbyshire and Nottinghamshire. On one day (9 April) more than one hundred were arrested as more than a thousand pickets besieged Cresswell Colliery in Derbyshire. Picket violence and clashes between pickets and the police became daily viewing on the TV screens across Britain. It is said that through the year that the strike lasted more than 10 000 miners were arrested and charged with a range of 'public order' offences. Violence occurred not only at the pit gates but also at and around the homes of working miners.

Confrontation at Ravenscraig

Ravenscraig is a major steel works in Scotland. The steel industry in Britain, as indeed worldwide, was still under threat, despite the massive pruning that had taken place under the chairmanship of Ian MacGregor. Capacity still exceeded the sales that could be achieved on the world market and one solution to this problem and maintain a viable industry would have been to close the Ravenscraig Works. Against this background, the workers at Ravenscraig feared that once the works was closed – and it was threatened with closure due to the shortage of coal supplies – it would never open again. Management would argue that the costs of starting up again – and it is an expensive business, due to lining collapse in the furnaces – would not be justified with a falling market for the products. Both management and workers at Ravenscraig were therefore determined to keep the works in production at all costs. A certain amount of coal was allowed into Ravenscraig, but it was said that this was not sufficient to maintain the furnaces in efficient production. The Scottish miners refused to increase coal deliveries to Ravenscraig via the normal route. As a result the management organised delivery of coal by road and this led to a major confrontation at the gates of the steel works at the beginning of May as coal lorries ran the gauntlet of massive pickets.

It was through the month of May that strife intensified almost everywhere. In that month 57 miners were accused of 'riotous assembly' at Mansfield, Mr. Scargill's wife was arrested on a Nottinghamshire picket line, extra police patrols moved into some pit villages to counter intimidation of working miners and 41 police and 28 pickets were hurt whilst 82 were arrested outside the Orgreave coking plant. Mr. Scargill was amongst those arrested on that occasion.

The first death

It was on 15 June 1984 that the first death occurred that could be directly attributed to picket action. A miner was killed under a lorry during picketing at the Ferrybridge power stations. Three days later eighty were injured, including twenty-eight police during running battles outside the Orgreave coking plant. This was said to be the strike's worst day of violence. The violence continued through to November, but the intensity slowly abated. However, the impact of violence took the headlines once again when on 30 November a South Wales taxi driver was killed by a concrete post dropped from a bridge as he was driving a working miner to his pit. Two strikers were charged and later convicted of this crime. There seems to be no doubt that this was the turning point so far as violence was concerned. Public revulsion was so great that it was obvious that continuing violence would only fuel the increasing antagonism to the strike throughout the country. The government had made its attitude very clear at this time. Pit gate battles had intensified because of the steady drift of miners back to work and the Prime Minister (Mrs. Thatcher) warned: 'Violence will not succeed.'

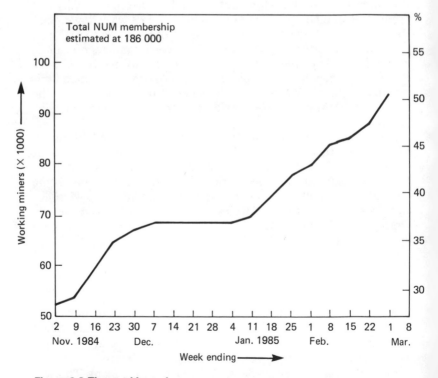

Figure 9.2 The working miners
Some 50 000 miners remained at work throughout the year-long strike. From the beginning of November 1984 there was a slow return to work, which accelerated rapidly once it was apparent that negotiations had broken down.

How not to negotiate

A series of meetings took place between the NCB and the NUM, but all ended without result. The key issue was the closure of uneconomic pits. The NCB insisted that it had, as part of its management role, both the right and the duty (under the Act setting it up) to manage, and so make the final decision with respect to closure. It was prepared to consult and had always done so, in accordance with established procedures, but the Board asserted it had the right to make the final decision. It must not be forgotten that there were fierce passions on both sides, and that the strike was much governed by emotion. Union loyalty was still a potent force.

There were a variety of peace initiatives. At the beginning of September Mr. Robert Maxwell, owner of the *Daily Mirror*, sought to bring about a reconciliation, but his effort was stillborn. A month later the special conciliation body set up by law to mediate in strikes tabled a plan that was rejected by the NUM. At this time another union working in the mining industry, known as Nacods, whose members were responsible for pit safety, threatened to strike, giving seven days notice to the NCB. No one could go underground without a member of Nacods being present, so a strike by this union would have closed all working pits down, thus bringing complete shut-down. However, a formula was agreed with the union and the threatened strike was called off. There was an attempt to build on the agreement that had been reached with Nacods in negotiation with the NUM, but the talks finally collapsed. Thus, at the end of October, the NCB asserted that 'it had nothing more to offer'. Nevertheless, the Trades Union Congress entered the arena, seeking to achieve a resolution of the problem through its secretary, Mr. Willis. Following a series of informal meetings with both the NCB and the NUM and finally with the Government, a TUC committee drew up a revised peace formula: two previous drafts had been rejected by the NUM. This was presented to the miners executive, meeting in London – we are now towards the end of February 1985 – and was once again rejected. As a result the Coal Board said: 'We have nowhere further to go.' Throughout this period the number of miners returning to work was steadily growing, as indicated in Figure 9.2, so that there was mounting pressure on the union to reach an agreement. It appeared that the prospect of negotiation held up the return to work, so at this point the Coal Board refused any further negotiation whatever. They took full page advertisements

in most of the daily and Sunday newspapers with a banner
headline:

This was our final word. We just have no further to go

As a result there was a record return to work – 3 807 in one day.
This was on the 26 February 1985 and two days later the Coal
Board were able to announce that more than half of the NUM
members were now back at work. The following Sunday, 3 March,
a delegate conference of the NUM called off the strike, with no
agreement on pit closures, the crucial issue throughout the dispute.

Over the period of the strike some seven hundred miners had
been dismissed by the NCB for a variety of offences associated
with the strike, ranging from the stealing of coal to damage to
NCB property and violence against other miners. There was a
demand for an amnesty for all miners so dismissed, but this had
been rejected. It seemed, as the strike was brought to an end, that
this issue was of far more importance to the miners on strike than
the issue of pit closures.

It would appear that the union negotiators, led by Mr. Scargill,
made a number of tactical errors, were intransigent and finally
found that they were completely unable to marshall the support of
the other unions for their cause. It is said that the breakdown in
negotiations at the end of October 1984 was a watershed in the
progress of the strike. It was the union's last real chance to
negotiate its way out of the rigid position it had taken up, but it
failed to take advantage of the opportunity that was there. Trade
union observers point to it as the moment when Mr. Scargill shed
the cloak of an industrial negotiator and came out into the open as
a political fighter. From then on the isolation of the NUM within
the trade union movement became ever more apparent and its
bargaining position grew progressively weaker as the drift back to
work accelerated. The strike entered a period of limbo, with no
peace initiative for nearly three months. Union funds were being
sequestrated and the NCB was offering a cash lure to miners who
went back to work before Christmas. So the strike ended in victory
for the government, who then did their best not to gloat. One
press comment:(3)

the strike ... has been farcical and momentous, cruel and
noble ... [the settlement] ground them down and out.

Parallels from the past

The last attempt at armed insurrection on the United Kingdom mainland is said to have been in 1839, when 7 000 miners descended on the Monmouthshire town of Newport, intending to capture it and set off a chain of insurrections in Birmingham and other towns.(4) It was a miserable failure. Bristling with arms which they had made themselves in secret workshops, the seven thousand revolutionaries cornered some thirty five soldiers and a number of special constables in the Westgate Hotel at Newport. They succeeded in wounding the mayor of Newport and a sergeant, but when the military returned fire they fled like hares, leaving 20 dead and an unknown number of wounded. Whilst their working conditions were atrocious it appears from the analysis given by Dr. Jones in his book that the real reason was revolutionary: they hated the owners, their managers and the police force.

The picture that we are given of the South Wales coal and iron fields at that time is of an area given over to lawlessness, drunkenness, criminality and every kind of violence. Violence was an essential part of any wage bargaining and the main instrument of organised labour was a secret terrorist organisation. Any miner who worked during a strike would be beaten to within an inch of his life and his house would be burned down. It was an early taste of what is now called 'workers' power'. Violence, of course, has been a significant feature of this present strike.

The next major issue involving the miners came in 1926, when there was a General Strike led by them, but that collapsed without achieving anything of significance. It did, however, leave the unions bitter and seriously divided, a situation that lasted for a decade or more. Once again, in 1985, the miners have been isolated in defeat, forced to go back without achieving the objectives they had fought for.

In the early 1970s, striking miners brought down the Heath government, and flying pickets were effective in closing down large areas of industry. Then, Arthur Scargill announced that 'the working class had only to flex its muscles and it could bring governments, employers, society to a complete standstill'.(5) But conditions have changed drastically in Britain since then. There is now a nationally coordinated police force, whose components, whilst retaining their individuality, can rapidly reinforce each other to deal with mass picketing wherever or whenever it occurs. In place of high employment there is heavy unemployment. This largely explains the reluctance of the other unions to support the miners with anything more than words. Yet again, whilst there was a massive energy shortage in the seventies, the 1980s are witnessing the biggest energy surplus of the century. Coal in abundance can be bought at less than half what it costs to mine it in Britain.

With the unions weak, with picketing under control, with fuel available, either by shifting to oil or moving the massive stocks of coal already above ground, there never was a point at which the government had seriously to consider cutting electricity supplies to industry or the home. So the strike failed.

Defeat is called victory

The reactions and statements of the various leaders of the miners as the strike was drawing to a close are an interesting commentary upon human nature. For instance, on the day that some 3 800 miners went back to work, one headline ran: 'And Arthur Scargill still calls it a flop!'(6) When the coalfield delegates decided by a majority vote (98 to 91) to return to work, Arthur Scargill came out of the meeting saying: 'Not a defeat for me'.(7) He said he felt terrific, and listed the strike's achievements: withdrawal of the plan to close five pits and put them in the new colliery review procedure, the Coal Board's failure to implement its 1984-85 pit closure programme and the mobilisation of the entire NUM including the 'magnificent women's support groups'.

The majority of the miners still on strike went back to work on Tuesday 5 March, many walking in procession led by bands and lodge banners. To quote:(8)

> They went back with banners flying, putting on a brave face for the watching world. For many miners, their year-long war of attrition ended in an almost carnival atmosphere, marching to work with local bands, amid cheering crowds.

But the news had been relegated to page two and the headline ran: 'Hiding defeat on the bitter road back'.

How much did it all cost?

The cost of the strike to the nation is most difficult to assess. Arthur Scargill, in the article to which we referred earlier (2) alleged that the cost to the British taxpayer was approaching £7 billion. More conservative estimates put the cost at around £3 billion, made up as follows:(3)

	£ million
Burning oil instead of coal:	1,200
Coal Board losses:	1,100
British Steel:	200
Social security – extra payments:	050
Extra policing (net of tax):	200
Lost income tax:	300
TOTAL:	3,050

In addition, of course, countless small traders in the mining communities must have suffered severely, whilst those firms who normally supply the Coal Board with materials and equipment must have had a bad year. But of course the money goes around and around. The NUM seems to have paid out at least £10 million on picketing and hardship funds. It is interesting to note that the strike hurt the economy far less than might have been expected, presumably because it was one of the least efficient industries. The country just exchanged a loss in one area for a loss in another!

If one looks at the coal industry itself, it is said that some sixty coal faces have been lost for ever whilst major markets have gone elsewhere and may never be recovered. What perhaps is of greatest concern is the legacy of bitterness and hate that may well remain. Reporters interviewing individual miners as the news broke that the strike was over reported as follows:(9)

Some even talked of violent reprisals. 'You watch the accident figures', said one miner. 'In a mine you depend on someone saying "watch your back" when something falls, or not pushing as a train goes past. There are going to be a few bad accidents.' It sounded grim, but it also sounded empty.

What of the future?

Industrial observers hope that the final outcome for this prolonged dispute will be cheaper energy in the UK. The strike has taken a year out of Mr. MacGregor's strategy to develop an industry that would produce competitively-priced coal. Before the strike the NCB was overproducing and could not sell its surplus abroad except at a loss-making price some two-thirds of that it was charging its largest British customer, the Central Electricity Generating Board. Its extra production only created extra losses. With 21 million tonnes of new capacity coming on stream by 1990 from the new pits at Selby and Belvoir, cutbacks at the older pits will have to be accelerated and will be severe, if a profitable industry is to be achieved.

We have seen earlier in Chapter 8 (Synthetic fuels – still a dream) that within the next decade synfuels may well begin to play a significant role and this will bring a substantial increase in the demand for coal. We would expect UK coal to become increasingly competitive on the world market and then it will have a price advantage over both oil and natural gas. Figure 9.3 illustrates the price trend over the past ten years or so for these three basic energy sources in the US, and the trend is very similar in the UK. It will be seen that whilst before the 1973 crisis the difference was marginal it now seems that coal will retain the price advantage it has gained. So the future looks bright if only the industry can be operated economically.

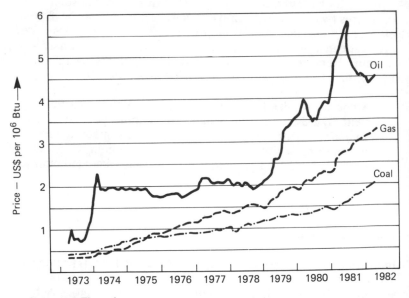

Figure 9.3 The price war
This graph, giving US average delivered prices to electric utilities for coal, fuel oil and natural gas, illustrates that coal is becoming increasingly competitive on world markets. (Source: Federal Energy Regulatory Commission.)

Conclusion

Despite this being the longest-ever strike, it does not appear to have had any substantial impact on the British economy. To a large extent this has been due to the fact that alternative viable energy sources were available and were utilised.

The fundamental issue in this disastrous strike, ignoring all the political overtones, was the right of management to manage. Now, for the first time in years, pit managers will feel that they have the authority to run their collieries. Before the strike it was the branch committees of the NUM who often decided which men worked on which shift and who got the bonus-earning jobs. This was done with the tacit approval of senior management and had the result that many union activists never went down the pit but spent all their time on union affairs. But during the strike Mr. MacGregor has restored power to the local managers. It was they who organised the bussing of working miners, ran local advertising campaigns and were encouraged to deal directly with the men who returned to work. We now expect that the managers will continue in that role, cutting out the union middle-men.

Another issue, not directly related to the mining industry, was the right of a man to go to his place of work without let or hindrance. The Nottinghamshire miners, who continued working throughout the strike, took the NUM to court with the result that the union was fined £200 000 and Mr. Scargill £1 000 for continuing to describe the strike as official. Union funds were sequestrated for the non-payment of the fine and a receiver was finally appointed. It may be said that the outcome has demonstrated that in modern society you can only go so far: you cannot hold a country to ransom. It was essential that the government win and be seen to have won. Economics will now prevail over politics and management will be allowed to manage. Whilst immediately disastrous, this strike, because of its outcome, may well have been a blessing in disguise, doing the British economy more good than harm in the long run.

References

1 Article: 'After victory, a new start for coal', *Economist*, 294, 9 March 1985, pp. 45-7.
2 Scargill, Arthur, 'A battle we had no choice but to fight', *The Observer*, London, 3 March 1985, p.10.

3 Lloyd, J. (Industrial Editor), 'It ground them down and out', *Financial Times*, 4 March 1985, p.23.
4 Jones, D.J.V., *The Newport Insurrection of 1839*, Oxford, 1985.
5 Editorial: 'Fall of King Ludd', *The Daily Telegraph*, London, 4 March 1985, p.14.
6 Norris, D., 'And Arthur Scargill still calls it a flop!', *Daily Mail*, London, 26 February 1985, p.1
7 Article by industrial correspondent, *The Daily Telegraph*, London, 4 March 1985, p.1.
8 Carter, Bryan, 'Hiding defeat on the bitter road back', *Daily Mail*, London, 6 March 1985, p.2.
9 Edwards, Clive, 'Traitors! The cry from a defeated army', *Daily Mail*, London, 4 March 1985, p.2.

Part Four

THE EMERGING
TECHNOLOGIES

10　RCA's slipped disc

The disc problems that we are now going to review relate to what is known as the *videodisc*. What is a videodisc? Even in this day and age that is a question which may still be asked and to answer it we have to relate it to that modern wonder television. The word 'video' describes the recording of photographic images and its major use is in relation to television. Photographic images have been recorded, first alone and then in conjunction with sound, for a great many years, the medium on which the record was preserved being photographic film. Then it was found possible to record both vision and sound together on a magnetic tape and we had what was called the 'videotape', the major users of this system being the broadcasting companies worldwide for the purpose of first recording and then transmitting their programmes. The basic difference between the two systems is that whereas the picture on film is brought to a screen using a projector, the picture recorded electronically on magnetic tape can be transferred electronically to a television transmitter, or to a television receiver.

However, whilst the broadcasting company had no problem with the cost of the apparatus that could read the videotape, the ordinary householder could well find the cost prohibitive and means were sought whereby the cost could be much reduced. Everyone was familiar with the gramophone record, a disc used to store sound in a form whereby it could be replayed cheaply and the manufacturers thought that a similar approach to the reproduction of vision might be equally cheap and popular – hence the videodisc. The magnetic tape record of sound and vision together, when marketed for domestic use, was called a videocassette. RCA, a major firm in the record business in the US, were pioneers in the development of the videodisc and at one time leaders in the market. The company coined the trade name 'Selectavision', having spent some fifteen years on secret development – they called it the 'Manhattan Project' – after another highly secret project with the same name, the development of the atomic bomb. But this was no 'bomb' taking sudden and devastating hold on the market. After five years and the expenditure of some US$500 million, RCA in April 1984 finally decided that this particular disc had 'slipped'. The problem was basically financial. Having spent some US$500 million on the sale of about five hundred thousand videodisc players, they had spent some US$1,000 per player, whilst selling the machines at around US$500. This difference includes development costs, which would not have been so significant could they have been spread over a much larger volume, but that was not to be. Now, why was it that they were not able to build up sales to the volume that had apparently been anticipated?

The story in headlines

A headline is very much like a cartoon, in that it condenses a theme into a short phrase. It can sometimes tell so much in so few words that we find it a very useful way in which to illustrate our stories. What our publisher calls the 'caption' at the head of this section is designed to do just that, as indeed are all our captions, and the writers of articles use the same technique. Quite often a headline also drives home the point being made very effectively. When we review the headlines on articles in the literature relating to RCA and their development of the videodisc, we find they run like this:

> The video disc fiasco
> One of decade's mangiest dogs
> RCA abandons video disc
> Technological star – commercial flop
> It's a product that should have succeeded
> Priority of a decade abandoned
> Never caught on like videocassettes
> Slipped disc – no surprise
> CBS to halt manufacturing video disc
> RCA abandons video disc

In a few headlines you already have the story and you see that what was evidently a very promising technical concept failed in the market. What went wrong, and why? Whilst the failure of their development programme was a major disaster, fortunately RCA were big enough to survive it. However, when we look at the history of this particular company, we find that the videodisc fiasco was not the first such. This suggests that unless RCA can come to terms with the very fast advances now being made in the technology relating to the field in which it works, the company may well 'slip' again. However, it is always possible that the lessons that are there have now been learned. It is those, of course, that *we* must now seek to learn, that being our purpose.

What is it all about?

As we pursue this particular story it is very necessary that we keep in mind the difference that there is between a videodisc and a videocassette. The videodisc has but one purpose – to be played. However the videocassette can be used for both playing and recording. Hence, whilst the machine used to play a videodisc is called a videodisc player, you can buy both videocassette players and videocassette recorders, the latter being somewhat more expensive than the player since they have a recording mechanism as well. The videocassette recorder can record either directly from a television set, thus recording programmes that are being transmitted, or from another videocassette. To achieve that, you had at one time to have another videocassette recorder to play the videocassette from which you wished to record, but now you can buy machines that combine both functions, accepting two cassettes at once.

When the video*disc* and the videodisc player were first introduced to the market, the video*cassette* player and the videocassette recorder were comparatively expensive, costing around US$1,000. It was on this basis that RCA and other manufacturers in the business surmised that in due course the videodisc player would replace the videocassette player. Much of the cost of the videocassette recorder lay in the recording/playing head, as it is called, because great precision is needed to get a good picture. But technological development, led by the Japanese, enabled mass production of a high-precision head, slashing the cost of the videocassette recorder to US$300. As a result the sales of the videocassette recorder doubled every year between 1981 and 1983. It was a tremendous market, over four million being sold in 1983. By contrast, sales of the videodisc player in that year were a mere 300,000, with RCA taking some 75 per cent of those sales. Looking forward to 1984, it was estimated that if the cost of the cheapest model in the videodisc player range was reduced to US$199 sales in that year could reach half a million. However, RCA decided not to follow that course. Instead they pulled out of the business and cut their losses. Other companies in this infant market, such as Zenith Radio and IBM, had done that earlier.(1)

What went wrong?

The videodisc was the pet project of the then chairman of RCA, Edgar Griffith and during his time it was the 'priority of the decade'. His successor, T. Bradshaw, who took over in 1981, came to the subject with a new mind and could therefore take a fresh and unbiased look at the project. He also had the courage to take hard decisions. Hence the decision to abandon the project.

The problem in the market lay, above all, in the fact that the videodisc player never caught on because of its inability to record from the television set. In addition, cassettes were considerably cheaper than discs. There were also other factors that contributed to the final demise of the disc, such as the rapid development of a rental market for cassettes.(2) This was not foreseen by RCA. Cassettes became available for costs as low as US$1 per day. Market analysts were not surprised at the final collapse of the video disc player, since some had been saying that it was long overdue. In retrospect some observers considered the system to be doomed from the very beginning (3) because of its reliance on a technology which, though simple and cheap, was flawed. The flaw lay in the inability to get really superb picture quality. This is not the first time that RCA has 'backed the wrong horse'. Over thirty years earlier RCA opted for its own 45 rpm records, rejecting the Columbia 33-1/3 rpm standard for the LP record. This led to a destructive fragmentation of the market. Later, when the costly but advanced laser technology came along, developed in the European market, RCA did not follow, but stayed with their outmoded needle technology.

Interestingly, those videodisc players using laser technology, an area which RCA has not entered, seem likely to hold their own, despite initial fears that they would become obsolete. Whilst they cost somewhat more, being priced in the shops at around US$700, their picture and sound quality is unmatched. Whilst it is true that at the higher price level the laser videodisc player may never have a mass appeal it is expected that even some video cassette player owners are likely to opt for the laser videodisc player, and it is expected that the market could grow quite significantly if and when the machine can be given a television recording facility. One of the pioneers in this area of laser technology, most appropriately named Pioneer Electric (of Japan) remain committed to the system and have actually been able to increase their sales of the videodisc player and the related discs. However, a Pioneer Electric spokesman has been quoted as saying that 'the failure of laser disc would mean a very dark future for Pioneer'. So what are *they* doing? They are not standing idly by letting events overtake them. They are known to be active in the next generation of videodisc players, said to be an 8mm video machine incorporating a camera and a recorder/player all in one compact package.(4) The market for this is expected to be very substantial and several other manufacturers, both in Japan and the US, are following a very similar line of development. But not RCA – slipping again?

Was it 'sudden death'?

Reading the Wall Street Journal in early April of 1984, when the news broke that RCA were abandoning the video disc player and it became a front page story, one might have been excused for thinking that it all came as a complete surprise to everybody concerned, but as we have said elsewhere this is never actually the case.(5) There are always plenty of warning signs if you will only look for them. Only a month before the news of the decision to cease production broke, RCA was planning to transfer its video disc player manufacturing operation in Bloomington, Indiana to another unspecified location. Since the new location was not specified, those astute enough might well have drawn the conclusion that this was indeed the end of the road, but at the time the market analysts did not seem to react. Three months earlier still, in January 1984, it was reported that video disc players 'are not going great guns but it will remain a profitable business for RCA'. Was this another piece of 'writing on the wall'? With hindsight, we can well say that the company was leading press and public towards the 'death' of the video disc player so far as it was concerned. We are told that when the line was discontinued there were some 12 000 players in stock with RCA and another 150 000 in the hands of the trade. However, since there are some 500 000 video disc players supplied by RCA in the hands of their customers, the company has undertaken to continue the pressing and distribution of the discs used in the machines 'for a few years'.

Once the 'death' was announced, the dealers began to wonder whether the RCA video disc player would become a collector's item in the course of time, but it seems that idea did not get very far, judging from the hurry they were in to return their unsold models to RCA, or to offer them as 'free gifts' along with other items costing five to ten times their price. But we are sure we do not need to tell our readers that nothing is ever free – not even the 'free lunch'!

Where did RCA go wrong? We have already mentioned their failure to seize on the appropriate technology. The company has been left behind in the marketplace time and again because it has failed to appreciate the speed with which changes can take place in electronic goods, because of the rapid advance in technology. Then they have not been able to recognise the appropriate forward-looking technology when it was there. These days there is no need to develop such technology yourself. It is often quicker and cheaper to license or purchase developments made by others. RCA failed completely to be aware of the requirements in the marketplace and the developments that were taking place there. They were 'out of touch'. No wonder, then, that they were left far behind. How far behind has been summed up in the phrase:(6)

It was like working on the Model-T Ford when the 1971 Cadillac is around the corner.

It is very evident that RCA failed to understand and comprehend the advances being made in electronic technology, even though that was its own field of activity. To sum up, we would say that RCA failed to recognise that the consumer considered the facility to record vital to his enjoyment, and lost some US$500 million discovering that simple fact – a fact plainly demonstrated in their own sales by the steady movement from the gramophone record to the cassette for the handling of music in the home.(7) The motivation for this was undoubtedly the ability to record, despite the fact that the quality of reproduction from cassette in the home has never reached that possible with the record. RCA sold both: why didn't they read the message?

Was it a strategic error?

It is as well to remember that RCA manufactured both the videodisc player and the videocassette recorder. They still have a major share in the market for videocassette recorders and that business remains profitable. Perhaps it was thought good policy not to 'put all your eggs in one basket'. That is good advice, but you still need to expand your choices with care. RCA were not the only company who started out developing both the video cassette and the video disc and it is interesting to compare their reaction to the market response with that of their competitors. As early as 1981 a short analysis on the subject was entitled, interestingly enough: 'Will discs slip?'(8) RCA gave their answer to this question some three years too late. On the other hand Sony decided to pull out of video disc development much earlier and went all out to develop the video tape and the video cassette. In the event that has proved a most profitable decision.

RCA launched their videodisc player in March 1981 and the initial market response was good, largely because it was priced in the shops at around US$500, whilst at that time the videocassette player and the videocassette recorder cost twice as much. Encouraged by this RCA increased their production target by some 50 per cent, planning to sell some three hundred thousand machines by the end of 1981, with the associated production of some three million discs for use on the machines. Also because of this initial success two other companies who had also invested very substantial sums in the development of disc systems, JVC of Japan and Philips of Holland, decided to go ahead and market their versions. Sony, on the other hand, withdrew from the field, saying that in their judgment the inability of the video disc system to record programmes from the TV would result in buyers for the home 'consigning discs to the scrapheap'. One wonders whether RCA were aware of this view and what notice they took of it. We suspect they ignored it, because at that time the video disc player was a 'pet project' of the then chairman of the company. It was this blind commitment, it seems, that prevented RCA from seeing where the videodisc was going. Whilst it is technically feasible to record programmes on disc – RCA did it to supply discs to users of their machines – the process is complex and expensive. It involved the use of laser technology and was very evidently going to be out of the reach of the consumer – because of price – for years to come. It is true that the disc had certain advantages over the cassette tape, such as:

1 They cost US$15, prerecorded, in 1981, about half the price of a cassette at that time.
2 There was much better quality of reproduction.
3 There was rapid access to any individual frame (which carries one picture).

However, improvements in cassette technology not only narrowed the price differential but made random access quicker.

This facility for random access is a very interesting feature. The disc has ten times the capacity of a cassette tape, yet access to any individual frame is almost instantaneous. But even this weakness in the cassette tape is likely to be overcome. Toshiba are developing a technology which uses a single loop of tape with several tracks. This single loop takes a mere 30 seconds to go round, and apart from using considerably less tape, which makes it cheaper, it begins to meet the major disadvantage of cassette tape, inability to offer rapid access to individual frames.

The disc may yet survive!

The way that technology develops in the most unexpected directions is truly amazing. At the same time that RCA was abandoning the manufacture of the video disc player we can read an article with the title 'Optical disks: looking up'.(9) The key to this change in course is the development of a one-box system combining audio, video and data storage technology. Pioneer, who were the first to market laser-read video discs had begun to market by the end of 1984 a videodisc player which can read both video discs, which carry films and television items and also audio discs, such as the new laser-read compact audio disc that carries music. Sony are also developing a single player for both compact audio discs and data-storage discs in conjunction with Philips. A compact optical (laser-read) audio disc can store up to 270 000 pages of text, more than ten times the present 3-1/2 inch magnetic floppy discs. The optical disc, for instance, could be the ideal substitute for encyclopaedias, reference books and maps. Publishers may well produce books both in the normal style, as this book but also, as an alternative, on an optical disc, giving the reader the choice. It is said that Sony are even planning a compact version for use on the dashboard of a car, so that maps and other guides can be consulted by the driver as required. Add the Sony development to the progress already made by Pioneer and you have the ultimate in 'magic boxes'. However, this development is unlikely to replace the videocassette recorder, the ordinary cassette player or the floppy disc systems in the immediate future, unless it can be made erasable and re-recordable. Such a system is now said to be coming on the market.(10) This achievement, which was expected to take a good many years, is rightly being hailed as a 'milestone for the industry'.

RCA could well draw a lesson from Sony, whose secret of

success is said to be:(11)

> Knowing what the public wants
> Giving it the very best in what it wants

What does the future hold?

It seems that video discs and computers used together could be a powerful combination indeed. Bring them together and the possibilities are endless. Before going on vacation one could study not only hotel rates, rail and airline schedules, but also see the location come alive on the screen. Major manufacturers such as General Motors and Ford are using video discs to train their dealers and teach their maintenance staff. Other applications include the automated salesman, such as the video screens one sees in multiple stores and airports, training manuals and the like. As the computer becomes more widely available there is no doubt that the potential of the disc can be more fully realised.(12)

Just to demonstrate the degree of development in this area, let us quote briefly from a technical description of a new disk drive designed to be used in conjunction with computers:(13)

> Shugart Corporation is the first American OEM company to announce a laser-based optical disk drive with the introduction of Optimer 1000, a device storing one gigabyte of information (one billion characters or about 400 000 typed pages of text) on one side of a removable 12in. disk.
> Using non-erasable laser technology, the Optimer 1000 provides up to 10 times more online storage capacity than comparably priced magnetic disk drives and has applications in micro and mini computers. It is the first in a family of optical disk drives from Shugart.

Note, as we said earlier, that the data is non-erasable. However it is said that this feature is considered desirable with accounts and the auditing of accounts and this device is said to be aimed at the lower end of the office market place.

In terms of the volume of data that can be stored, we have a quantitative leap. If the floppy disc can carry a hundred pages, then the optical disc can carry a thousand books, including an entire encyclopaedia and telephone directories for several cities.(14). A single optical disc (termed a compact disc) will be equivalent to some fifteen hundred floppy disks or fifty Winchester hard disks. This innovation is already on the market, complete with a portable player incorporating a single 'chip' for control and only a little larger than the disc itself. And who has pioneered this development? Yes, you guessed it — Sony!

Conclusion

It is very evident, as we consider this story of the RCA venture into the videodisc player market, that prolonged experience is no safeguard. It is still possible to 'back the wrong horse', as they say. This means that those venturing into new fields, whether from an established base or not, are always liable to do just that. The real lesson, therefore, is not that mistakes can be avoided. Often they cannot. The lesson rather is that we must learn from the mistakes of others and not multiply mistake upon mistake. If we are going down the wrong path, let us recognise that and have the courage to abandon it before it is too late. We see, too, that new technology and rapid innovation need not be a danger. Provided the situation can be seen for what it is, it can be taken advantage of and profits made. Whilst RCA had to abandon the videodisc player market, at least one firm still survives, largely by pioneering and further technological development may well lead to a resurgence of interest in the video disc by the general public in the process of time.

References

1 Article: 'Videodiscs: what stunted the growth of an infant industry?', *Business Week*, 30 January 1985, p.63.
2 Article: 'Phase out videodisc players', *Wall Street Jnl.*, 5 April 1984, p.3:1.
3 Article: 'Slipped disc: no surprise', *Wall Street Jnl.*, 12 April 1984, p.31:2.
4 Article: 'Pioneer electric: still committed to videodiscs after a wobbly start', *Business Week*, 24 January 1983, pp.60-1.
5 Kharbanda, O.P. and Stallworthy, E.A. *'Corporate Failure: Its prediction, panacea and prevention'*, McGraw-Hill, 1985.
6 Article: 'The anatomy of RCA's Videodisk failure', *Business Week*, 23 April 1984, p.89.
7 Article in *Fortune*, 110, 24 December 1984, p.81.
8 Article: 'Video development — will discs slip?', *Economist*, 280, 15 August 1981, p.69.

9   Article: 'Optical disks: looking up', *Economist*, 290, 3 March 1984, p.85.
10 Article: 'Here comes the erasable laser disc', *Fortune*, 111, 4 March 1985, p. 100.
11 Article: 'What makes Sony run?', *Readers Digest*, (Indian edn), February 1985, p. 60.
12 Article: 'Compact discs: Will they work as well as they play?, *Economist*, 294, 2 February 1985, p.75.
13 Article: 'Light works on disk drive', *Computing Equipment*, UK, Vol.2, No.2, February 1985, p.32.
14 Article: 'Optical discs: thanks for the memory', *Newsweek*, 21 January 1985, p.3.

11 Cable television – the oversold revolution

Whilst cable television is a worldwide phenomenon we dare not assume that all our readers are familiar with the term and what it implies. So let us say, first of all, that whilst the normal television set has an antenna and receives its programmes from broadcasting stations that radiate a range of programmes, with cable television the programmes reach the home via a cable, however they are first received. Because television programmes are radiated using very high frequencies their range is usually quite limited: limited to some 100 kilometres at the most, although there are freak situations where the range can be substantially greater than that. With cable television the station that transmits the programmes may not only provide its own programmes, but also via its own television antenna a number of broadcast programmes. In Europe at least it can extend significantly the number of stations available, because it can install a high and very efficient antenna system, that no ordinary householder could afford. But the quality of reception of course falls off with the more distant stations. It is said that the choice will increase greatly and quality be much improved as and when direct satellite transmissions become available to a wider audience, something that is already beginning to happen, as we shall see.

The story in headlines

Let us adopt this device once more to illustrate what has been happening with cable television over the past few years. A random selection of headlines runs thus:

Growth is slowing
Interest cooling off
Earnings drop sharply
Crowded new world of TV
Cable shakeout begins
Financial tombstone

It is very evident from these headlines, culled from the technical press, that cable television is not prospering as was expected and the reasons for this are most interesting. As we follow the story of cable television and its growth worldwide, you will see some of these headlines clothed with facts and figures.

How it all began

Cable television, when the idea was first mooted, was thought to be the answer to all the entertainment and educational needs of the television user. It was probably oversold, but an excess of enthusiasm is by no means the only reason why it has not developed as was at first expected. As with anything new and novel, there was great excitement among the public and the advertising created an anxiety not to be left out. The cable television companies declared that it would be 'first come, first served', thus implying that those who did not rush in would have to wait a long time. But that initial interest and excitement has now dissipated, at least in many of the developed countries. What has been termed the 'cable revolution' has more recently been transplanted into the developing countries, at least in their urban areas, but it remains to be seen whether it will ever prosper there.

If we may take Bombay as an example in this, the first cable television installations were carried out in a clandestine manner and even now there are no regulations regarding the installation and operation of cable television. The transmitting station would be installed at a central location in a high rise building and there was widespread and unauthorised use of videocassettes. This approach led to the mushrooming of what we might call 'one man shows' all over the city. However, despite the initial enthusiasm among potential users, in the end there were only a few thousand subscribers from among a million owners of television sets. There was no centralised system, so that the cable television company installed a complete facility just to serve a block of perhaps a hundred flats. If the company was fortunate in its location, it might be able to serve a group of high rise buildings adjacent to one another. This meant that almost invariably it was never possible to secure sufficient subscribers to 'break even'. In addition, the market was fragmented, with quite a number of individuals, often of the 'fly by night' type, seeking to 'make a fast buck', as they say. Their promises, largely verbal, were thrown to the winds when they realised that the potential was not there. In addition, much of the material being used on video cassette had been pirated or otherwise illegally obtained and there was the constant risk of seizure. This is the picture of the development in just one city, but it is typical of what has been happening in the developing countries, where regulation has been minimal or non-existent.

Is cable television growing?

If we turn to the developed countries, where there is a degree of regulation, we see that there has been significant penetration, as indicated in Figure 11.1.(1) But whilst some European countries have largely caught up with the US and Canada in terms of the development of cable television, others are virtually free. It is curious that the smaller the country, the larger is the extent of cable television usage. This arises most probably from the fact that the larger countries do not have ready access to foreign programmes, whereas the cable company in the smaller countries, surrounded by other countries, can easily pick up a wide range of alternative programmes. Italy has no cable television and is likely to remain that way because the country is served by a number of private commercial television stations, thus leaving no real scope for the cable television company. Belgium, heading the list in Figure 11.1, with the largest percentage of homes served by cable television, has a very wide choice of programmes via that system. In the southern half of Belgium, which is French-speaking, cable television viewers have a choice of French, Dutch, German and Luxembourg channels as well as their own. It is expected that they will be receiving BBC programmes from the UK once the copyright dispute has been resolved. In The Netherlands those living in the west of the country already get that service, since it is possible to receive the broadcast programmes across the North Sea with a suitable, tall antenna for most of the time. The advent of cable television in The Netherlands was stimulated by the desire of local councils to get rid of the masses of unsightly TV aerials on the roofs of houses in urban areas.

The future of cable television is going to be largely determined by national policy, which in many countries has still to be defined.

The position is changing very rapidly, the introduction of fibre
optic cables on a commercial scale threatening yet another drastic
revolution in the approach. Fibre optic cables have a very high
carrying capacity and there is now talk of using such cabling not
only to introduce television into the home, but also for a wide
range of other services. In Great Britain, following an act of
parliament legislating for the issuing of franchises and with the
introduction of fibre optic cables, cable television may well get a
new lease of life. For instance, in Coventry plans are afoot to
connect up 16 000 homes.(2) This is for the initial trials only. If
successful, the system could be rapidly extended. Coventry has
been chosen because its underground telephone system was almost
completely renewed after the Second World War. This means that
the new cables can be fed through existing ducts, minimising the
amount of excavation required for cable laying. Figure 11.2 shows
two satellite dishes for the service being installed on the roof of the
Telephone Exchange in the centre of Coventry. These will home
in on two satellites orbiting some 23 000 miles above the earth.
These are ECS-1 (European Community Satellite) and Intelsat V.
Subscribers to the service should be able to receive as many as 16
different programmes, assuming that they have that number of

	TV sets	Cable TV
	%	%
Belgium	95	68
Holland	96	60
Denmark	95	60
Sweden	98	52
Switzerland	89	48
Ireland	90	39
West Germany	95	38
France	90	37
Norway	95	24
Great Britain	96	11
Austria	92	5
Finland	95	5

Figure 11.1. Cable TV penetration in developed countries
It all began in the US and Canada, but some European countries are now
catching up. Belgium heads the list of European countries with cable TV.

channels available on their television set.

Another factor creating problems is that of copyright. Then there is the question of advertising revenues and the fact that television advertising standards vary quite markedly from country to country. Whilst you might think that a picture, supported by words in a foreign language, might nevertheless go a long way

Figure 11.2 Satellite dish for cable TV
In this photograph we see two satellite dishes being installed in preparation for a cable TV service in Coventry, in the UK. (With thanks for permission to publish from the photographer, Mr Trevor J. Bryant of Coventry.)

towards advertising a product, it appears that there are only three pictures which mean the same thing in any language: boy-meets-girl, a baby's smile and a traffic jam. Gestures can have very different meanings in different countries, as we have explained at length elsewhere.(3)

The economics are elementary!

The success or failure of cable television is fundamentally a matter of economics. If a cable television project can pay for itself and make a reasonable profit for the sponsor, then it will flourish. What then are the economics of the case? In almost every case, it seems, the economics are suspect. A rich London suburb should be an ideal area for cable television. If, however, such an ideal case is analysed, it seems that the investor would have to wait at least five years before his investment began to make a profit.(4) Yet companies are still seeking to enter the business in Britain.

Even in the States it appears that the prospects are not good, with some of the American cable television companies talking of getting out of the business. Economic calculations show once again that they are not going to make a profit if they keep all the promises that have been made about the service to be provided. Initial cost estimates have doubled, expected subscribers have failed to materialise and the advertisers have disappeared. Typical of the American companies now 'wanting out' is Warner Amex Cable, which was successful in securing one of the biggest franchises ever.(5) That company lost US$70 million on cable television in 1983. It is now trying to curtail its operations in Dallas and Milwaukee, installing one service cable instead of two, thus halving the number of promised channels to 54. The company is also suspending the celebrated *Qube* system, two-way television and community programmes made by and for the local community. Having learnt the hard way, the chairman of the company probably speaks for the entire industry when he says:

> The companies oversold their wares to get franchises but did so in good faith. Cable is a new and uncertain business. Warner's own research [a self-serving but interesting study of six big cable systems] shows that customers are confused by having too many channels. The average household, with 30 to 70 channels to choose from, used only 9 channels a week, and any system offering above 40 was likely to have many empty.

He went on to add that during 1983 a number of programming

services had failed due to slow response from advertisers and the threat of competition from other techniques. Nevertheless optimists still abound. According to one estimate cable television is now available to more than two-thirds of all homes in the US and of these over 40 per cent actually have it.(6) This usage is expected to rise to 70 per cent.

Another expert shares the pessimism of the chairman of Warner Amex, agreeing that cable television is not in good shape. It has had tremendous growth in the US, but most of the enthusiasts have now signed up and further growth is suspect. The system needs large numbers of subscribers if it is to operate at a profit and the advertiser just stays away in the absence of impressive audience statistics. The cable television companies are also faced with loss of revenue due to the 'theft' of their services, by for instance a user running cable to a neighbour. One estimate places such losses as high as US$500 million a year.

The customer is king

With cable television the customer can choose. He can choose, first of all, whether or not he will have it at all and if he has it, he still chooses what he is going to look at. If the customer has television and nothing else, then the provision of cable television offers him a wider choice than he had before.

But of course he has to pay for that choice, a payment which has to be justified in terms of its value or interest to the user. If our potential cable television user already has or purchases a videocassette recorder then his choice is materially widened, with or without cable television. He can record programmes from the television to view when he wishes but in addition, and most importantly, he can purchase or hire videocassettes with recorded films and programmes, or even exchange such cassettes with his friends. Now the choice is very much his. He is no longer limited in choice by either the television stations available to him, or by the content of the channels which a cable television company may bring to him.

In terms of cost, payment for the provision of cable television is generally in terms of a monthly subscription over an agreed contract period: in effect, a fixed charge. With the videocassette the customer pays only for what he wants, when he wants it, whether he purchases cassettes or hires them. He can most probably widen his choice considerably at minimal cost if he hires, or records programmes himself, or copies from another cassette.

The legality of these last two steps is doubtful and the law on such matters varies from country to country, but since the law, if it is there, cannot be enforced, the cost remains nominal. Quality may vary, but people do not usually seek to retain and store programmes. More usually they will record a new programme over the old, so that the initial cost of a videocassette, some US$20, gets spread over a number of viewing opportunities and the cost per programme soon becomes minimal and of much the same order as the cost of rental, around US$1 per day of usage. Thus the owner of a videocassette recorder finds that he gets better value from the facilities that the machine offers than he ever can from cable television. In addition, with the new films, the user finds that the film becomes available on cassette many months and even years before it is released for use via cable television.(7). There is no doubt at all that the average user opts for the videocassette, rather than cable television. This can be demonstrated not only by the slow growth of cable television, but also by the dramatic growth in income that Hollywood is getting from the sale of videocassettes, thus:

Year	Income US$ million	Percentage of total income
1980	20	1
1983	625	14
1988	1130	16

The last set of figures is of course an estimate.

The domestic satellite dish

Cable television is not only threatened by the desire of the user for choice and the fact that he can make such a choice, but also by the rapid growth of knowledge in the field of electronics and the ever-increasing ability to apply that knowledge – now into space itself. There is no doubt that we are in the midst of an electronics revolution and one development that seems likely to have a major impact on the average householder is the direct-broadcast satellite. The use of satellites for the transmission of television programmes, telephone messages and electronic data across the world is now a commonplace, but till now the transmissions via satellite have been received by official bodies such as the post office, or by public corporations set up for the purpose, who then distribute the data to the ultimate user. In this way we are all familiar with the fact that, for instance, a talk by the President of the United States can be seen worldwide *as it is given* and we are able to view news items on the television screen shortly after their happening. But those involved in satellite broadcasting are now proposing to go a major step further. For instance, it is proposed to put several direct-broadcast satellites into orbit, probably by 1986. Their broadcasts would be receivable over very wide areas, such as the whole of Europe, and anyone able to install a dish aerial about a metre across would be able to receive the programmes. Not only is this a serious threat to cable television, but governments would find that they had lost control over what their citizens were able to see. For this reason it is very possible that governments will intervene, in order that they may have the power of censorship. One method of intervention would be to insist that all such programmes were channelled via cable television, banning the use of the dish aerial by the private citizen. It is expected, for instance, that some such step may well be taken in Britain, and if that came to pass it would of course provide a boost for cable television.(8) But let us not forget that analysis of consumer use by Warner to which we referred earlier. The satellite may well multiply the availability of programmes, but does the average householder want to look at them? In addition, the barrier of language is likely to intervene.

When we consider what the average user would wish to look at, it seems very evident that he does not actually wish to look at advertising. At the moment it is largely a matter of compulsion, the advertisements interspersed within the programme being watched. Cable television has to attract advertising revenue if it is to prosper, but a new remote control device is now on the market, called the 'zapper', which can switch channels during commercials whilst the viewer stays seated. Advertisers see this as offering a substantial threat to the penetration of their advertisements and their reluctance to use television as an advertising medium grows.

The impact of government regulation

Certain countries are contemplating the regulation of cable television and Britain seems to be taking the lead in this. This means, of course, that their proposals are likely to be used as a model by others. A recent *White Paper*, a proposal document issued by the British government as a prelude to legislation, includes provisions that would reduce the rate of return on cable television investment to a level lower than that currently obtaining in the US. Cable television is not a real alternative in Britain for the reception of television programmes, because not only is the television set already in nearly every home but almost invariably it is possible to receive an excellent picture. Very few areas suffer from the inability to receive television programmes, with the result that cable television is hardly an attractive alternative for that purpose.

Another factor influencing the British market for cable television is the widespread use there of the videocassette recorder. The penetration is so high that the residual market would not sustain a range of programmes via cable. The proposals in the *White Paper*, which have now become law, restrict any individual franchise to 100 000 outlets, which is barely economic. One area where cable transmission could find a wide market, data transmission, has been limited to two companies only, British Telecom, the state organisation now privatised, and a public company – or we should now say *another* public company called Mercury. This denies what could be a really lucrative market to the cable television companies. Both British Telecom and Mercury are busy installing optical cable countrywide, to increase the volume and quality of data transmission via the telephone lines – and this could easily include television transmissions. A similar approach is likely to be followed in many other countries in Europe, with the telecommunication authorities improving and enlarging their existing cable networks. The first European satellite, ECS-1, has been operative since mid-1983, but private companies are not allowed to pick up and use the signals without permission from the telecommunication authorities. The dominance of the governmental authorities in this area throughout Europe must continue to curb the expansion of cable television there.

Cut-throat competition

Given the choice, the cable television companies prefer to operate in the larger cities, where a large number of subscribers can be connected for a minimum cost in terms of cable. Elsewhere, what is called subscription television has been used. This is a single-channel television service which broadcasts scrambled programmes. A decoder, for which the user has to pay, is used in conjunction with the television set to view the programme. But this business has not really prospered. For instance, Oak Industries Incorporated, a giant in this field in the US, ceased operation in Dallas and Phoenix after losing nearly half of their subscribers. The business only thrived whilst there were no cabled transmissions. Once cable arrived in the area, single channel pay-television could not compete.

So far as the US is concerned, fierce competition between the various cable television companies has not helped matters. In some metropolitan areas, such as New York City and Washington DC, negotiations have gone on for years, the municipality waiting for the best offer.(9) Cities are courted by the cable companies and various devious tactics are employed to get the franchise. There is a prescribed franchise fee of 5 per cent of the gross revenue, but payments of up to 10 per cent are not uncommon. In Sacramento the cable television company agreed to plant 20 000 trees in order to win the franchise.

Is there a future for cable television?

In our judgment cable television has had its day. The novelty has worn off. Whilst there may be scope in countries where it has not yet made an impact, we doubt it, because of the steady growth of the use of the videocassette recorder worldwide. The user has such a wide choice once a videocassette recorder comes into the home that he is no longer interested in the alternatives that cable television can offer. It also has to be remembered that the growth in the number of programmes available does not bring with it a wide range of quality programmes.

When television first came in, the possession of a television set was of course the 'in thing', although that particular idiom had not gained currency in those far-off days. But the quality of reception was very poor and many of the programmes were also of a low standard. As a result many became disillusioned and got rid of their television sets – but they kept their television antenna installed on the house top that they might be seen to be 'keeping up with the Joneses'. We believe that in like manner many will become disillusioned when they see the *quality* of the mass of material that comes on offer via cable television.

Conclusion

Once again we see that in a new and growing market, demand remains the crucial factor and the customer is king. Many companies failed to realise this, just saw a new market and sought to 'jump on the bandwagon'. But they were soon thrown off again. It seems that in the developing world at least the market rapidly reached saturation point, the possibility of a much wider choice not being a sufficient lure. Even in an affluent society people still look for 'value for money' and no significant benefit has been brought to the user through cable television.

References

1 Article: 'The cabling of Europe: in the shadow of the satellite', *Economist*, 288, 13 August 1983, p.49.
2 Irvine, C., 'Cable TV will tune in to space', *Coventry Evening Telegraph*, 25 February 1985, p.1.
3 Stallworthy, E.A. and Kharbanda, O.P., *International Construction: the Role of Project Management*, Gower, 1985. See the section 'Communications the link' in Chapter 8.
4 Article: 'Cable TV: the overpriced revolution', *Economist*, 286, 19 March 1983, p.41.
5 Article: 'Cable television: channels to burn', *Economist*, 290, 28 January 1984, p.31.
6 Article: 'The crowded new world of TV', *Fortune*, 110, 17 September 1984, p.156+.
7 Article: 'The competition looks on', *Time* (US edn), 24 December 1984, p.53.
8 Article: 'Cable television: Getting the revolution to roll', *Economist*, 287, 30 April 1983, p.37.
9 Article: 'Cutting through the delays in cable franchising', *Business Week*, 16 May 1983, pp.22-3.

12   That stupid computer!

Most of our readers no doubt come into contact with the activities of the computer these days, at least indirectly, since they are widely used to prepare accounts, render invoices and pursue late payments. We have all heard of, if not experienced, the computer system that sends you a monthly reminder that you owe US$0.00 (or its equivalent in your own country) until you find a 'listening human' to tell your troubles to. Another aspect that gives rise to a lot of irritation is the apparent slowness of response. Getting off the mailing list, for instance, can take a very long time.

When it comes to the computer in the home, the major use to date seems to be as a toy, despite all the advertising. Its use as an educator or business tool in the home still seems slow in coming. As one Atari salesman said bluntly:(1)

> There is only so far you can go with intimidation and telling the public that if you don't buy your kid a computer he'll grow up to be an idiot.

The clever computer

Most certainly the development and introduction of the computer has brought about a revolution in our lifetime. With the advances still being made there seems to be no end to the possibilities. Business operations have been revolutionised and the lifestyle of the individual in a great many countries has been transformed to an extent no one even imagined a decade ago. Certainly the computer is a very wonderful piece of machinery, that can do a wide range of different operations far faster and with greater precision than any human, but let us not forget the human element that lies behind it – *all the time!* The effective operation of the computer is wholly dependent upon the human who designed it and then the human who operates it. We can be stupid at times – a stupidity that is then reflected in the operations of the computer. It is as simple as that. Whilst many people tend to personalise the computer and give it a mind of its own, as we have done in the title to this chapter, in fact that is a very misguided assessment of the situation. The example we have already given to you – the monthly reminder that you owe nothing – is a programming fault, *not* a computer fault and there are many other examples that could be cited. For instance, many routine procedures such as the bulk mailing of magazines have been computerised with considerable savings in time and money. Just as we write this chapter we have received four copies of the identical issue of the same magazine, the covers being addressed as given in Figure 12.1. It is very evident that this is the result of faulty input, but how that has arisen rather puzzles us. A renewal form has to be completed every year, but if we have filled the form up slightly differently each time, one would have thought that the entry of the 'new' address should have brought about cancellation of the old. Of course, the fallibility of computers in terms of their human operators is well recognised, as is shown by a note in the catalogue from a book mail order house, Daedalus Books, of Washington

---

The systemic computer

C ENG	MANAGING DIRECTOR
OM P KHARBANDA	O P KHARBANDA
O P KHARBANDA & ASSOC	O P KHARBANDA & ASSOCIATES
501 OLYMPUS	501 OLYMPUS ALTAMOUNT RD
BOMBAY, 400 026	BOMBAY,
INDIA	400026 INDIA
MANAGING DIRECTOR	MANAGING DIRECTOR
DR O P KHARBANDA	C P KHARBANDA
OP KHARBANDA & ASSOC	OP KHARBANDA & ASSOCS
501 OLYMPUS, ALTAMOUNT RD	501 OLYMPUS ALTAMOUNT ROAD
BOMBAY, 400 026	BOMBAY, 400 026
INDIA	INDIA

Figure 12.1 The address roll
The above four names and addresses are, of course, all the same to the human eye, but the computer as programmed sees them as four different people.

DC. They give a good-natured warning to their customers:

> As if we wouldn't mess things up well enough by ourselves, Daedalus now has a computer to help.

How thoughtful to warn us! Mercifully, the company went on to promise that a human being will remain available to answer any questions about its computer-written invoices. So, if you *do* get repeated reminders to pay up your arrears of US$0.00, we trust that you will be able to telephone a human being somewhere to explain that both time and money could be saved by modifying the computer program slightly. If they wish to keep in touch, perhaps they should instruct the computer in such circumstances to send you a friendly message, such as: 'We are happy to have you as a satisfied customer with no arrears but we trust that is not because you have stopped buying our books.'

Of course, such examples of faulty programming could be multiplied and they have given rise to what is now a classic in the computer world, the term *GIGO*, an acronym for 'garbage in, garbage out'. The use of the word 'garbage' rather than 'rubbish' tells us where the phrase originated – in the US. The problem is that a simple error, such as entering the wrong figure, can play havoc, since the final result has a fallacious sanctity, being incorporated in a 'printout'. For reasons which still mystify us, a computer printout has an authority all its own.

Another aspect that might well be much more serious in the long run is that reliance on the machine stops people thinking. This is already very apparent with the electronic calculator, now in the hands of every schoolchild in the West – and a great many grownups. The till in almost every shop not only notes the cost, but calculates the change to be given. The result of this is that there is hardly anyone anywhere any more who can even add and subtract, let alone do multiplication sums. In similar fashion computerisation of planning and control may be damaging productivity in the long term, since reliance on printout data has displaced human thinking. The subjective approach is completely neglected, yet subjective assessments of developing situations are all important to their proper resolution.(2)

The saga of Silicon Valley

A certain industrial area in California has become known worldwide as *Silicon Valley* because it has been seen as the birthplace and centre of the electronics industry in the US, an industry built around what is called the 'silicon chip'. We dare not attempt to describe or define the silicon chip for you. Let us just say for the uninitiated that the silicon chip is a very complex but extremely small device that can be given a program and a memory and is therefore at the heart of every computer. And not only computers! Every washing machine, dishwasher and many toys now have a silicon chip as part of their operating mechanism, to program the routine through which they go to perform their functions.

The electronics industry, centred in Silicon Valley, has grown extremely rapidly, supported very largely by a phenomenal growth in the demand for the 'personal computer', made possible by the advent of the silicon chip. Growth through the eighties was estimated to be at the rate of 50 per cent per year, and the industry expanded to meet the expected demand, but it failed to material-ise. In addition, everyone was trying to 'get in on the act'. As a result, the number of different personal computers on the market multiplied, from just a handful some five years earlier to nearly two hundred different models. And they were indeed all different: that was one of the major handicaps in this market. Competition became ferocious and many firms collapsed. Fred Hoar, a former *Apple* executive – *Apple* is the trade name for one particular model of microcomputer – did not mince his words when he said: 'The personal computer industry has reached a new chapter in its history: Chapter 11.' Chapter 11, of course, is a particular section of the Bankruptcy Act in the US which is often used by companies threatened with insolvency. The market is full of ailing companies.(3) The state of the industry can be well illustrated by citing a few examples: some of the names you will recognise, some you will never have heard of.

1   *Atari*
    This company is known worldwide as a maker of video games, but it ran up losses eventually totalling US$653 million and has now been acquired by Jack Tramiel, a former Commodore president.

2   *Cavilan Computer*
    This company raised US$23.9 million of venture capital two years ago, launched a lap-size computer but was slow to develop an improved model. It has had to lay off 210 out of 280 workers and needs additional capital.

3   *Convergent Technologies*
    Introduced its lap-sized computer *Workslate* in 1983, but

couldn't cope with the demand due to production snags. Lost US$6.5 million in one quarter and stopped making *Workslate* to concentrate on desk-top office computers.

4 *Diasonics*
A maker of diagnostic equipment, the company took in US$123 million in one of the largest stock offerings ever, but lost US$104 million.

5 *Eagle Computer*
Developed a computer compatible with the IBM range but was taken to court by IBM for copying its software. Dealers stopped stocking the machine and in the process the company 'lost a lot of ground' and do not have the capital resources to 'repurchase it'.

6 *Mindset Corporation*
Announced its first personal computer in March 1984, some years later than its competitors. The model was well received but could find no space in dealers showrooms.

7 *Trilogy*
Founded in 1980 by Gene Amdahl, a former IBM engineer, the plan was to build a new supercomputer using a revolutionary semi-conductor chip that would be much faster than the conventional chip, but the company discovered that 'it was just too much to bite off'. Losing US$73.7 million in the first half of 1984, it abandoned the project and restricted its production to conventional chips.

8 *Visicomp*
This company produced a pioneering business program called *Visicalc*, but ruinous competition and copycat products have prevented it from coming into its own.

What is the meaning of this apparent collapse of an industry? Is the 'high-tech boom', as it has been called, now over? It would seem so, if we believe the newspaper reporters. Thus:(4)

> There has been a steady stream of reports of ominous developments in Silicon Valley and the other high tech enclaves in New England and the Sun Belt states. America's vaunted leadership in high technology, the wellspring of innovation for the entire industrial sector, is eroding rapidly in every major electronics market.

There are many who still view Silicon Valley as the promised land, but there have been too many failures for the trend to be ignored. It is very obvious, as the reasons given for failure are studied, that supply has far exceeded demand, especially in the area of the 'home computer', bringing a price war that many companies just could not survive.

Homeless home computers!

The magazine *Fortune* made home computers one of its 'catastrophes of the year' for 1984.(5) From 1980 onwards the sales of home computers grew very rapidly, practically doubling every year till 1983. Sales for 1984 in the US were of the same order as for 1983, namely some 5 million, but it appears that the market had reached saturation point. But all the makers had planned to meet a rapidly growing market.(6) With supply far exceeding demand, the various manufacturers entered into a 'price war' in an endeavour to maintain and improve their market share. Over a period of some eighteen months prices were slashed by as much as 75 per cent, sending a shock wave through the industry and causing very heavy losses for major companies, such as Texas Instruments and Warner Communications (owners of the Atari computer company). The dramatic fall in prices is illustrated in Figure 12.2. As will be seen, the basic price of some home computers dropped below US$100.(7) This meant that for some

Make	Home computer pricing			
	Earlier US$	December 1981 US$	December 1982 US$	June 1983 US$
TI 99/4A:	825	399	199	99
Commodore VIC 20:	—	299	199	89
Atari 400:	600	399	299	99
Radio Shack Colour:	—	499	299	199
Timex Sinclair 1000:	—	99	99	29

Figure 12.2 A price collapse
The above listing of the shop prices for a few of the home computers on the market demonstrates very clearly the way in which prices fell to match the competition.

companies it was impossible to carry on. It was not only a question of price: there was also much mismanagement and poor planning. Texas Instruments, for instance, seeking to pull their market share up from 25 per cent to 45 per cent, shipped equipment to dealers far in excess of their requirements. To quote:

> They opened the factory doors and flooded the market until the retailers couldn't take any more.

The collapse of Osborne, whose home computer had found widespread technical acceptance, can be traced directly to an overcrowded market, linked to a mistake in sales policy.(8) The company announced a new improved model well before they were able to bring it onto the market. The sale of their machines collapsed as those keen to buy the Osborne waited for the new model to appear. Running out of funds, the company had to apply for protection under Chapter 11.

The malaise is widespread. Commodore International, the largest home computer company in the US, suffered a 94 per cent drop in profits in 1984. Sales in the second quarter fell from US$431 million to US$333 million, and profits from US$50 million to US$3 million.(9) This was as a result of the slowdown in sales on the US market. It would appear that the US consumer has become disenchanted with the home computer. Further price reductions, such as announced for a new computer by Atari, are not expected to generate an increased volume of sales. The leader, Apple, also seems to be suffering from overstocking, there having been minimal shipments since Christmas 1984. Christmas is the peak time for home computer sales. The Xerox Corporation has abandoned its plans for a 'briefcase computer' for similar reasons: estimated lack of demand. All in all, a sorry story.

All this is centred on the US market, but elsewhere similar things are happening. A home computer 'craze' is tending to grow in many developing countries, but companies there seem hardly to understand what it is all about. If we may take India as an example since it is typical, let us look at just one of the metropolitan cities, Bombay. In a city of many millions there are probably a few thousand personal or home computers in homes or office, but of these well over half are not being used: many because they cannot be serviced. Most were purchased without any consideration at all as to their end use and those who have got them do not know what to do with them. Having purchased the computer, only then do they begin to find out what they can do with it. This applies not merely to private but also to 'small business' use.(10) Thus there is a tremendous waste of materials and human resources – a 'mini' disaster!

The impact of crime and fraud

Another area where the computer makes the headlines with distressing frequency is in connection with crime and fraud. Just to illustrate what is happening, the Federal Bureau of Investigation (FBI) in the US seized four teenagers who allegedly tapped into two computers at NASA's Marshall Space Flight Center in Huntsville, Alabama. At the Slavenburg Bank, in Rotterdam, some insiders using secret computer codes transferred some US$65 million to a private account overseas over a period of two years before the theft was detected. Since hundreds of billions of dollars are transferred across national boundaries every day, it will be appreciated that the stakes are very high indeed. Yet the technological safeguards are apparently primitive and the operating procedures poorly defined.(11) Whilst an average bank robbery is estimated to net some US$20 000, in sharp contrast the average sum involved in electronic fraud is some US$500 000. Yet the chance of detection and prosecution is much less.

The development of theft and fraud using computer techniques has developed to such a degree that a new job description has appeared: Computer Security Consultant. According to Harry Wood, a computer security consultant based in Washington DC:

> Given the pace of technological change in the financial industry and the growth of home computers, the risks are very high.

This is illustrated by the fact that the total losses due to computer crime are estimated to run at more than a billion dollars a year in the US alone. A survey by the American Bank Association amongst 283 companies and public agencies disclosed that 25 per cent had suffered 'known and verifiable losses'. The legislators are finally seeking to deal with computer crime and a law has recently been passed in the US that makes computer trespassing, theft and fraud specific offences. However, computer crime still seems to be relatively easy and often goes undetected for long periods of time. Indeed, one wonders to what extent computer crime *is* detected, seeing that the various safeguards can be so readily bypassed.

The extent of the literature on the subject of computer crime is perhaps one indication of its widespread nature. Typical of the titles are:

> International Computer Crime – a Growing Threat
> Electronic Fraud: the Crime of the Future
> Insuring against Electronic Bandits
> High Technology Miscreants Beware
> Common Sense and Computer Security

The last title heads an article which makes the point that management policies and controls may be much better deterrents to computer crime than either laws or technical gadgets.(12) There are even full length books on the subject (13) and articles with thought-provoking headlines such as 'Computer theft boom' (14) and 'The revenge of the hackers'.(15) That last reminds us of another aspect that is now beginning to gain prominence: the possibility of employee revenge. A recent report by International Resource Development Inc., a market research firm located in Norwalk, CT, in the US advises that deliberate harmful acts by employees were cited as the next greatest concern following accidental or unintentional mishaps by workers in their survey.(16) Whilst disgruntled employees have always been able to take it out on a company if they really put their minds to it, this has suddenly been made a lot easier by a powerful accomplice, the microcomputer. Before the micro, knowledge of computers was limited to a select few: now millions of individuals are familiar with their use and, if so desired, their abuse.

The soft steal

Despite the prevalence of computer crime in various forms, managements do not yet seem to take it very seriously. Even when the perpetrators are caught, many companies seem reluctant to take action. They prefer to write off the loss rather than prosecute in order to save themselves embarrassment.(17) According to Jay Bloombecker, director of the National Centre for Computer Crime Data, out of the thousands of computer crimes that are committed only a hundred cases are pending. Statistics of that sort are by no means a deterrent. In addition, the law on the subject is by no means clear. Whilst it is a crime to steal tangible property, such as a computer, it may not be a crime to steal an intangible item, such as information, which can be more expensive than the computer itself. But in any event, even if laws are enacted in an attempt to deal with the problem, they will have to be implemented if they are to be effective. The computer raiders are often bright young people and society, instead of regarding them as criminals tends to admire them. In fact some one hundred and thirty of the most devoted among them met in November 1984 for the first time ever.(18) It seems that most of these bright 'kids' have now grown out of the pranksterism with which it all started and wish to set an example for the next generation. One of these 'hackers', now a teacher, said: 'It's one thing for a high school kid to show off how he can dial the phone for free. It's quite another thing for an adult to go around encouraging school kids to steal'. Those attending this meeting included:

Lee Felsenstein   – designer of the Osborne 1.
Richard Greenblatt – who developed the LISP machine for artificial intelligence research.
Burrell Smith   – an Apple repairman who built the Macintosh.

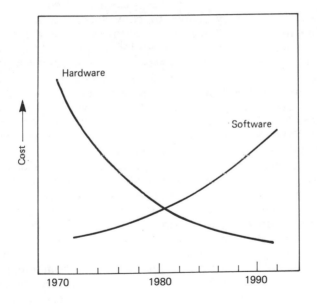

Figure 12.3 The cost revolution
The graph, which is diagrammatic only, makes the point that for the average user the cost of the software in setting up an installation may soon exceed the cost of the hardware.

John Draper   — who developed a system for making free
                        phone calls by using a toy whistle
                        from a breakfast cereal box to imitate
                        the tone used by AT&T for long
                        distance calls.

Security remains the basic problem, since 'lock and key' is not the
remedy. The computer can still be entered via the telephone line
with a little ingenuity. The problem is actually growing, since the
steady advance in technology continually opens up new possibilities to the ingenious thief.

Even more serious, in some respects, than the invasion of the
computer to steal either data or money is the piracy of software
programs. It seems that it will not be too long before the cost of
the software (the programs used on the computer) will be more
than the cost of the hardware (the computer itself) as we have
illustrated graphically in Figure 12.3. In this context the piracy of
software is a threat to the continuing healthy development of the
computer industry. To illustrate the problem, a program costing
say US$500, stored on a floppy disk, can be rented for perhaps
US$100.(19) It is very simple to copy such programs before
returning them so that the rental business, as in the case of
videocassettes, encourages and even invites piracy. One market
research consultant, Jean L. Yates, estimates that such illegal
copying, which is construed as an infringement of copyright,
probably results in lost business of upwards of US$500 million a
year to the companies designing and selling such software. Once
again, the law is not a great help, since ownership is not clearly
defined. The concept of property in relation to a software program
has yet to be firmly established but the sooner the better in view of
the rapid growth and increasing importance of this sector of the
business. It is already more than US$2 billion per annum, and
seems to be growing at the rate of about 50 per cent per year. The
United Computer Corporation, one of the most aggressive advertisers in the software rental business in the US has been sued for
piracy by MicroPro, the developer of the word processing program
trademarked *Wordstar*, which claims some 45 per cent of the world
market. Whichever way the case finally goes it is bound to have a
tremendous impact on the fortunes of the industry. If piracy
cannot be effectively prevented, then many of the smaller companies are going to go out of business and those who stay in
business will have to charge much more than they otherwise would
for their programs to legitimate purchasers. The basic question
being raised and not yet settled is whether copying of a rented

program is a violation of copyright. In a case involving Apple Computer and the Franklin Computer Corporation, the court cast doubt on the validity of copyright in software. Apple, who were suing for infringement of copyright, have gone to appeal however. Lotus Development Corporation filed a US$10 million 'theft' suit against another company for making unauthorised copies of its popular program called '1-2-3', for use in their branch offices. However the suit was settled out of court. The high price being charged for '1-2-3' was an incentive for piracy.(20) According to Peter Brown, a lawyer, the copyright law in the US permits 'fair use'. That means, he says, that 'users are allowed to make backup copies for their own use, but they are not allowed to duplicate programs or lend them out'.

Some firms have introduced 'copy prevention' devices that make programs much more difficult to copy. But since this prevents even legitimate copying, such as is done for 'back-up' purposes, it has been largely abandoned. Secret passwords have been tried in an attempt to eliminate copying, but these can always be broken by determined 'hackers'. Computer fraud is undoubtedly 'big business' worldwide and it probably costs the US computer industry alone many billions of dollars a year.

Conclusion

Our survey of the computer industry illustrates that technology in this particular field is progressing faster than the ability of the average human to comprehend it or to cope with it. As a result the social and legal implications of its use have not been fully understood and the user is unable to cope with the hidden potential. This allows the 'above average' person, such as the 'hacker', to take advantage of the situation. Hence an article with the title 'Man, meet machine' states bluntly:(21)

> Computer designers are still groping their way towards an understanding of how people respond to computers.

It is useless to suggest that the development and use of this new technology be slowed down so that people can catch up. So, once again, management must meet and cope with the situation confronting it. The theme we shall pursue in the next chapter takes a very different technology, but we shall see very similar problems confronting management as a consequence of its development.

References

1　Wallis, L., 'What's the use of home computers?', *Across the Board*, October 1984, pp.37-44.

2　McGarrow, R.E., 'Ironies of the computer age', *Business Horizons*, (USA), September/October 1984, p. 34.

3　Article: 'Sad tales of Silicon Valley', *Time*, 3 April 1984, pp.42-3.

4　Ball, I, 'Honeymoon is over for US. high-tech', *The Daily Telegraph* (London), 6 March 1985, p.5.

5　Article in *Fortune*, 110, 24 December 1984.

6　Article: 'Shake-out in the hardware wars', *Time*, 27 June 1983, p.41.

7　Uttal, B., 'Sudden shake-up in home computers', *Fortune*, 108, 11 July 1983, pp.105-6.

8　Article: 'Osborne's demise', *Duns Monthly*, October 1983, p.14.

9　Article: 'Commodore International', *Financial Times*, London, 30 January 1985, p.13.

10　Personal conversation with Mr. Vivek Kharbanda, Vice-President, Data Corp, Bombay, March 1985.

11　Reily, Ann, 'Computer crackdown', *Fortune*, 110, 17 September 1984, pp.103-4.

12　Buss, M.D.J. and Lynn, M.S., 'Common sense and computer security', *Harvard Business Review*, 62, March/April 1984, pp.112-121.

13　Klemen, A. and Sizer, R., *The Computer in Court*, Gower, 1982.

14　Budiansky, S., 'Computer theft boom', *Nature*, 309, 21 June 1984, p. 658.

15　Ugnibene, P.J., 'Computer saboteurs', *Science Digest*, 92, July 1984, pp. 58-61.

16　Article: 'Will employee revenge damage your computer?', *Computer Equipment*, March 1985, p. 45.

17　Article: 'Computer security: what can be done', *Business Week*, 26 September 1983, pp.80-82.

18　Article: 'Let us now praise some famous hackers: a new view of some much-maligned electronic pioneers', *Time*, (US edn), 3 December 1984, p. 76.

19　Article: 'Software rentals: piracy is the hot new issue', *Business Week*, 1 August 1983, pp.62-3.

20　Article: 'Software piracy', *Chemical Business*, May 1984, p. 46.

21　Article: 'Man, meet machine', *Economist*, 293, 27 October 1984, p. 87.

13 Genetic engineering – growing pains

Genetic engineering is a very new discipline, one of the newest amongst those that have sprung to life in this age of fast-developing technology. So new is the phrase that it cannot yet be found in the dictionary. However, it is possible to assess its meaning by evaluating each of the two words separately. The dictionary tells us that 'genetic' is 'of, in, concerning origin'. Engineering will hardly require definition for our readers, but for the sake of completeness that is defined as the 'application of science for the control and use of power, especially by means of machines'. So now you should be able to set up your own definition of 'genetic engineering'. It has to do with origins. Life begins in the genes and its development is controlled by the genes. A gene is a unit of heredity in the chromosome and each unit, or gene, is said to control a particular characteristic of the form of life to which it relates.

Genetic engineering can be said to have been discovered about ten years ago now and at first it was seen as a way of manipulating microbes to make them perform the particular function which the scientist had in view, but it has rapidly moved on and a major area of activity is now the potential manipulation of the human genes. The process is carried out *in vivo* and *in vitro*.(1) That is a technical way of saying 'in the body or in the test-tube'.

The story in headlines

A multitude of articles and technical papers have appeared on various aspects of our subject and once again perhaps the best way of introducing you to the complexities of genetic engineering is to present you with a long list of headlines. So:

The boom in genetic engineering
The moral dilemma
The birthpangs of a new science
Life for sale
Shaping life in the laboratory
Whose baby am I?
A host of ethical problems
Scientific opportunities and dangers
Genetic millionairing
Experiments halted
The risks are real
Altering heredity
Military gene project stirs furore
The promise and perils
International regulations
Splicing a regulatory body

We hope that you now have some idea of the ground that we have to cover if we are going to assess the progress, the prospects and the perils for this new science. Although so new, some areas are already facing disaster and perhaps the reasons for that have already become apparent. Genetic engineering operates in a 'high risk area' in more senses than one.

As we have said and as our headlines indicate, the literature on the subject is growing rapidly and though it is still a new and novel subject UNIDO (United Nations Industrial and Development Organisation) are helping to set up an International Centre for Genetic Engineering and Biotechnology, initially at Trieste in Italy and New Delhi in India, with affiliated centres elsewhere. UNIDO have also started publishing an excellent survey of the current literature and developments in the field, called the *Genetic Engineering and Biotechnology Monitor*. This survey, started in February 1982, is being published quarterly. In accordance with our usual practice, having introduced another specialised word to you – biotechnology – we should explain it. The prefix 'bio' is in effect another word for 'life' or 'living beings' (from the greek *bios* = *human life*) so that biotechnology is the technology of living things.

First the boom

The firm *Genetech* was founded in 1976 by Venture Capitalist, a certain Robert Swanson and a biochemist at the University of

California, Herbert Boyer. After four years of obscurity it suddenly came to life as it were with an offer of US$36 million of stock. At that point it was only one of a number of companies offering little more than the promise of a range of novel products, such as interferon, which it was proposed to manufacture from yeast cells. This particular announcement alone raised its stock by US$7 a share. The demand for its stock was in fact phenomenal. Within minutes of its coming on offer the demand brought the price up from a par value of US$35 a share to US$89 a share, with brokers rationing the shares to their customers. Wall Street had never seen such speculative fever, and that for a relatively obscure company.(2)

What caused this tremendous interest? Well, the antiviral agent interferon was said to be a possible weapon against cancer. In addition, a number of other possible products on the horizon included vaccines against hepatitis and malaria, low-calorie sugar, self-fertilising food crops, fuels and plastics manufactured from waste products. The public could recognise the potential in such developments although they understood nothing of the techniques by which these marvels were to be achieved. The techniques, then only in the laboratory stage at best, and sometimes only an idea in the mind of a research chemist, seemed within reach through adaptations of gene splicing, or recombinant DNA (deoxyribonucleic acid) processing. This is genetic engineering and other possibilities in that field include the modifying of the hereditary mechanism of micro-organisms or cells, the fusion of cells, DNA synthesis and the creation of hybridomas, long-lived cells that would produce antibiotics. All these developments had the most exciting commercial possibilities. Of them all, gene splicing has been heralded as a 'compass for the explorer', a powerful tool for first examining and then changing the machinery of heredity. The technique is said to be the most important scientific development since the splitting of the atom – and everyone knows what a revolution that has led to and the scares that it has generated.

Gene splicing was developed in the seventies at a number of universities and it seemed to be *the* technology for the eighties, much as plastics were of the forties, transistors of the fifties, computers in the sixties and microcompouters in the seventies. Even the usually conservative journal the *Economist* hailed biotechnology as 'one of the biggest industrial opportunities of the late twentieth century'. Typical of the companies pioneering in this field at this point were:

Cetus Corporation
Founded in 1971 by a physician, biochemist and Nobel

Laureate in physics, Donald Glaser, the company uses gene splicing and other techniques to modify microorganisms in order to produce commercial chemicals such as ethylene oxide and alcohol.

Biogen SA
This company, based in Geneva, is research-oriented, being founded in 1978 by businessmen and scientists, including a Nobel Laureate in chemistry, Walter Gilbert. The major investors were Schering-Plough and Inco (formerly International Nickel). It was this company that produced the first gene-spliced interferon-like human protein in 1980.

Genex Corporation
Started in 1977 by a molecular biologist, a major investor being the Koppers Company. The objective is to produce industrial chemicals using gene-splicing techniques.

These companies are typical of the many.

But questions come

Much of the work in this field involves basic and fundamental research, which normally has a long gestation period. Because of this it has attracted young, brilliant scientists and engineers across a range of disciplines. Bringing scientists, chemists and engineers together in commercial organisations has encouraged much cross-fertilisation and many new concepts have been born, but any commercial investment demands a relatively quick return. It was also the case that much of the basic research was being carried out at universities, which not only raised a number of questions, but brought conflict. Research at universities is almost invariably carried out at the expense of the taxpayer, yet it seemed that the direction of such research might be governed by commercial considerations. Should a research group take up a basic question like the origin of cancer, or should it try to isolate a new tranquilliser? The second choice has more immediate commercial possibilities than the first.

Another problem is the matter of secrecy and commercial rivalry. Research work at universities should be published that all may benefit, but what happens when researchers at a university start cooperating with a colleague in a commercial organisation – or with colleagues in two rival organisations? Will there be a free exchange of information and specimens? It was questions such as these, raised by faculty members at Harvard that led to a decision not to take part in such commercial ventures, although it would have welcomed the cash it would have brought. Stanford University, following a somewhat similar course, advised its members to use 'caution and deliberation' in dealing with companies involved in genetic engineering. Such conflicts of interest have already brought a series of legal disputes. For instance, the University of California has secured US$350,000 through the courts from Genetech. This is in lieu of the work on a hormone that induces human growth that a researcher from the university brought to Genetech when he joined that company. Another dispute revolves around the allegation that a set of cells used by Genetech to produce a certain type of interferon was first created at the University College of Southern California. Boyer, who is a co-founder of Genetech, is still a senior researcher at the university, acting as a consultant to the firm one day a week. He owns nearly a million shares in that company, which at the conservative price of US$40 a share means that his interest is worth US$40 million – but the share price has topped US$89! His colleagues at the university are both jealous of his apparent good fortune and irritated at having to work with him. It is even surmised that his commercial connections may have cost Boyer a Nobel prize, but we do not suppose that he would be much concerned about that.

What are the risks?

The financial questions surrounding this fundamental research is but one aspect of the problems that are beginning to confront those seeking to commercialise the discoveries that are being made. The biochemist Paul Berg of Stanford University, in the course of his work in this field, planned to insert the simian virus SV40, originally found in monkeys, into the bacterium escherichia coli (E.coli), found in the human intestine. Research had already established that SV40, harmless to monkeys, where it originated, was cancerous in mice, hamsters and test-tube cultures of human cells. What then would happen if the modified E.coli escaped from Berg's laboratory, established itself in the human gut and kept on multiplying? It could well be a sort of time bomb that would eventually explode, leading to the death of millions. The implications were felt to be too serious and the experiment was dropped.

   Here is a powerful tool that may well do wonders for the benefit of mankind, but some slight mishap and mankind could well be destroyed. Some very fundamental questions are raised once the possible implications of genetic engineering are appreciated and the answers are largely unknown. The illustration we have just given was of a known risk, because experimentation had already disclosed that there *was* a risk, but what about other experiments which at this point in time seem to be quite innocuous? How can we be sure that there are not hidden risks, waiting to be disclosed and that will come to light only when the new material has been spread abroad? It has been said, apparently with truth, that this new technology may 'profoundly affect the lives of tens of millions of people'. For well or for ill? It is very evident that until knowledge in this field has increased very considerably, a high degree of caution and restraint is very necessary.

That the risks associated with the continuing developments in genetic engineering are very real is further demonstrated as we learn of the work of Professor Yuri Ovchinnikov, a leading Soviet expert in genetic engineering and engaged in research with a view to using recombinant DNA to create a new generation of biological weapons. The poor safety record displayed by Soviet research scientists whilst working on the development of new germ weapons could well constitute a serious threat in itself. Is it any wonder, therefore, that articles are continually being written with titles such as 'Averting Genetic Warfare' (3) and 'The risks are real'.(4) Typical of the fears expressed by eminent scientists, who are those we would expect to have a realistic appreciation as to what is involved, are those of another Nobel Laureate, David Baltimore. He feels that genetic engineering could well bring about a society that severely restricts the civil rights of the individual. What *is* the price of progress?

The patent problem

Genetic engineering has also proved a fertile if controversial area for patents. Initially the US Patent Office refused to accept applications for patents involving genetic engineering on the ground that a new life form was not patentable. However, in 1980 the US Supreme Court overturned this decision and that led to a great number of patent applications, patents and lawsuits about patents. In giving the ruling from the Supreme Court in 1980 Chief Justice Warren Burger declared that no one can 'deter the scientific mind from probing into the unknown any more than Canute could command the tides'. Be that as it may, the arguments continue unabated, new ideas are continually being generated, new questions are raised as the older ones get answered: it is a process of development that will inevitably go on ... and on. But whilst it is exciting, fascinating, daring, a crossing of new frontiers, will it ever be profitable?

The growing pains

Genetic engineering, more particularly as it has moved out of the university laboratory into the commercial world, has brought with it a number of political and ethical problems for which there seems no easy solution.(5) The possibility of experiments which may have far-reaching consequences at present unknown has led to furious debate and the halting of many experiments proposed by the scientists involved. But there is the hidden threat in that it is very easy for such work to be carried out in secrecy. This avoids public debate and any restrictions that might then be imposed.

To take but one example in this field, genetic engineering offers increasingly sophisticated tools for controlling and monitoring procreation, with benefit – so far as is known at the moment – to both mother and child. But such research brings forward fundamental questions of ethics in view of the unrestrained curiosity of the medical researchers.(6) Complex questions are raised that involve not only the scientists themselves, but politicians, theologians and philosophers. Typical of such questions are those relating to what is popularly called the 'test-tube baby'. This uses *in vitro* fertilisation (IVF). Then the questions come:

Should spare embryos be kept in cold storage?
Should all surplus embryos be disposed of?
Should scientists be allowed to continue with such experiments?
Should the foetus be tampered with?

Typical of the 'tampering' that is possible is a series of experiments by Dr. Martin Kline at University College, Los Angeles in 1980. He removed human bone marrow, treated it and then transplanted it – that is, returned it to a human body. No harm was done, so far as is known, but the experiment failed. Earlier trials with animals had also failed. The project was then denied any further government grant by the University Review Board because of the ethical questions that were being raised by such experimentation.

The possibilities that are opened up by the developments in genetic engineering are perhaps best displayed by the numerous books that have been written on the subject. Their titles illustrate both the dreams and the complexity of the subject. We have 'The eighth day of creation' to illustrate the dreams (7) and 'Genetic Prophecy – Beyond the Double Helix' to illustrate the complexity.(8) A review of the former book summed its message up thus:(9)

> Biotechnology is moving beyond gene splicing with secondary supply and information industries developing: manpower shortages, patent and licensing issues may pose problems.

It is very evident that the commercialisation of the discoveries that are being made is not going to be easy. Whilst genetic engineering seems to hold much promise, the approach to its commercialisation is unusual. There seems to be a continual seeking for publicity, not only among those new to the industry, but also by the pioneers. Genetech, for instance, seems to put out some startling announcement every month and appears to be continually striving to maintain what is called a 'high profile'.

The second book mentioned above has also been fully reviewed in the technical press.(10) That review considers that whilst genetics has a role in predicting and preventing disease, the possibilities for such applications may be overstated. The last chapter in the book has the title 'The perils of prophecy'. The particular prophecy referred to is that made possible by pre-natal genetic screening. Whilst this may be useful it is seen to be fraught with dangers. Society seems obsessed with the concept and may compel screening even before the validity of the testing techniques has been fully established.

A profile of failure

Many companies who have entered the field of genetic engineering have not only come but gone. This has been a common fate for those striving to make a profit in this most uncertain field of endeavour. To illustrate what can happen we thought that we would trace the road to failure of one such firm. Those that fail are usually under-capitalised and research-oriented and the company whose history we will review is typical in this.(11) Armos was founded in June 1980 by two ex-employees of Genetech, an industry leader. Armos was set up with a capital of US$1.5 million provided by its founders, the name having been derived from the greek word for 'harmony'. By the end of the year about a dozen senior scientists with supporting staff had started operations in a leased warehouse. By late 1981 the company had succeeded in attracting some venture capital and the research team got down to the serious work of developing animal vaccines, which was going to be their 'forte'. The team that had been assembled was talented, but had been taken from the academic world. There was no positive managerial direction, the co-founders being part of the research team.

In the absence of a full-time competent managing director, rivalries and jealousies arose between the team members. The co-founders suspected that there was a lack of loyalty within the team and started opening personal mail and monitoring telephone conversations. The 'recipe for disaster' that was already being brewed took a turn for the worse when part-time outside consultants were called in to advise. In desperation what was called 'The Manhattan Project' was launched in the Spring of 1982 to bring a promising product quickly to commercial availability. But that took much longer than had been expected and the company was unable to raise the further funds needed to bring their work through to a successful conclusion. The inevitable result was of course the collapse of the enterprise.

Those who have analysed what went on have criticised, in particular, the management style of the co-founders. It is said that neither of them appreciated the realities of the situation. Whilst Sheehan has been described as 'pleasant but remote and aloof' Carlock is seen as 'flamboyant and confrontational'. Yet months before the final crisis Carlock was being very down-to-earth, saying: 'It's awfully tempting to grow but we don't want to build a palace until we have sales. We want to build a company based on sales rather than on contract revenues'. When one remembers that they began their operations in a warehouse that comment is significant. But sales were nowhere in sight. With the future very much in doubt, Carlock said in March 1982 'I think we've come up with a winner'. This was when the company was already in deep trouble but the statement may well have been designed to lift the spirits of the Armos team. But time was already running out and in August 1982 Armos filed for Chapter 11 with debts of US$1.7 million and assets of around a million dollars.

The failure of Armos and many similar companies can be traced directly to a breakdown in the venture capital system, associated with a fundamental failure in management. The significance of certain basic aspects of management have been stressed by us time and again.(12, 13) Management is indeed the crux. Whilst it is true that the initial assessment of the capital required to get the business going was much too low, this is not necessarily a management failure. Research is notoriously difficult to evaluate in terms of the time that it will take to achieve a result. But, having convinced prospective investors that you have a good idea and a talented team, to secure continuing support you also have to demonstrate managerial ability. In this particular area managerial ability lies not only in a recognition that the first estimates of the time required to develop the product are proving low, but a positive approach to the handling of that situation. This calls for a series of financial assessments, including appraisal of the cash flow, revised projections, a modified corporate strategy and the like. In other words, not only a presentation of the problem, but an outline of the way in which it will be handled. It is this positive approach that will attract further financial support. It was this that Armos lacked, together with many other firms who have fallen by the wayside with them.

The changing pattern in the financing of such projects has indeed been very real. Before 1982 some US$600 million had been raised for investment. Through 1983 the investing public remained enthusiastic and a further US$400 million was raised, but disenchantment came in 1984, when the public support fell to a mere US$12 million.(14) Centocor got only US$5 million, whilst it was calling for US$15 million. Public confidence was further eroded by companies such as Storage Technology, and Armos, whom we mentioned above, going bankrupt. Some of the major chemical companies, such as DuPont and W.R. Grace are however buying stock in genetic engineering companies and this provides another source of funds.

A two-edged sword

Genetic engineering is still very new and full of potential. Some companies, after years of intensive research and product development, are on the brink of reaping the rewards for their efforts. The developments in prospect may well unlock the mysteries of cancer, heart disease and genetic defects, but at the same time visions are conjured up of a new 'super race' bred in test-tubes.(15) Then comes the dread thought: what happens if a mistake is made: will we have a generation of stupid humans? Whilst the benefits can indeed be great, the risks are also very great.

This has led to the industry being threatened by the political, philosophical and ethical issues with which it has thus become associated. We have seen something similar in relation to the discovery of atomic energy, to which this new phase of discovery has indeed been likened more than once. But in drawing the parallel let us not forget what has actually happened to atomic energy since its discovery. The most intense development was generated by the desire to have a weapon of war, and that still remains the case. The peaceful use of atomic energy has become bogged down in a wide range of environmental, technical and financial problems, with its vast potential remaining largely untapped. You will remember that we dealt with some of those problems in Chapter 7 (The Nuclear Stalemate). We suspect that the parallel is all too real and that the fruits of genetic engineering – the beneficial fruits at least – are not going to be enjoyed in the near future, if at all.

It seems as if the investment market is beginning to come to a somewhat similar conclusion.(14) As a result several companies that have been floated recently have been under-suscribed. Biogen SA of Switzerland went to the market for US$60 million, but only managed to secure US$25 million, whilst Hybritech of San Diego could only raise about half of the US$80 million that it was seeking. As a result of this decline in interest, the share values of many companies in the business have fallen well below the initial price, as illustrated in Figure 13.1.(17) All these companies originated in Silicon Valley. Payoff, it must be remembered,

	Share prices	
Company	Initial price US$	Market price (end 1984) US$
Amgen	18.00	4.25
Biogen	23.00	5.25
California Biotechnology	12.00	5.25
Centocor	14.00	10.25
Cetus	23.00	10.00
Collaborative Research	11.00	5.25
Genetech	35.00	50.00
Genex	9.50	8.00
Hybritech	11.00	15.50
Molecular Genetic	9.00	6.50

Figure 13.1 The collapse in share prices
The companies in our list have gone against the trend: the exception proves the rule. Genetech shares would have been higher still, but for the fact the number of shares has been increased by splitting.

comes not from basic research but from the successful development of profitable products. In the case of the one exceptionally
successful company listed in Figure 13.1, it cost nearly US$60
million to get the product *Interferon* to the marketplace. The very
expensive and long drawn out gestation period that is the inevitable accompaniment to this type of development has an adverse
effect on the initial profits and investors become disenchanted.
Then finally, even with those products that have been manufactured and marketed, the market response has been well below
what was anticipated and forecast. To take but one illustration of
this, *Humulin* is a genetically engineered insulin, but by late 1982
it had only captured a mere five per cent of the world insulin
market. The risks are indeed great.

Conclusion

It is evident that genetic engineering demands the setting up of
elaborate research organisations with a wide range of facilities and
a high degree of expertise. This is very expensive in itself, but the
expense does not stop there. The product, once developed, has to
be proved and sold and this is also a very expensive operation. It is
very evident that two quite different and distinct types of mentality
are called for: the research mentality and the business or finance
mentality. The research scientists who *have* to be deeply involved
in the initial product development are far too busy with that to
start worrying about such mundane matters as finance. Whilst they
may well be very anxious to get answers, the impelling reason is
not financial, but curiosity and a desire to succeed – with the
research, not with the business. The cost just does not enter into
their assessments of progress. In a sense it cannot: they would no
longer be good researchers if it did.

As a result of this conflict of interest a great many firms have
already come to grief and many more will follow. The obvious
solution to the problem is for the researcher to team up with the
financial entrepreneur. Where that *has* happened, success has
followed. Good business management is essential if disaster is to
be avoided.

Time also plays a very significant role, because time costs
money. The researcher is incurably optimistic and will almost
invariably under-estimate the length of time things will take and
hence how much money is needed. This is inevitable, in that the
researcher *has* to be optimistic, otherwise he would not be a good
researcher. So the research mind has to be allied with the more

cautious, critical and calculating approach adopted by the good manager.(18)

It is always a long, long way from the laboratory bench to the commercialised product, and the more novel the concept the further the distance that has to be travelled. Genetic engineering is a radical departure from all the generally known and understood forms of engineering and its early rapturous welcome had no economic basis. It was purely emotional and when the 'chickens came home to roost' as the saying goes, the failure of many companies who had entered this new field of endeavour was inevitable. It should also have been expected, for all the warning signs were there from the very beginning, but it seems they were not seen by the many. A few companies have of course entered into genetic engineering with a sound appreciation of the problems and plans to meet and overcome them, but they are very much the exception. As developments continue, regulation is likely to develop and multiply, just as it did with nuclear power, and the impact of this on the industry has yet to be seen, for it is early days yet.

References

1 Kirk, R.E. and Othmer, D.F., *Encyclopaedia of Chemical Technology,* (3rd edn), Vol. 11, John Wiley, 1980.

2 Article: 'Shaping life in the lab: and profiting from gene splicing', *Time,* (Pacific edn), 9 March 1981, pp.30-39.

3 Asinof, R., 'Averting genetic warfare', *Eventual Action,* 16, June 1984, pp.16-22.

4 Wright, S., 'Genetic engineering: the risks are real', *Christianity & Crisis,* 43, 19 September 1983, pp.329-33.

5 Comprehensive Report in *Chemical and Engineering News,* 62, 13 August 1984, pp.10-63.

6 Article: 'The birthpangs of a new science', *Economist,* 292, 14 July 1984, pp.79-83.

7 Judson, H.F., *The Eighth Day of Creation,* Simon & Schuster, New York, 1979.

8 Harsanyl, Z. and Hutton, R., *Genetic Prophecy: Beyond the Double Helix,* Wade Publishers, 1981.

9 Book review: 'Genetic engineering industry has growing pains', *Chemical and Engineering News,* 59, 6 April 1981, pp.17-22.

10 Book review: 'The promise and perils of genetic prophecy', *Chemical and Engineering News,* 60, 2 August 1982, pp.23-4.

11   Fox, J.L., 'Armos: Profile of a biotechnology firm's failure', *Chemical and Engineering News*, 60, 13 September 1982, pp.8-12.

12   Stallworthy, E.A. and Kharbanda, O.P., *Total Project Management: from Concept to Completion*, Gower, 1983.

13   Kharbanda, O.P. and Stallworthy, E.A., *Corporate Failure: Its Prediction, Panacea and Prevention*, McGraw Hill, 1985.

14   Article: 'Biotechnology companies: bugbears', *Economist*, 293, 1 December 1984, p. 94.

15   Cover feature: 'The gene doctors', *Newsweek*, 5 March 1984.

16   Article: 'The glamour goes from biotech: investors' enthusiasm running out?', *Economist*, 291, 2 June 1984, p.78.

17   Article: 'Dream delayed, dream denied', *Forbes*, 134, 17 December 1984, pp. 36-7.

18   Therrian, L. and A. Hall, 'A laurette in science – but not in business', *Business Week*, 31 December 1984, p.34+ (2 pages).

Part Five

THE END – DISASTER!

14 A giant is humbled

There can be no doubt that the construction industry offers much scope for enterprise and industry and that there is considerable opportunity for profits, since it is a growing industry worldwide. Nevertheless there are many casualties, since the law of the 'survival of the fittest' undoubtedly prevails. The industry has certain inherent risks, since typically the annual turnover of a construction company is usually some ten times the capital employed, whilst the workload can be very erratic. We now propose to look at three major contractors in the construction industry, one of whom was virtually wiped out, one who survived only because construction was but a small part of its worldwide activities, whilst the third, manufacturing construction equipment, had a meteoric rise, only for the business to collapse almost overnight. In this chapter we look at the first of these three cases.

A company of repute

Once upon a time there was a American construction company called the *Chemical Construction Corporation*, popularly known as Chemico. The company, active in the process plant construction field, worked worldwide and grew fast, in common with many other American construction companies, in the postwar construction boom that followed World War II. Its history is somewhat difficult to follow, since it changed hands several times. This is currently a common feature in the corporate world, acquisition, merger and takeover being a device for growth. The companies the subject of acquisition can be doing well, but more usually lack something – often good management or finance. Chemico did indeed change hands several times, the last change being in 1973, when it was taken over by *Aerojet General Corporation*, a subsidiary of the *General Tire and Rubber Co.* for a sum of around US$20 million. At the time Aerojet were seeking to diversify. Chemico's annual sales were running at around US$100 million and the company had a good profit record, although it had suffered a modest loss a year earlier.

Companies that are 'on the brink' in terms of profits are often a 'good buy', since they can usually be acquired rather cheaply. But for the takeover to be a success and bring a substantial turnaround in profits, there must be synergy between the new owner and his purchase. The past experience of Chemico in this area had not been too happy. Each time they had been taken over in the past they had been required to fall in line with a new and different management style: there was no synergy.

At the time of their takeover by Aerojet, Chemico had a considerable backlog of work including the Arzew contract in Algeria, which they had just signed. This was almost certainly the largest single contract Chemico had ever undertaken, and the volume of prospective work could well have been the deciding factor when Aerojet were considering the aquisition. Chemico had to fall into line with the current Aerojet management philosophy and as a result it was split into several autonomous divisions, according to its various lines of business. An Aerojet vice-president was installed as chief executive, but was soon replaced when he failed to produce results. This course of action badly demoralised the senior staff of Chemico, who were not only disturbed by the violent action 'at the top', but also felt that the formation of a series of 'little companies' not only increased overheads substantially but also reduced the effectiveness of the company as a whole. As a result many of the senior executives left, whilst others were asked to leave. In addition, and this was very serious, the project team for the Arzew contract, a major petro-chemical installation for Algeria, consisting of some twenty-five people, broke up and many of its members also left Chemico. All this had serious consequences, making a major impact on the ability of the company to complete its contracts, but was it the cause of the eventual disaster? We do not think so. We believe that the roots of failure went much deeper, but to demonstrate that we have to go back in time.

How did it all begin?

We need to go back to Bombay in the early fifties, when it was decided to build a fertiliser plant at Trombay, a suburb of Bombay, adjacent to existing petroleum refineries who would supply the necessary feedstock: naphtha in this case. By the early sixties the project had developed to the stage where the foreign exchange component of the total cost was to come from a US aid loan, this necessitating the use of an American contractor for the design of the plant. Chemico were chosen as the main contractor for Trombay I, as the project was titled, whilst the owner, the *Fertiliser Corporation of India* (FCI) as it was then called, was going to undertake the civil engineering and mechanical erection under the direction of Chemico. This was in line with Indian government policy, which had the objective of not only minimising the foreign exchange costs, but also of developing the necessary expertise locally, so that future plants could be handled without external help.

Scheduled for completion in 1963, Trombay I was finally commissioned in 1966. The cost had escalated from a first estimate of Rs.247 million to Rs.378 million. Once in operation, the plant did not work too well and just a year after commissioning a rehabilitation scheme was under way. It is our view that the overruns in time and cost were due largely to the nature of the contract, which split the responsibility for the project. Just to illustrate what happens in such a situation, FCI, as civil contractors, had to provide the compressor foundations to Chemico design. On completion, they were rejected by Chemico, who alleged poor workmanship and demanded that they be demolished and rebuilt. They threatened that if this were not done they would relinquish their responsibility for the running plant. Disputes of this nature delayed the project for many months. An expert committee from the Central Water and Power Commission examined the technical issue and decided that all was in order. They concluded that much unnecessary controversy could have been avoided by closer cooperation between contractor and owner, but in retrospect it appears that Chemico, falling behind with their own work, used this issue as a scapegoat and excuse, thus covering their own lapses.

The audit report

Following the unsatisfactory conclusion of the contract, there was an investigation, first by the Committee on Public Undertakings and then later by the Bedi Commission. Their reports raised the following questions:

1   What was the root cause of the three-year delay: delays in the execution of work by FCI, or delays in the supply of drawing and equipment by Chemico?
2   Why was there no penalty for delayed completion?
3   Why were the general manager and the financial director of FCI not associated with the discussions with Chemico?
4   Did the FCI managing director act entirely in the interests of his company?
5   Is a five per cent retention sufficient to ensure that guarantees will be met?
6   Why was the claim totalling some US$1 million against Chemico dropped?
7   Why was no spares contract included with the main plant contract?
8   Why was there no action against Chemico's admitted 'over-invoicing' against shipment in order to secure larger payments?

These questions, to which there were no satisfactory answers, demonstrate very clearly what went wrong with this particular contract. It also appears that apart from the many irregularities in the arrangements made with the contractor, there was a complete lack of communication and coordination between owner and contractor. Finally, it appears that Chemico went off 'scot free', leaving behind a very defective plant. It should have been their responsibility to ensure that it met the operational and production guarantees that must have been made when the contract was first entered into.

Whilst the several disputes between Chemico and FCI were referred to international arbitration and the proceedings have long been completed, the results have never been announced because FCI failed to pay the arbitration fees. Meanwhile the relationships between the two parties were so strained that there was charge and countercharge in the press. Chemico even went so far as to take a full page advertisement in some of the leading Indian newspapers justifying its stance and putting the entire blame on FCI. A sorry story.

Now we go to Algeria

Natural gas is a product of major importance in world energy economics and large volumes are transported over long distances from producer to user. For the economic transportation of the gas across the oceans of the world, it is necessary to liquefy it. This means cooling the gas to a very low temperature at source and then keeping it at that temperature whilst it is stored and transferred to specially designed ships that keep it liquid by continuing to refrigerate it whilst it is shipped across the world.

The first such installation in Algeria, built at Arzew and known as LNG-1, was a six-train unit that was finally commissioned in 1978. When completed it was heralded as 'the world's largest liquefied natural gas (LNG) project'.(1) But its construction had a chequered history and a dramatic aftermath, which we can highlight as follows:

Mar. 1972 The US government authorises the first long-term imports of LNG, over a 20-year period.

Mar.1973 EXIM and other banks approve a US$ 402 million financial package for a series of projects to enable the import into the US of one billion cubic feet per day of LNG from Algeria.

Apr. 1973 Chemico are awarded a contract to build a plant for the liquefaction of this gas, estimated to cost US$350 million. Work to start in May 1973, scheduled completion April 1976, with full production by mid-1977.

Nov. 1975 Sonatrach, the owner, cancels the Chemico contract.

Jan. 1976 Sonatrach concludes a contract on a cost-plus basis with the Bechtel International Corporation for the completion of the plant.

May 1976 The US Securities and Exchange Commission announces that Chemico may not have properly accounted for some US$15 million paid to it in connection with the contract.

July 1976 Sonatrach sues the General Tire and Rubber Co. (owners of Chemico) for US$45 million, alleging that three of its subsidiaries improperly used 'payoffs' whilst securing the contract.

Feb. 1977 Algeria concerned about the cost overrun, the failure of US companies to meet their commitments and the slowness of the US Federal Power Commission to act on the application for the LNG import contract.

July 1979 Arzew LNG project finally completed by Bechtel.

The contract with Chemico was cancelled by Sonatrach alleging 'total incompetence and poor performance'. The project at that time was already 7 months behind schedule and Sonatrach were under contract, with heavy penalties for delay, to supply the LNG

to the El Paso National Gas Company. Thus for them timely
completion was vital and delay extremely costly.

A lost future

The cancellation of a contract is a very rare occurrence, never
undertaken lightly. It is a most drastic comment on the performance of the contractor and since it is very public, the news soon
spreads the world over and the future business of that company
will inevitably suffer.

Reputable contractors pride themselves on the fact that much of
the work they secure is 'repeat business' from satisfied customers
and the need to have satisfied customers is a major incentive
towards efficient performance. In the present case the initial
contract was to be one of a series. LNG-1 was to be followed by
LNG-2, LNG-3 and so on over the years. Once experience has
been gained on the first project, and with a satisfied customer, it is
highly likely that further contracts will also be secured by the same
contractor. He has an in-built advantage as compared with any
other contractor, since he already has local experience. Chemico
were fortunate indeed to secure LNG-1 against stiff global competition. There is no doubt that had they performed well they
would have been in an extremely strong position in relation to the
subsequent contracts. Their 'know-how' in relation to conditions
in Algeria, by no means the easiest in the world, would have been
a great advantage. Contracts worth billions of dollars were in
prospect that would have given the company an assured future.
But that was not to be.

On cancellation of the contract with Chemico, Bechtel were
called in to 'rescue' the situation. They must have quickly established a high degree of credibility for good performance since even
before the completion of LNG-1 they had been awarded further
contracts worth some US$2 billion by the same client. Whilst
cancellation is very serious for the contractor, it is equally serious
for the owner, since there is an inevitable loss of several months in
completion whilst the new contractor takes over. There is also a
substantial financial loss, since all the benefits of the initial
competitive bid will have disappeared and a lot of the work will
have to be done again. It is therefore certain that for Sonatrach
cancellation was the last resort, yet they took it. Their reasons
were simple. In their view 'Chemico never completely engaged in
the project: never put adequate personnel and equipment on the
project'. It appears that Chemico's bid was too low in relation to
the difficult conditions prevailing in Algeria, where there were

many formalities in respect of customs clearance and frequent labour unrest. The contract offered a fixed fee together with a ceiling price for the materials and construction work and a modest escalation clause. It would appear that as the contract proceeded, Chemico began to realise that they would lose heavily on the contract. The fact that the company changed hands on the heels of concluding the contract did not help, since this resulted in the team who had first developed the project and assessed the costs being disbanded. The new team had not been involved in the initial contract negotiations and hence had no commitment. Everything that went wrong, and in particular the underestimating, could be laid at the door of those who had departed. Fearing heavy losses, Chemico in effect abandoned the project, thus precipitating a situation where the owner had no option but to cancel.

Whilst LNG-1 was a difficult contract and the biggest that Chemico had ever undertaken, the major change in management structure must have made a substantial contribution to the final disaster. The new owners, an aerospace company, sought to impose their management style on a construction company operating in a field of which they had no previous experience. The resultant demoralisation of the personnel meant that the management became disrupted and ineffective, communication with the owner suffering to such an extent that they were not even on speaking terms.

Allegations of improper conduct

Following upon the cancellation of the Algerian contract a series of investigations took place in the US. As a result the contract figured as part of a major suit by the US Securities and Exchange Commission (SEC) against Chemico's parent company, the General Tire and Rubber Company that was begun in 1976. The action was part of a post-Watergate drive to expose questionable corporate payments. This particular suit covered the broadest array of charges that the SEC had brought against any company. The charges that were made included:

1   A possible US$15 million paid by Chemico in connection with the Algerian contract.
2   Illegal and improper payments 'in excess of several million dollars' for political campaigns since the early sixties.
3   A payment (through 'overbilling') of US$500 000 to a consultant in Morocco, shared with three cabinet ministers, to secure

a tyre plant expansion.

4   Illegal payments in Chile to directors and consultants, achieved
    through a reduction in profits, in order to obtain price in-
    creases and also to maintain their monopoly there.
5   A US$300 000 'nominal' payment to government officials and
    others in Mexico to obtain certain favours.
6   Payment to a consultant in Romania to obtain approval for the
    building of a plant there.
7   A payment of US$150 000 between 1971 and 1973 to 'get off
    the Arab black list'.
8   Numerous gratuities and other benefits to military officers and
    civilian employees of executive government agencies in the US
    with whom it had contracts.

Quite a list! How were such payments made? The story goes that it
was largely achieved through over-invoicing, recording losses on
profits, the creation of 'slush funds' and cash 'doled out' by the
president of General Tire and Rubber Company from a wall safe
in his office. But what concerns us is the first item in the list, the
payment alleged to have been made by Chemico to secure the
Algerian contract. Perhaps this explains why their deplorable
record in India appeared to have no influence on their ability to
secure this major contract in Algeria.

The end of the road

The name Chemico no longer features in the listings of construction contractors. This is hardly to be wondered at, since one would
not expect the mishandling of the projects in India and Algeria to
be isolated instances. Indeed, a news item (2) alleged that the
Russian government was going to Geneva to seek arbitration in
respect of ammonia plants built by Chemico in the USSR. It
appears that Chemico were seeking relief from their performance
guarantees, their reason being a poor job of plant installation by
the Russians. That echoes what happened at Trombay. However
Chemico, when confronted with the news, denied all knowledge of
such plans for arbitration. They did however acknowledge that a
number of contractual matters were still outstanding in relation to
their Russian contracts, which they were seeking to resolve by
discussion. It would appear that the Russians, like the Indians
before them, had lost all confidence in negotiation.

LNG-1 was inaugurated in February 1978, some eight months
behind Chemico's originally scheduled completion date of mid-

1977. That must be counted a major achievement, seeing that Chemico were said to be already seven months late when Bechtel took over. How did Bechtel succeed where Chemico had failed. We have dealt with this at length elsewhere (3) but it can be summed up as the ability to learn from experience. All contractors — indeed, everyone — make mistakes, but those who succeed are those who learn from their mistakes. They listen to the voice of experience. This Bechtel most certainly have done, in the persons of their project managers. The project manager is the key figure in any project and his competence in the field of human relations is fundamental to his success. He does not stand alone and *cannot* stand alone. He heads a *team* and the project director heads a number of teams. Success lies in making sure that all the credit goes to the team. At the end of the day the project manager stands aside and lets his team 'take a bow'. Thus we find the chairman of Bechtel, Mr. S.D. Bechtel Jr., is reported as saying when the plant was inaugurated, and the world was looking on:(4)

> I am proud of our Bechtel people at Arzew. They can take great satisfaction in knowing they have done an outstanding job in helping Algeria develop this vital natural gas resource.

Conclusion

A basic precondition for success in contracting is that the contractor must work *with* the owner, or client. Both will then benefit, repeat orders will follow for the contractor and there is a continuous harmonious relationship. In India and again in Russia Chemico seem to have set themselves in *opposition* to their clients and when they adopted the same stance in Algeria the client, by cancelling their contract, brought about their collapse and disappearance from the contracting field worldwide.

It is clear that Chemico did not learn from experience. We, however, are writing this book so that our readers may learn from the experience of others. Integrity in the conduct of business is an essential to success, with sharp practice leading only to short-term advantage. Had Chemico faced up to their responsibilities at Trombay, they would have been better equipped to cope with the problems that were to come in Algeria.

References

1 Bechtel Brief, October 1979, 'Bechtel's project managers:

Roger Elton directed the world's largest LNG project'. Bechtel Briefs are published monthly by the Public Relations Department of Bechtel, PO Box 3965, San Francisco, CA 94119, USA.

2   Article in *Chemical Week,* published in New York, 20 February 1980.

3   Kharbanda, O.P. and Stallworthy, E.A., *How to Learn from Project Disasters: True-life Stories with a Moral for Management,* Gower, 1983, 273 pp.

4   Bechtel Brief, March 1978. 'Algeria's new LNG plant: fuel for US homes and industries'. For publication details see Reference 1 above.

15   The IBH fiasco

IBH Holdings, once Europe's largest construction company, started small, but it grew too fast and then got caught up in the 'whirlpool' of recession. Its founder got caught up too, finally pleading to fraud charges and being committed to prison. But that is the end of our story and we should start at the beginning.

Horst-Dieter Esch founded IBH Holdings whilst Germany was in recession, in 1974. He was but 30 years old and had little capital, but that was compensated for by plenty of boldness and imagination. In some five years, by early 1980, IBH ranked third amongst the international construction equipment companies, standing alongside giants in the field such as Caterpillar and Komatsu. The expansion was achieved largely by acquiring troubled construction equipment manufacturers at cheap prices, together with a very aggressive marketing policy. Esch, a welder's son, was materially helped in his ambitious plans by an equally ambitious and friendly banker, the aristocratic Ferdinand von Galen, a leading partner in Schroder, Munchmeyer, Hengst & Co. (SMH), a private bank with their headquarters in Frankfurt.

Apart from his ambition to build an international empire in the construction equipment business, Esch was a very persuasive salesman. Certain multinational engineering and construction companies took up part of the equity in IBH, an association which assisted the business interests of IBH, in that it further established the credibility of the company. As a result of his efforts five such companies held some 70 per cent of the IBH stock, as shown overleaf:(1)

	Holding %	Consideration US$
General Motors: *	19.6	60
Dallah Establishment:	19.6	
Powell Duffryn: **	13.2	30
Babcock International:	10.1	
Schroder, Munchmeyer, Hengst & Co.:	9.1	

* This was against Esch's purchase of GM's Terex Division, whose headquarters were in Ohio, in the US.
** This was against Esch's purchase of Powell Duffryn's Hymac Division, which made excavators.

From all this, Esch's skill as a financial negotiator is very apparent. For the purchase of the subsidiary Terex from General Motors all he gave was a promissory note for around US$250 million. The Dallah Establishment is a Saudi industrial and trading company, and he must have sold IBH well to encourage them to invest in a company so different from their normal line of business. Similarly, whilst Babcock International, a British engineering company, carries out major construction works and so used construction equipment such as was sold and hired by IBH, there was no obvious reason why they should invest in the company. In offering some of the equity to his bankers (SMH) he may well have laid a successful trap for them in connection with further borrowing, far beyond what was normal in the banking world, but we shall come to that later.

In furtherance of his objective of making IBH one of the largest construction equipment groups in the world, Esch went on what we might call a 'shopping spree', but in the process he seems to have acquired a large number of loss-making companies both in and allied to the construction industry. Since some of the equity was held by *users* of such equipment, Esch must have expected that their business would come his way.

Incautious bank funding

Thanks to the personal relationship which existed between Esch and the banker von Galen, SMH, through its subsidiaries and other companies under its control, lent some DM900 million (say US$335 million) to the IBH group against a balance sheet totalling some US$820 million, excluding the SMH's Luxembourg operations.(2) This was far in excess of what was permissible under German law, whereby a bank is required to limit outstanding loans to any borrower to 75 per cent of the paid-up capital. This restriction would have limited the loans by the bank to IBH to some US$35 million. The amount loaned was some ten times that – yet IBH was still crying out for funds.

By this time IBH were in trouble and that meant that the bank was in trouble too, since their fortunes were so intimately connected. They were likened to 'two climbers roped together on a steep mountainside – if one suddenly fell, he would drag the other along'.(1) That is exactly what happened, though it was the bank that fell first. But there is no doubt that the bank fell because of its commitment to IBH. That fall was so sudden that there was no chance whatever to retrieve the situation. It has been noted elsewhere (3) that although such company collapses *appear* to be sudden they can always be foreseen. Those 'in the know' – and in this present case that *must* include both Esch and von Galen – must have seen trouble coming. The overambitious growth of IBH, fuelled by the bank's reckless lending, must have been seen as such, whilst the bank had lent out far more than was proper in view of its resources. It was this that led to the downfall of both companies and it was a situation that did not come overnight. It was developed over a period of years and analysis of the several balance sheets would have demonstrated what was happening.

However, IBH was a private company, so no balance sheets were available to the outside observer for scrutiny. So far as can be judged from such information as has been published, it would appear that the company broke even in 1981, made a loss of some US$85 million in 1982, later reduced to US$45 million, perhaps through General Motors waiving the US$40 million still owed to them for Terex. The losses in 1983 were presumably far greater than those for 1982, but there is no definite information. It would appear that none of the major German banks were willing to get involved with IBH and it was this that led Esch to cultivate his friend von Galen. Von Galen was fully aware of the limitation imposed by German law, since he concealed what was happening by routing money to IBH in ways that hid the ultimate destination of the funds. However, it appears that the German regulatory authorities had some inkling that something was wrong and von Galen sensed this and took the initiative by going to them and disclosing to them what had been done. This was on 1 November 1983. Esch returned from a trip to New York the following day to learn that his bank was in trouble. A consortium of banks took over SBH with the blessing of the official authorities. They were able to save the bank but not von Galen and his three banking partners, who were personally liable for the losses to the full extent of their private fortunes. The collapse of SBH did not necessarily imply the immediate collapse of IBH, but once the problems of that company became public knowledge, other German banks that had been doing business with IBH, although only in a small way, cancelled any outstanding lines of credit. IBH had therefore to apply for court protection under the German bankruptcy laws. In a desperate bid for rescue, Esch proposed to pay his creditors 40 cents to the dollar over some eighteen months. The outlook for the IBH stockholders was of course poor indeed and the shares of Powell Duffryn and Babcock International, both UK based companies, fell by several points on the London Stock Exchange. It is interesting to note that, as compared with his friend von Galen, Esch, whilst chief executive and prime mover in all that had happened, was only liable to the extent of his stake in IBH, since that was a joint stock company.

Was there a loophole in the law?

This affair shows us how easy it is to hoodwink the regulatory authorities by a device as simple as using different addresses for borrowers who were actually all interrelated. Even the bank's head office in Berlin failed to notice that SMH had nearly a third of its assets at risk to one customer. The incident also brought home to the German authorities that what had happened in Italy, as demonstrated by the exploits of the late Roberto Calvi, could also happen in Germany.(2) Doubts about Luxembourg as a place to conduct financial transactions were also raised, since it was in Luxembourg that a holding company of the late Roberto Calvi's Banco Ambrosiano had defaulted on their loans, and now von Galen had used companies in Luxembourg to conceal *his* transactions.

Whilst it seems that the government in Germany is not going to be rushed into a change in the law, bankers do expect the Finance Ministry in Bonn to be less sympathetic to any suggestion that the proposed five-year transition period for the bringing of holding companies into the consolidated accounts of the parent banks might be extended. Also as a result of the IBH/SMH affair the money market rates to the smaller German banks operating from Luxembourg have been raised. Whether SMH did indeed exceed its authorised limits seems to be a matter of interpretation. In West Germany no bank can extend loans exceeding 75 per cent of its equity to any one customer. That means that SMH, with a capital of DM110 million, could lend up to DM83 million to any one customer. But through what we might call the 'back door', a factoring company in which both IBH and SMH had a 49.6 per cent stake, and hence not consolidated with the bank's accounts, IBH was loaned several million more deutschmarks. But over and above that, the SMH subsidiary in Luxembourg, with total assets of DM1,100 million, lent IBH and its associates a further DM500 million. Such lending was within the law in Luxembourg, but was far in excess of what was allowed under German law. Such a loan would also be outside the new West German law now being drafted. It seems, therefore, that businessmen of acumen can always find a 'loophole' in the law to protect themselves when they are taking actions which are most certainly against the spirit and intent of the law.

Picking up the pieces

The IBH salvage plan submitted to his bankers by Esch envisaged his retaining the German companies in the group, notably Hano-mag and Zwettelmeyer, two companies which accounted for about a third of the total group turnover in 1982 of DM2.5 billion. He further proposed to dispose of the American and British com-panies, the two biggest of these being Terex and Hymac, leaving the French and Brazilian companies in the group to sort out their own problems in accordance with the regulations of their respec-tive countries.

The Brazilian company, a subsidiary of Terex in the States, claimed to have a workload sufficient to enable it to carry on without any support from the parent company. For the French companies the collapse could not have come at a worse time, since in France the organisation CIRI, the government's industrial reconstruction committee, was in the process of finalising a financial rescue package for the four French subsidiaries – Macu-Meudon, HP Industries, Derruppe Industries and IBH-Paris. These together had made a loss of US$12.5 million in 1982 on total sales of US$88 million. Once the troubles of their parent became known to their subsidiaries in France, they wanted to 'go it alone' and of course the French government was keen to help them, since that would save some 1,100 jobs. But the construction equipment industry in France was already in deep trouble. Poclain, one of the leaders, had made a loss of US$25 million in 1982 and was expecting an even bigger loss in 1983. The firm of Richier had already been rescued by the government earlier in 1983. It is a true saying that troubles never come singly, and we expect you can now see why.

In Britain, the two companies there (Terex in Scotland and Hymac in Wales) were put into receivership. In addition, the world's biggest distributor of construction equipment, Blackford Hodge, was put at risk because it was getting nearly half its sales through Terex. Drop a little pebble in a pool and the ripples can go far and wide!

One's loss is another's gain

Naturally enough the main shareholders in IBH, General Motors, the Dallah Establishment, Powell Duffryn and Babcock International lost all, but they were all large enough to sustain the shock. But they had suffered too much to come to the rescue, seeing no possibility of salvaging any part of their original investment. On the other hand, the collapse of IBH must ultimately benefit its competitors, mainly Caterpillar and Komatsu. In the short run, however, they suffered, having to face a price war as IBH unloaded its stocks in order to get cash to pay its creditors. However, they must eventually benefit by the removal of a major competitor. There could also be some nice pickings, since both the European and American assets of IBH could prove attractive to other companies in the business.

The final drama

The rescue plan put forward by Esch was not acceptable to the banks who had come to the aid of SMH and so he had to resign. His objective, naturally enough, was to keep the group intact, although much reduced in size. Above all, Terex, the group's pride and joy, bought from General Motors in 1980, was to be kept. Terex had factories both in the US and in Scotland in the UK. Too small to be viable before IBH bought it, it would still be unable to continue on its own. However, such a company could be an ideal aquisition for a major company in the construction equipment business, such as Komatsu of Japan, just as it had been for IBH. Komatsu are second only to Caterpillar in the world market, and Terex could serve them as a firm base in the European construction equipment market. So there are potential purchasers who have every prospect of making a success of individual sections of the group, as it is broken up. The bank, SMH, also had buyers, including West Germany's biggest bank, the Deutsche Bank, because of course its loans to IBH were only a part of its business. SMH had been very successful in its securities operations, which in some sections quadrupled profits in 1983.(4)

Following the several participants in their chequered career, we see matters coming to a head in the year 1984. The main events of that year are best seen if we present them in chronological order, thus:

February: On suspicion of inflated sales figures and camouflaged inventories, the headquarters of IBH were searched. General Motors (the former owner and still a major creditor of Terex Corporation, a part of IBH Holdings) agreed to provide cash in return for its use of the Terex name and designs by a new construction equipment manufacturer to be formed by General Motors in Scotland. To this end, General Motors was negotiating to buy back Terex Limited in Scotland from the receivers in charge of IBH Holdings.

March: Esch taken into custody pending investigation of certain irregularities. The warrant was issued on the basis of a strong suspicion that Esch had given fraudulent assurances to Dallah Establishment, the Saudi Arabian investment group who had become one of his major stockholders.

August: Files of General Motors, Frankfurt, confiscated in an investigation of suspected irregularities in the capital increase of IBH.

September: The IBH receiver demands US$46.5 million from General Motors in view of the capital increase that GM had made in IBH during the period 1980-82. It was this that was partly responsible for the collapse of IBH.

November: Esch sentenced to three and a half years in prison after he had pleaded guilty to fraud charges – falsifying the balance sheet and defrauding investors in IBH.

Conclusion

It seems that the 'fall of the house of Esch' could have been prevented if it had not been built up so fast and had stood on a somewhat firmer financial foundation. The freedom to get loans in excess of what was appropriate in the circumstances led inevitably to disaster. The fact that all this happened in the midst of recession only made matters worse, bringing the collapse somewhat earlier than would have been the case in better times.

We will also remind our readers that the old adage, 'honesty is the best policy', remains true even today. Government regulations grow in complexity but they have their purpose and should be heeded.

References

1   Ball, R., 'The fall of the house of Esch', *Fortune*, 108, 12 December 1983, pp.105-6.
2   Article: 'IBH Holdings: after the fall', *Economist*, 289, 12 November 1983.
3   Kharbanda, O.P. and Stallworthy, E.A. *Corporate Failure: Its Prediction, Panacea and Prevention*, McGraw-Hill, 1985.
4   Article: 'The house that Horst built', *Economist*, 289, 3 December 1983, p.74.

16   A desert dream

We all have dreams, but it is indeed rare for our dreams to come true. We now want to look at a dream that led to disaster. This particular dream goes back to 1968, when Sueyuki Wakasugi, then a top official in the Mitsui Group, unique in that it was established in the seventeenth century and is perhaps the oldest trading company in the world, was driving through the hot barren wasteland near Abadan, some 700 km south of Tehran. He saw something quite picturesque – the gas flaring at the distant oilfields.

This sight led Wakasugi to dream of converting Iran's wasting resource, natural gas, into profitable petrochemicals through the use of Mitsui technology. There were a few years of gestation, then his dream led to the birth of the most expensive and the most embarrassing investment ever undertaken by a Japanese company.(1) Now, two oil crises (1973 and 1979), one revolution (in Iran, 1978) and one war (between Iraq and Iran, 1980-) later, Wakasugi's dream has turned into a nightmare. After three years spent in feasibility studies, construction started on site in Iran in 1976. The project was reported to be 85 per cent complete and within six months of completion in March 1979, when work on site had to be stopped due to the Iranian revolution.

Scope of the project

The project as finally agreed consisted of a world-scale ethylene cracker, with a capacity of 330 000 tonnes per annum of ethylene, together with other derivatives and liquefied petroleum gas. A 50:50 joint venture company was formed between the National Iranian Oil Company and the Iran Chemical Company, a Japanese investment company in the Mitsui Group formed specifically for the purpose of investing in this project in Iran. The plant was to be built at Bandar Shahpur, renamed Bandar Khomeini after the revolution. (Bandar is the persian word for 'harbour' or 'port'.) The project made technical, commercial and even political sense. A waste resource was to be converted into valuable products for which there was not only a direct need within Iran itself, but also an increasing world demand at the time the project was planned. Mitsui not only provided the necessary initiative but also the technology and the finance. In addition they underwrote the marketing of a substantial proportion of the finished products, since the Iranian domestic market was not all that large. It was a project patently in the best interests of both the main parties involved and, if it had been brought to a successful conclusion, both would have been well satisfied.

After the revolution

As we said above, work on the project stopped when the revolution came in March 1979. However, the revolution as such over, construction of the complex was resumed in the summer of 1980 after protracted negotiations. However, work had to be halted again in October of that same year because of the outbreak of the Iraq-Iran War and the aerial bombing of the worksite. From then on there had been sporadic resumptions of work, only for it to be stopped again when bombing was renewed. We do not need to pursue its history further, nor even to wonder whether it will ever be completed and come into commercial production, because our interest is not so much the project as the impact it had upon the Mitsui Group back in Japan. We have a project, initially financially sound, that was bedevilled first by a revolution and then by a war. What happened in financial terms?

The cost

The initial cost of the project was estimated at about US$500 million. This cost was to be shared equally between the two partners, since they each had a half-share in the company formed to build and run the plant. By 1979, with the project 85 per cent complete, the estimated cost had risen to more than US$1 billion, at least double the initial estimate. This is by no means surprising – to us, at least. It happens quite often, as we have demonstrated elsewhere.(2) This meant that the financial contribution required of the Mitsui Group had risen from US$250 million to US$500 million, with no end in sight. There was some very tough negotiations, and the Iran government finally agreed to provide all the further finance required to complete the project. But the plant would have to be completed before Mitsui could even begin to think of any return on their massive investment, and they were still committed to providing technical support. The possible final cost of the project is of course still an unknown. An estimate three years later (3) indicated that some US$3.6 billion had already been spent and that a further US$2 billion would be required to get the plant repaired, rehabilitated and working. Of course, this would make the final cost some twelve times the original estimate and the project could no longer be assessed in normal financial terms. To make any sense of the financial calculations, the Iran government will have to write off most of the cost, to give the operating company a reasonable base from which to begin. This has happened often enough with nationalised companies in the past, but the Mitsui Group has a 50 per cent interest in this particular company. We doubt, however, whether they will ever share in any ostensible profits such as might then be shown in the accounts.

Mitsui 'on the hook'

This joint venture between Iran and Japan began in the private sector. It was conceived and then nurtured by the Mitsui Group and it seems that in the beginning they thought it such a good deal that they kept it all to themselves. The government were not consulted. This approach was in sharp contrast to that adopted by the joint ventures for petrochemical complexes entered into by Mitsubishi in Saudi Arabia and Sumitomo at Singapore. Both of these were declared 'national projects' from the very start. They were approved by the government beforehand and as government-sponsored projects they enjoyed financial and other support from the Japanese government.

When the Iranian project ran into trouble it was burdened with interest payments then running as high as US$450 000 *per day*. Apart from loss of 'face', Mitsui stood to lose some US$68 million in hard cash, this representing the uninsured portion of the project. This came at a time when the overall prospects for the Group were none too good. So – this was in December 1978 – the then Chairman of Mitsui, Yoshido Ikedo, suggested that real political determination was now needed to deal with a very serious situation. He therefore requested the Japanese Prime Minister to declare the project a 'national project'. The reaction of the government was that, whilst they were prepared to 'pitch in', they were not willing to bail Mitsui out. As for declaring the project a 'national project', why should they? The government had not been consulted as had been the case with the other two projects termed 'national projects'.(1)

One of the pre-requisites to declaring a project a 'national project' was that a number of different Japanese companies were to be involved, but here there was only one – Mitsui. To overcome this particular hurdle, Mitsui persuaded some 70 other Japanese companies and 20 banks to invest a total of US$23 million in the project. This was designed to secure government support. At the same time, representatives from MITI and the Ministry of Finance, who had underwritten the project, visited Iran. They concluded that, whilst the project did not have a very bright economic future the Japanese government would be the biggest loser, since they had insured the project.

As a result of all this 'wheeling and dealing' the project was finally declared a 'national project', the Japanese government together with the Export-Import Bank agreeing to help to salvage the project by investing in it. This was in October 1979. Their total new investment at that time was some US$440 million, of which US$88 million had been found by the Japanese government and the rest by the Import-Export Bank and some other commercial banks. At this same time the estimated cost of the project had risen to US$3.2 billion.

A further complexity was the incident of the American hostages at Tehran. When this happened Japan, in order to safeguard its venture, would not join with the US in imposing sanctions against Iran. Construction was delayed whilst tense bargaining took place in Tokyo, Tehran and Washington. Then, following further bombing of the plant by Iraq all 750 Japanese workers transferred from the site to Tehran. Were they, too, hostages?

By the end of this year (1980) Japan felt it had to decide whether to pull out with a potential loss of US$1.4 billion or come up with a further US$80million or more to keep the project afloat. It is at this point that a Mitsui executive declares: 'If we continue we will fall into hell. If we withdraw we fall into hell.' Iran was pressing Japan to pay half the construction costs incurred before suspension, some US$120 million, together with the costs of repatriating the Japanese workers and the interest payments on loans and salaries for 1 400 Iranians. Don't forget that Mitsui had a 50 per cent stake in the project and should therefore have borne 50 per cent of the cost. The Vice-Minister for International Affairs back in Japan, Naohiri Amaya, declared:

> Japan must not give up the project ... it will decide the destiny of relations between Japan and the Middle East.

Whilst we have headed this section of our story 'Mitsui on the hook' it is now very evident that it is the Japanese government that is 'on the hook', having taken over much of the financial burden.

The political impact

The history of this particular project illustrates very clearly the problems of risk analysis when it comes to political judgments. Just two years prior to the revolution Iran was considered to be politically stable: one of the most stable countries in the Middle East and a prime area for industrial development. This must also have been the considered opinion of those shrewd Japanese businessmen who put their money into the venture, or they would never have begun. Of course, there was strong motivation for the project in that the Japanese were thereby making sure of a crude oil entitlement. This was undoubtedly the main factor and a fundamental pre-requisite to Mitsui investing in this billion-dollar project. But that too was very dependent upon political stability.

Whilst the project was considered to be financially sound in the beginning, it is also true that Japanese investment in Iran and elsewhere in the Middle East has been dictated mainly by the desire to ensure an uninterrupted supply of crude oil and related products.(4) This is the object of 'entitlements', as they are called, and this was an integral part of the contract entered into for this project. This basic motivation behind such Japanese investment has been confirmed by independent Western observers.(5)

We have to remember that we are now looking at Japan's biggest single foreign investment. The Japanese consortium decided in April 1983 that they would not make any further investment, despite Iran's insistence that Mitsui should increase their investment to cover their share of the enormous cost overrun, both present and future.(3) Any further investment had to be viewed against falling oil production and a large reduction in the oil revenues accruing to Iran. Also, as a result of the Iraq-Iran War and the destruction that had occurred at the Abadan Refinery, that cheap gas feedstock had also largely disappeared.

All these factors brought Mitsui to the conclusion that enough was enough. The last straw apparently was an Iranian veto on a plan to pay off the Iranian workers for the duration of the war. The Japanese government had also backed out, refusing to pay the US$94 million that they had agreed to provide earlier. Mitsui, to protect their own interest in the project, continue to express their determination to complete the project, but they at the same time resolutely refused to commit any more funds.

In the meantime, of course, the international scene had changed quite drastically. In view of the limited domestic market, the bulk of the products from the complex were to have been exported, but now two other world-scale petrochemical complexes have been completed, one in Saudi Arabia and the other in Singapore, and are taking up the market long before Bandar Khomeini is finished, *if* at all. In addition, looking only at the Near and Far East, further projects in China, India, Indonesia, Malaysia and Thailand are in advanced stages of planning. Except for those in India and China, these plants will all be making the bulk of their products for export. Since there is still general overcapacity in petrochemicals worldwide, the gravity of this in relation to Bandar Khomeini is apparent. There is no longer a market. They are going to be far too late. This is a continuing dilemma for both parties. However, the motivation appears to remain political, rather than economic. Iran, as a matter of national pride, may well want to see the project completed and producing, although there is now every likelihood that it will be abandoned.

What of the future?

Mitsui did not collapse, as did Chemico when confronted with a major project disaster (the case dealt with in Chapter 14). This is in part due, of course, to government intervention and also in part because of national attitudes and policy. The banks in Japan play a very protective role, and this is to be seen here. Mitsui were able to get wide support from the banks when they saw that they had to spread the risk in order to get the Japanese government to intervene.

But have Mitsui learnt any lessons as a result of this disastrous venture? It would seem so, since they have now pulled out of a number of other overseas ventures. One interesting development is the share that Mitsui has taken in an Australian North West Shelf LNG Export project. They have a one-sixth share only, whilst Mitsubishi have another sixth share. So no longer are they seeking to have it all. It is also interesting to note that their Japanese partner is in fact a competitor.

We have taken a look at this particular project to see what lessons there are for us. It is very clear that disaster came primarily because the political situation changed drastically overnight. Could that have been foreseen? The answer to that is simple and direct: it is no. The future cannot be predicted, however much economists would like us to believe that it can. This is therefore a 'fact of life' that we have to reckon with, but cannot avoid. For example, only a few months before the oil crisis of 1973, the pundits were full of predictions, but they were all rosy ones. They saw no change coming. But, once the change came, they pointed out that their predictions had been qualified. So they still professed to be right. It is somewhat like the weather-man telling us that there is a 10 per cent chance of it raining today. Whether it rains or not he is right! However, having heard his forecast and seeing that the possibility of rain was less that 50 per cent, we made our judgments, went out without an umbrella – and got wet!

So did Mitsui.

Conclusion

The experience of Mitsui in Iran makes it very clear that the future *cannot* be forecast. Intuition, or what some call the 'sixth sense', is often better than any technical forecast, but even that often fails. Except for the 'politics' the project would have been completed very satisfactorily, an end that was ardently desired by *both* the parties, even after the change in government. But once war intervened, it would have been far better and cheaper to abandon the project. Mitsui did indeed seek to do this, but the government in Iran still wished to carry the project through to completion, presumably for reasons of prestige, since it was very apparent that it could never be a financial success. Thus economic considerations were put far into the background.

References

1   Wiegner, K.K., 'Saving skin but losing face' Forbes, 124, 74ff., 15 Oct. 1979.
2   Kharbanda, O.P. and Stallworthy, E.A., *How to Learn from Project Disasters: True-life Stories with a Moral for Management,* Gower, 1983.
3   Editorial: 'Mitsui moves to a showdown', *Economist,* 279, 2 May 1981, pp.79-80.

194 THE END – DISASTER!

4 El-Zaim, I., 'Japanese corporate strategy and orientations', *Arab Economist*, 2, December 1978, pp. 5-32.
5 Report: 'Middle East industrialisation', published by the Royal Institute of International Affairs, 1980.

Part Six

MANAGEMENT IS THE KEY

17 The power of politics

It should be realised that 'politics' is not confined to governments and their actions, or even the relations between governments, the public and companies. Politics – what we might call internal politics – play a role within most companies. Those in a company seeking to 'get to the top', will often manoeuvre and manipulate where they can, 'pull strings', curry favour and so on. This is never good for a company when it occurs. It is often counter-productive and usually destructive. But apart from emphasising how undesirable such activities are, we do not propose to enter further into that aspect of management. We are more concerned with the activities of governments and the way in which these activities impinge on companies and the projects they implement. The case studies that we have developed and analysed in the earlier chapters have given us a number of examples where governmental action has been a major contribution to final disaster. If we are to prevent and avoid disaster, then it is important to appreciate the way in which governments work and act in relation to industry. Their actions are always politically motivated: that is why we speak of the 'power of politics'.

Beware red tape

One outstanding and continuing feature of all governments is what may be called the bureaucratic approach. So close, so constant, is the relationship between bureaucracy and government that it has been enshrined in the dictionaries. For instance, the *Concise Oxford Dictionary* defines it thus:

> **bureaucracy:** government by central administration: officialdom or officials of such government.

bureaucrat: (esp. *unimaginative*) official in bureaucracy.

The italics are ours. It is this concept that is the constant image of the bureaucrat and in this way bureaucracy is equated with inefficiency, constant delay and completely unimaginative handling of business and people.

Another term synonymous with unimaginative bureaucracy is the phrase 'red tape', although it seems to have fallen out of fashion. The term derives from the red ribbon that lawyers used at one time to bind their documents together, and 'red tape' refers to the legalistic approach to a subject so often adopted by the bureaucrat, which seems to the onlooker merely a device to avoid doing anything constructive – or, indeed, doing anything at all.

So important is this aspect of bureaucracy that a full length book has been devoted to the subject.(1) This book makes the point that whilst 'red tape' is almost universally hated, yet it seems to get everywhere. The writer poses what is for him a mystery – and for us too: how is it that something so unpopular can be so widespread and enduring? He can give us no explanation, it appears, but he concludes:

> Red tape has thus taken its place with death and taxes as an inevitability of life. It may be even more endurable than they are ...

It seems then that bureaucracy and its most irritating manifestation, red tape, are something that we will never be able to avoid and must therefore learn to live with. It is a constraint that we must work within when running a company or developing a project. Due recognition of the impact of bureaucracy, its potential and the development of techniques to minimise its effects are thus an integral part of proper project management.

The impact of regulation

An essential element in project management, and vital to success, is cost control. The impact of government regulation has now become a most significant factor in cost, often taking it out of the control of management. Whilst caring governments may well spew out a multitude of regulations, their implementation costs money. When they are issued and have to be implemented during the lifetime of a project, they inevitably undermine the estimates of cost that have been prepared and can well make a significant contribution to ultimate disaster.

In Chapter 7 when dealing with the present situation in relation to the development of nuclear power plants, we said little about the impact of the multitude of regulations that have been and still are being issued by governmental authorities, largely with a view to protecting the public, chiefly because we have said it all before.(2) One reviewer of that book got to the heart of the matter, we feel, in making the following comment:(3)

> Here it must be said that people insist on being warmed, air conditioned and attaining ever higher standards of living, oblivious of the continually increasing amount of the earth's surface which must be torn up to meet their 'just' aspirations. Nuclear power is bound to come, declare the authors, but to meet the costs, environmental demands will have to be reduced ... It must have been noticed that the profitable explorations of deep sea and dense forest by naturalists, some of whom spearhead the environmental protests, make a good living by selling their services to television and glossy book publishers. They could not do so, except by using the sophisticated equipment manufactured in great industrial conglomerations.

This comment highlights the inherent conflict that exists and will continue to exist whilst we have an industrially-orientated society. People wish to enjoy the fruits of industrial development and technological innovation, but they are most reluctant to pay the price. Regulation is, of course, a part of that price.

The statistics of regulation

When it comes to assessing the impact of regulation upon industry, we go to the United States, since not only do the States have a highly regulated society, but the statistics are fairly readily available. There were said to be some fifty-five Federal Agencies manned by some eighty thousand bureaucrats in 1979, and we would expect that figure to have grown since then. The cost of preparing regulations, monitoring their application and complying with them is estimated to exceed US$100 billion per year in the US alone, some 95 per cent of that cost being borne by industry, the balance by the taxpayer. But of course the taxpayer pays all in the end, since the cost of complying with the regulations is ultimately reflected in the prices he pays for goods or services. What the figure is worldwide we hardly dare to speculate – US$250 billion a year?

But this is only what we might call the visible cost of regulation. There is much that is hidden, including such things as companies failing because of the regulatory burden, innovation stifled and productivity reduced because of the time and effort taken in complying with the regulations, completing all the forms of application, making returns and the like.

Let us be quite clear as to the implications. No one would wish to dispute the need for pure water, clean air and the protection of the environment. These are the prime objectives of regulation. But there must be a proper balancing of need and risk both in establishing and enforcing regulations, if all initiative and innovation is not to be strangled at birth. The need for a balanced approach is now beginning to be seen.

Regulating the regulators

In the past we have seen what amounts to a war between the regulatory bodies and industry at large. But as we saw, one of the consequences of the Bhopal disaster was to cause the American management to start urging further regulation. We suggested that companies should adopt a much more open policy and let their neighbours know what they were doing. This has the result of opening up a debate in which the government departments can be joined, bringing the questions and the problems into reasoned public discussion. Once a constructive dialogue is built up between the two key parties – those drafting the regulations and those who have to obey them – real progress to the benefit of all can be made. One government official, an economist who spent some four years on an in-depth study of the impact of regulations has made two suggestions which we think have great merit:(4)

1 Each regulation *must* be accompanied by an economic impact statement.
2 Every regulatory agency should be constantly reviewed to determine its continuing usefulness.

If such an analytical approach were adopted, the community and the environment could be well protected at less exorbitant cost.

Bureaucratic rule

Bureaucrats, by definition, as we saw at the beginning of this chapter, relate to government. They are its officials. But as we also said, bureaucrats are by no means confined to government circles. They are everywhere. Let us see where that thought leads us. Let us first consider the bureaucrats in government. Peter Drucker, styled by many as a 'management guru', is convinced that government – any government – is totally incompetent as an industrial manager. His advice to governments, if they would improve in this respect, is to follow a three-point formula:(5)

1   Clear and specific goals
2   Set priorities
3   Abandonment

He adds movingly, from his own personal experience, that the last of the above three pieces of advice is the toughest to carry out, the most novel, and yet the most important of the three. What is 'abandonment'? It means bringing something to an end once its purpose has been served. A good example is to be found in what are called the 'sunset' laws in the US. These are laws setting up a government agency, but where, within the same law, the agency and its programme is terminated after a given time. That is, we feel, a very sensible approach, but there are a multitude of cases where an agency long survives its usefulness. We feel we brought you one example in Chapter 8, when we were discussing the attempts made in the US to develop synthetic fuels. The Synfuel Corporation, set up by Act of Congress, now has a life of its own and it seems, you will remember, that Congress finds great difficulty in closing it down, even although there is a general feeling that it is serving no useful purpose. This may change.

The role of government

We want to look at bureaucracy in industry, but before we do that let us define the role of government and its bureaucrats. Speaking of government performance worldwide, Peter Drucker feels that it has been miserable indeed, except in certain specific fields. His major indictments of government are:(6)

*   Government can only wage war and inflate the currency
*   Government is utterly incompetent as an industrial manager

* Government is all-powerful, yet it has no effective control over its own organs of administration
* Government has failed in key areas which are their affair, such as creating a welfare state, good urban development, education and public transport
* Government has failed to create a new and happy society

These are all incontrovertible statements: any one of us, wherever we are in this wide world, have only to look around is to see that it *is* so.

Many attempts have been made from time to time to alter the system. Politicians of various persuasions come and go, but the situation remains almost unchanged. Indeed, one wonders at times whether it is getting worse, rather than better. This being so, it has to be recognised that government agencies, whatever the country, are the very last place from which to run a project or operate a company. The bureaucrat must never be placed in a position where he has to manage. Since governments, these days, are becoming more and more involved in industrial activity by way of initiation and finance, they have to be told that they *must not* provide the management. They *must* leave all that to the professionals. They must call in the consulting engineer, the manufacturer, the contractor and leave the actual work in private hands. A project run by bureaucrats is doomed from the start.

Bureaucracy in industry

Since, as Peter Drucker dares to assert, 'government is utterly incompetent as an industrial manager' and any government consists, at least in managerial circles, of bureaucrats, it must be accepted that a bureaucratic approach to project management would be a recipe for disaster. According to our own experience, bureaucracy is never seen in the smaller organisation. It only springs to life as an organisation grows in size.

We must not confuse regulation with bureaucracy. Regulation is both necessary and desirable, even in the smallest of companies and with every project, whatever its size. Can we illustrate that with an example from the field of project cost control? For successful project cost control good commitment control is vital. In connection with the creation of commitments there is one rule that is basic and that is incorporated in the financial rules of practically every company. That rule is very simple:

No commitment may be entered into with an outside company without prior *written* authorisation

The rule is of course supported by further regulations defining who may or may not issue such written authorisations, or orders, at various levels of management according to the amount involved. In the bureaucratic system that is the end. But in a normal company the rule is broken in an emergency, the individual assuming an authority that is not really his for the benefit of the project. Provided there is no abuse, such a situation can be accepted by management – but not by bureaucrats.

Government intervention

Governments, it seems, cannot stand aloof when projects collapse and companies fail. There are of course many examples of this worldwide, some so well-known as to be notorious. For governments, far too much is too often at stake. Unemployment is a major concern and collapse in one area or sector of the economy can often lead to collapse in others. Then there is the matter of what is called 'public confidence': the anxiety of governments to prevent bank failures is an example of that. However, we question very much the value of continuing government support. There is always the danger that poor management will be shielded from the consequences of its own shortcomings. After all, at the point in time when government comes to the rescue, the very fact that it *needs* to come to the rescue is an indication that something is sadly wrong – almost inevitably, with management. It is hardly our role to advise governments, but I suppose we have already passed on one piece of advice: that their administrators should not become involved in industrial managerial activity. Perhaps, then, it is also worth saying that whilst governments may well feel in certain circumstances that their political ends are served by saving projects or companies, they should take great care to see that they are not perpetuating bad management. So far as the objectives of this book are concerned, we would advise those initiating projects and wishing to see them brought to a successful conclusion, not to seek government intervention if it can possibly be avoided. In certain circumstances government finance may be acceptable and even welcome, but it must be reiterated that the project that is so supported should still be allowed to 'go its own way'. The bureaucrats must resist the temptation to intervene.

... and the lack of it

Probably one of the best examples of an effective relationship between government and management is to be found in the history of the relationship between British Leyland and the UK government. British Leyland was a conglomerate manufacturing a wide range of automobiles, lorries and buses and its survival was considered vital to the continuing growth of British industry. Successive governments had pumped millions into the company, but it continued on a downhill path, unable to compete effectively either in the home market or abroad. It therefore became a massive loss maker. In 1978 Sir Michael Edwardes was appointed chairman and chief executive, and both ran and ruled the company for some five years. He has written a book about his experiences with the most descriptive title: *Back from the Brink*, which means we are able to have an 'inside view' of all that went on.(7) It is a fascinating story, but for the moment all we wish to assess is the relationship between Sir Michael, his management and the government that appointed him.

Summing up the five years of his management, during which he succeeded in turning the company around, so that it was making a profit rather than massive losses, we see that Sir Michael managed to continue to have government support throughout, despite much opposition. The policy of the government in power at the time was to 'privatise' the nationalised companies wherever that was possible. However, that did not happen with British Leyland during the tenure of Sir Michael Edwardes, although one very successful division, Jaguar Cars, has been sold off to the public since he left. After some eighteen months in office, Sir Michael's assessment of the position was brief and candid:

> Management simply lost control of the situation. Models were not, or could not be updated. Quality and production fell to unacceptable levels, and disputes reached four or five times the sort of level that a 'continuous production' industry can stand ... Britain and the world blamed the unions, and turned their back on British Leyland products. But the real blame lay with management, for they failed in their duty to manage.

Sir Michael must have been quite persuasive within government circles, seeing that the government was in effect choosing between pumping more and more money in to keep British Leyland going, or cutting their losses. However, what is of immediate interest to us is the relationship that was maintained between government and management, despite the massive financial stake that the government had in the company. The government of the day was led by Mrs. Margaret Thatcher, and she expressed the government view thus:

> I never want to take on another BL. We shouldn't be in it at all, but now we're in it we have to choose the time and we have to back Michael Edwardes' judgment. He's the manager, I'm not the manager . . .

Despite being so closely involved and so desperately committed, Mrs. Thatcher never showed the slightest inclination to interfere in matters of detail in relation to British Leyland, not even in issues such as employee relations, which were of prime importance to the government. Thus they exemplified a basic principle of management: if you have a dog, don't bark yourself. The technical term is management by delegation. If all governments adopted a similar approach to the projects with which they were financially involved, there would be fewer disasters.

Conclusion

Government intervention and regulation *may* lead to the failure of a company or a project, unless they are used with great discretion. However well intentioned, intervention and regulation rarely achieve the objectives in view. The function of government is to govern: *not* manage. The latter function must be left to competent managers if disaster is to be prevented.

References

1 Kaufman, H., *Red Tape: Its Origin, Uses and Abuses,* Brookings Institution, 1977.
2 Kharbanda, O.P. and Stallworthy, E.A., *How to learn from project disasters: True-life Stories with a Moral for Management,* Gower, 1983.
3 Tebby, J.M. 'Book review', *General Engineer,* July/August 1983, pp.180-3.
4 Weidenbaum, M.L., 'Time to control runaway regulation', *Readers Digest,* (US edn), June 1979, pp. 98-102.
5 Drucker, P.F., *The Changing World of the Executive,* Allied Publishers, 1982.

6   Sapre, S.A., *Of Clouds and Clocks in Administration,* Directorate of Government Printing and Stationery, Bombay, 1973.
7   Edwardes. M., *Back from the Brink: an Apocalyptic Experience,* Collins, 1983.

18 Man and management

The subject of management has attracted an enormous amount of literature. Both academic and industrial circles have contributed extensively to the ever-growing literature on management. This is all to the good and a perusal of what has been written should make us wiser. Certainly the practising manager with experience may benefit, but a manager just entering the field could well be completely bewildered and confused, unable to see the wood for the trees.

Keep it simple, stupid

In view of the volume of information, a simple down-to-earth book on the basics of management (1) is to be welcomed. This book names three foundation blocks for good management:

1 Back-to-basics management
2 Interpersonal relations
3 Effective communication

Back-to-basics management comprises the assimilation of news, information and comment. This leads to knowledge. Knowledge, when meditated upon, leads to understanding. Understanding, associated with commitment and discipline *is* back-to-basics management.

The academician enjoys research and writes on management subjects primarily for the sake of knowledge. Theories galore are developed, but of what use are all these theories unless they can be put into practice. For the academician a theory may be an end in itself, but for those involved in management it is the practice that matters. It is only through practice that managers achieve results and thereby become effective in their business life. We are reminded of a saying with much wisdom in it:

> Knowledge without practice accompanying it is superior to practice without knowledge. Practice with knowledge is superior to knowledge without practice accompanying it.
>
> – Yoga Vasishtha

We think that this theme, central to successful management, is well summed up by the acronym: KISS – Keep It Simple, Stupid! This acronym has been at the heart of all our writing on management, exemplified, we feel, by a chapter that had the title: Simple *is* beautiful.(2) It is a well-established fact, little though we may like to hear it, that humans are not good at processing large streams of new data – this being perhaps the only area, apart from speed, where a computer has the edge over the human. Further, it has been established that the most we can hold in our short-term memory, immediately accessible, without forgetting something, is six or seven items of data. Well, here again practice seems well ahead of theory. The companies who excel have not only realised what is needful but have held fast to the 'KISS' principle despite the enormous pressures on them to complicate things. Whilst complication serves to impress, it usually fails to 'deliver the goods'.

Simple rules

Having recognised the need to get back to basics, what are these? Let us turn to an industrial manager who is also active in academic circles, having an MBA in management and a PhD in economics for an answer. He is currently a senior institute staff member at IBM Corporation's Information Systems Management Institute. According to him the present complex and competitive business world requires managers with a broad range of skills and a highly developed acuity in *personal* as well as business matters.(3) An effective manager must be able, inter alia, to:

> Make financial decisions
> Perceive the needs of the marketplace
> Implement latest technological developments
> Communicate well with his people
> Motivate his people in order to accomplish company's goals

But of course the manager does not stand alone. Results are achieved by teams, rather than individuals operating on their own. Good managers are not 'doers', but rather the developers and encouragers of 'doers'. This latter function is all-important and makes the greatest contribution of all to good management and its end result, the success of the company.

How does this come about? A team brings together all the qualities for success: qualities which any one individual could never possess. An expert has identified eight key team roles essential to effectiveness, each of these being associated with a particular personality.(4) We set out this relationship thus:

1	Leader	Calm, confident, controlled
2	Office Worker	Conservative, dutiful, predictable
3	Completer	Painstaking, orderly, conscientious, anxious
4	The monitor	Sober, unemotional, prudent
5	Designer	Individualistic, orderly, conscientious
6	Searcher	Extroverted, enthusiastic, curious
7	Shaper	Highly strung, outgoing, dynamic
8	Operator	Socially oriented, mild, sensitive

You can, we are sure, identify these roles in your particular company. The 'leader' will be the chairman or chief executive, the searcher the salesman, whilst a 'monitor' type makes a good inspector. With an optimum mix, a team can achieve far more than the individuals, operating singly, could accomplish: this is called synergy, literally meaning that the combined effect of the team exceeds the sum of their individual efforts. This comes as a result of their good interpersonal relations – one of the three foundation blocks for good management noted by us at the beginning of this chapter.

The leader's role

Teams *have* to have a leader, whether we think of our team as the company as a whole, or as a group within it. Successful companies will have a multiplicity of teams each with its own leader: we call them managers whether or not they have that title in the organisation to which they belong. But it is a valid point that many of the qualities required in a good manager are mutually exclusive. He is called upon to be highly intelligent – but not too clever. He must be forceful – yet sensitive to people's feelings. He must be dynamic – whilst exercising patience. A fluent communicator, yet a good listener. What a man! And if you find such a rarity, what do you do when he steps under a bus or a competitor steals him away? Nevertheless, let us assume that we have competent managers. It is they who have to build a team around them. And 'build' is the operative word. Individuals *can* grow in their jobs, assume greater responsibility and thrive, if they are working in a collaborative, team-oriented climate. One writer on this aspect of our subject puts it thus:(5)

> The task is not to change people. People are perfectly alright the way they are. The task is not to motivate people. People are inherently self-starting. The task is to remove those things that demotivate them, to get them out of their way. Or, more precisely, to create those kinds of organisational structures that allow workers to get at problems and act in some independent ways so they can develop their skills solving problems related to their own jobs.

This particular author sees the team as a potential resource for problem solving. The key to his approach is to encourage that which is in opposition – be it an individual, a department or a union – to function *as part of the team*. Thus the full potential of the organisation is achieved and progress will be made.

Putting theory into practice

Japan has emerged from the ashes to reach the top of the industrial league of nations in about three decades, a remarkable achievement by any standard. Experts ascribe this miracle primarily to the Japanese style of management, which has been the subject of a host of books and articles in recent years. Developed and developing countries alike have been exhorted to look to Japan and learn.(6, 7) Having begun as a mere 'imitator', Japan is now seen as the great example for imitation. What a role reversal! Thanks to their productivity, which has steadily increased over the years, together with harmonious management-worker relationships, Japan has come to dominate industry after industry. So impressive has been the progress of Japan in the industrial sphere that the US now seeks to emulate the Japanese style of management. This has its own irony, since most of the so-called Japanese concepts originated in the US. This situation has been most tersely summed up by the co-founder of the Honda Motor Company as follows: 'Japanese and American management is 95 per cent the same and different in all important respects.' What are these differences?

In Japan, men (and women) are the focus of all that is done. The individual is at the centre of it all and family life merges into that of the corporation. Parents are involved at the time of hiring and they are even rewarded for their offspring's achievements. All decisions are by consensus, so important is each individual's role seen to be. No one is left out of anything. This assures commitment, so essential to proper performance, and brings with it a harmonious work team: an approach which guarantees success. Salary is related to seniority, but promotion is on merit. This can lead to what some would consider a paradox: the head of a group receiving a lower salary than some of his team. Director and worker usually wear the same uniform and eat in the same canteen. This ensures a basic work formula: 'us *plus* them', rather than 'us *vs.* them', the attitude that prevails in most of the rest of the world. Excellent human relations are the result which, combined with long hours and complete dedication, has been a major factor in taking Japan where it is today.

Further, Japanese workers and managers are encouraged to continue learning throughout their working career. Specialists broaden their knowledge of allied fields and with considerable job rotation, can step into another's shoes at short notice. A Japanese worker may well spend some five hundred days in training during a ten-year working span. This cross fertilisation, achieved through job rotation and training, encourages creativity and leads to a spate of suggestions for the improvement of quality and productivity. Individuals and groups are recognised and rewarded for such achievements and share the financial gains that follow as a result.

So, what is the lesson for us? It should be clear that no management style, however effective, can be transplanted from one country to another with a very different culture, different values, and a different background. But whilst the Japanese system cannot be directly imitated it can be adapted and its principles used to strengthen current practice. To do this calls for in-depth study not only of the individual situation in any particular country, but also the situation in the individual company, for not only countries but also companies have a culture, as we have seen. One of the most interesting exercises in this field is happening in the UK, where Japanese companies have been setting up factories over the past few years. They have introduced their own management style with a high degree of success, but they have had the advantage of starting with a green field site. They have not, as yet, attempted to reform an existing, long-established company in that country. A basic element in their approach has been to agree with the unions that one union only represent *all* those employed at the factory. They have also been successful in agreeing 'no-strike' provisions.

The West can learn a lot from the Far East in matters related to productivity and labour turnover. This is typified by Japan, although other countries in that area seem to be learning fast. Both subjects have lately been the cause of considerable concern in most of the industrialised countries of the West and merit very serious attention, but many of the Japanese management practices are specific to Japan and *cannot* be transferred to other countries, as a recent survey established with some degree of certainty.(8)

The importance of the individual

Having seen that management is the crux of a successful company, having recognised that management is made up of men and women organised into teams, it is but logical to turn to a consideration of those men and women. We have also seen that the Japanese miracle is largely due to the emphasis placed on the individual. There they seem to have taken to heart the concept:(9)

To plan – for one year	– is to plant seed
– for ten years	– is to plant trees
– for a lifetime	– is to develop a *man*

Yet whilst in Japan so much emphasis is placed on the individual, the individual Japanese identifies himself *completely* with his company. In introducing himself, your visitor does not say, for instance, 'I am an engineer' but 'I am a Matushita man'. This association between the individual and the company goes so deep that one can tell the difference between a Mitsui manager and a Mitsubishi manager. Such is the identity of the person with the organisation.

In the West, however, attitudes are entirely different. Listen to the plaint of an auto worker there:(9)

> You really begin to wonder. What price do they put on me? Look at the price they put on the machine. When that machine breaks down, there's somebody out there to fix it right away. If I break down, I'm pushed over to the other side

until another man takes my place. The only thing they have on their mind is to keep that line running.

The management mentality that creates a situation where a worker is moved to make such statements is of course well on the road to disaster. The individual matters: he matters very much.

Nevertheless, despite the importance of the team and the quality of the individuals who make up that team, it still seems that it is the quality of the man (or woman) who leads a company that is all-important. This seems to be completely independent of the quality of the rest of the men and women who also work for the company. An outstanding personality *below* the top cannot bring success. He is a team member in the wrong place, a recipe for disaster rather than success. The chief executive more than anybody else will make or break a company. So, coming to assess potential disaster, never fail to look closely and very, very carefully at the chief executive. Let us do just that.

The principle of delegation

Having considered both the importance of the chief executive and his relationship with his team, let us ask the question: what are the qualities and characteristics that should be seen in the chief executive? What sort of a manager will he (or she) be?

Does the chief executive sit back and order everybody around? Does he hire and fire? Does he have a 4-hour day or a 16-hour day? A great deal has been written on this subject and we propose to present you with a brief outline of the man. May we continue to use the masculine gender, just to make it a little easier? We *do* recognise that women as well as men can make very good managers.

Let us see, first of all, how he sees himself. To take an instance, James F. Bere, chairman of the Borg-Warner Corporation is clear and precise:(10)

> The job [of the top executive] is not to make decisions ... it is to put good people in place and judge if they are making good decisions. You give them the power. When they come in and say, 'How do I do something', I say: 'That's your problem ...

This is called the principle of delegation, a basic principle in good management. All the textbooks tell us that effective delegation is the key to good management.

Now let us see the chief executive of the eighties as others see him. We are told that he should be a sort of 'ferryman', a transporter of persons and ideas from one place to another. Thus the chief executive is seen as having the following qualities:(11)

1 Ability to move easily between the past, present and future of the company.
2 Show his team a clear and convincing route to the company's objective.
3 Set an example to follow. Practice, not just preach.
4 Be a guide, counsellor and mentor to others in the company.
5 Put forward new ideas and get their acceptance.
6 Learn from success and also from failures – own and others.
7 Foresee technological changes and set strategies accordingly.
8 Self-achiever and also achieve results through others.

The 'ferryman' will constantly ask basic questions concerning his company, such as: Where are we now? How did we get here? Where must we be tomorrow? How do we get there? As we have reviewed the range of case studies, we have seen that if only these questions had been asked and answered at the right moment, practically all of the disastrous situations that we have studied would never have arisen.

Coping with potential disaster

Our theme is disaster: we see projects and companies in trouble. We have seen how and why they get into trouble. What is still more important is to find an answer to the question: how are they to get out of trouble? We have seen that most of the factors that got them into trouble had their roots in poor management: management that could not cope with the numerous problems besetting them from within and from without. And management, poor or good, starts at the top, with the chief executive, or the project manager, if we are looking at a specific project. This means, therefore, that where there is poor management, the only way to change the situation is by changing the chief executive. That may well lead to many other changes, but change must *start* at the top. This is the basic, major and most significant step if disaster is to be averted. How the change is to be achieved will depend upon circumstances. Sometimes it will be just a change in the project team, but at other times it will mean a change of contractor.

Such a change at the top has an immediate and salutary effect on all those involved: the bankers, the investors and the employees at all levels. A positive, 'we are going to do something' attitude is established, and this is essential to success. It is the vacillating approach that gets nowhere. Apart from its symbolic importance, the new chief executive is expected to develop new strategies, change direction – alter things, hopefully for the better. Everyone remembers the old adage: a new broom sweeps clean.

When we turn from single projects to companies, it is an open question whether or not top management as a whole should change as well as the chief executive. There is no consensus and both approaches – change the man at the top and change the board – have been followed with success. If we go back to the example of British Leyland, which we quoted in the previous chapter, the management was not subject to drastic change, but Sir Michael's achievement there was that he drew startlingly good performances out of people who until then had been doing most things wrong.

More recently, however, Sir Michael has taken over as chief executive of another ailing company, Dunlop, and there he has insisted on a wholesale clearout of the main board. It is interesting to note the reaction of the Dunlop workforce to that drastic action. Dunlop have a major factory in Coventry and the last time he wielded power in Coventry two factories closed. Yet a union leader there seems to have few doubts about the new chairman. He doesn't see that clearout as an ugly portent. His comment is:(12)

> It was necessary to prune the company from the top and he did it. I don't think he will chop jobs here. We have so much work and we have a good set-up, with successful local management and no industrial relations problems. I think Edwardes is the man to invest in and capitalise on that set-up.

We see that the workforce, as well as the management, sees itself as part of an integrated, small, self-sufficient unit. Just to close out this particular story, Dunlop has now been bought out by BTR. This company had to treble its initial offer before it succeeded and the final terms can be considered a real success for Sir Michael.

Conclusion

Good management is at the heart of any and every successful

company, essential if a company is to prevent failure and ultimate collapse. It is as essential as breathing! Whilst the literature on the subject is vast, we see that but a few simple, basic truths need to be recognised and applied for success to follow. Whilst company management is obviously teamwork the role of *one* individual is crucial – the chief executive. His ability is the key to success and lack of ability will spell disaster.

References

1   Culligan, M.J., Deakins, S. and Young, A.H., *Back to Basics Management: the Lost Craft of Leadership*, Gower, 1983.
2   Kharbanda, O.P., Stallworthy, E.A. and Williams, L.F., *Project Cost Control in Action*, Gower, 1980.
3   Winters, R.J., *It's Different When You Manage*, Lexington Books, 1975.
4   Belbin, R.M., *Management Teams: Why They Succeed or Fail*, Heinemann, 1981
5   Bennett, D., *Successful Team Building Through TA*, Amacom, 1975.
6   Pascale, R.T. and Athos, A.G., *The Art of Japanese Management: Applications for American Executives*, Simon and Schuster.
7   Kharbanda, O.P., 'Look east, young man', *Swagat*, September 1984, pp.49-51. (*Swagat* is an Indian Airlines publication.)
8   Everett, J.E. and Stening, B.W., 'Japanese and British managerial colleagues: how they view one another', *Joint Management Studies*, 20, pp 467-75.
9   Stuart-Kotze, R. and Roskin, R., *Success Guide to Managerial Achievement*, Reston Publishing, 1983.
10 Article: 'Turnover at the top: why executives are losing their jobs so quickly', *Business Week*, 19 December 1983, pp. 56-62.
11 Marlow, H., *Success – Individual, Corporate and National – Profile for the Eighties and Beyond*, Institute of Personnel Management, (US) 1984.
12 Walters, Peter, 'Workforce fate in lap of Little Moe', *Evening Telegraph*, Coventry, UK, 20 November 1984, p.6.
13 Walters, Peter, 'Workforce fate in lap of Little Moe', *Evening Telegraph*, Coventry, UK, 20 November 1984, p.6.

19 Prevention is possible

We now come to the crux of our subject, the prevention of disaster, an aspect which has been sadly neglected. All the emphasis in the literature on the subject has been on prediction. The prime purpose of prediction seems to be to guide and assist those considering investment, not those running the company. The neglect of the concept of prevention is well illustrated in what has become a standard work in the field, Altman's book *Corporate Financial Distress: a Complete Guide to Predicting, Avoiding and Dealing with Bankruptcy.*(1) Despite the title, not one of his 12 chapters include the words 'avoiding' or 'prevention', nor are they to be found in his subject index. Most of the book is devoted to the techniques of prediction, with a little on the legal and investment implications of bankruptcy. This is in harmony with the general tenor of the published literature. Argenti, however, whose approach we have commended in earlier chapters, whilst making no such claim in the title, does in fact devote a few pages to the matter of prevention.(2) We do have a whole book devoted to corporate recovery,(3) but even that book starts out:

> Corporate recovery is about the management of firms in crisis, firms that will become insolvent unless appropriate management actions are taken to effect a turnaround in their financial performance.

The book starts with crisis, and deals with 'turnaround strategies': that is, it tells us how to act once the crisis has arrived: the concept of warding off crisis is not there. Yet surely that is by far the better course.

Having noted that the body of knowledge, as published, on the subject of the prevention of business failure is sparse indeed, one

217

wonders why. Perhaps it is because the relevant knowledge rests with but a few individuals, who have had to learn from bitter experience, having been personally involved in a business failure, or an attempt to turnaround a collapsing company. That could well bring them to the resolve never to have such a thing happen again, and to develop their own technique of prevention in company management.

Another aspect is that such knowledge is extremely valuable, so perhaps those with the appropriate knowledge are keeping it to themselves. That such knowledge is worth a great deal of money is demonstrated by the careers of those having the skill to turnaround companies in trouble. Sir Michael Edwardes, whose work we also discussed in earlier chapters, is an outstanding example.

Act sooner rather than later

We assert that disaster can be prevented if the right action is taken. Our approach to the problem is based upon the premise that it is always a direct consequence of poor management. Of course, there can be external factors, outside the control of company management, that threaten a company's existence and some of these have been discussed at length previously, but we nevertheless maintain that management is the crux, and that sound management holds the key to the prevention of corporate collapse. In fact, we feel that is what good management is all about.

We have said it before and we now repeat, that disaster hardly ever comes suddenly. It develops steadily and there are stages in that development to be clearly discerned. Slatter has drawn attention to this and has also set out the corresponding response - when the management is poor.(4) We ourselves would analyse these stages thus:

Stage reached	*Management response*
1 Hidden crisis	– early warning signals ignored
2 Denial of crisis	– no action, crisis explained away
3 Organisation begins to disintegrate	– some action, too little and too late
4 Collapse	– too late – the damage has been done

A constant characteristic of poor management is its inability to make quick decisions. But when crisis comes, the decision-making process further deteriorates. This means that a poor management just is not capable of effecting drastic change, a process that demands a series of constructive and often unpleasant decisions. Hence in such a situation it becomes imperative to change the management – above all, to change the chief executive. Good management would take effective action during stages 1 and 2 above, with the result that Stages 3 and 4 most probably never occur. The early warning signals would have been acted upon.

'Early warning' signals

Whilst we believe that all the various pointers we have discussed are suspect to some degree, in that they have their limitations, there is a saying with a degree of wisdom in it, that 'half a loaf is better than no bread'. We would therefore recommend that the senior executive should initiate a regular assessment of company status using the academic or commercial assessments available to him. He should never – just never – think that he is, as it were, above that. We all have our 'blind spots', and an impartial appraisal, such as is offered in such systems, is a 'check-up' that may well pay off. For instance, it is routine these days for senior management to have an annual health checkup, where a wide range of 'indicators' are measured. The sensible executive does not say, 'I'm fit – I don't need a checkup'. No, he meekly submits and awaits the verdict with interest.

This is where the Argenti A-score approach can help. It offers an analytical assessment of the management 'style', but one doubts whether the senior executive can carry out such an assessment on his own. Self-criticism is most difficult. Perhaps this is where the management consultant should be called in, to offer an impartial outsider's assessment. In any event, the achievement of a turn-around will be a slow and painful process – but at least early action brings with it the promise of ultimate success.

The company accounts

All company accounts have to be audited before they are published. It is the duty of the auditor to at least qualify the published accounts with footnotes that highlight any discrepancy or unusual accounting practice that is being newly adopted, even although the practice may be perfectly legal. But unfortunately such qualifications are rare indeed and by the time the auditor introduces a footnote all the world knows that something is sadly wrong.

In the UK there is a qualification that can be made to the accounts by the auditor that is designed specifically to assess the status of a company. It is called the 'going concern qualification'.(5) The first thing we notice is that between 1977 and 1983, with quoted companies, only some 25 per cent were qualified on a going concern basis and of those some 70 percent had obvious problems – so there it was no news. However, the curious thing is that most of those companies so qualified and under threat did *not* fail. On the other hand, three quarters of quoted companies failing over the same period were not qualified on a going concern basis before bankruptcy. This illustrates, we feel, that where the auditor, and hence the directors of the company, were alive to the situation, something positive must have been done to avert disaster.

This raises the next question: were the auditors of all those other companies failing in their job? Not necessarily. We have to remember that the auditor is not in business to forecast bankruptcies and, as such, we should not expect him to be efficient and as reliable as those using techniques, such as the PAS score, that have been specifically developed for the purpose. When preparing the accounts of a company, there is behind it all the basic assumption that the company is going to continue, which makes it difficult for the auditor to make an unbiased assessment of the likelihood of his client's ceasing to be a going concern. Exhortations to the auditor to 'consider whether there are reasonable grounds for accepting that the financial statements, on which he is reporting, should have been prepared on a going concern basis' (APC auditing guideline ED, para 1), together with lists of obvious symptoms are not in themselves much help to the auditor seeking to make a very difficult probability assessment. Once again, there is no doubt that the application of reliable PAS score and associated techniques such as we have discussed to management and draft accounts during audit via a microcomputer could undoubtedly help overcome the statistical risk assessment problems faced by the auditor and could also aid audit planning. It gives an unbiased assessment of the situation, which is what is wanted. The slowness in applying such techniques leads one to the belief that, in essence, people 'don't want to know'. A human failing, but not of much help to failing companies.

However, when it comes to prevention, the published accounts really play only a minor role, since they present the historic picture only. They tell us what was going on six months ago, whereas what we really wish to know is the state of the company today.

The need for positive action

When we come to consider the potential for preventive action *within* the company, we must look first to the management of the company. The management will be the first to know of the company's likely troubles and they are also the best placed to do something about it. Signs of trouble will not escape the attention of even the poorest management: the problem with a poor management is that it ignores the warning signs. A poor management team is likely to go to extreme lengths to hide the true state of affairs, since they know well enough that it is all their fault. Perhaps it is here that the neutral comment on the situation provided by a commercial company analysis could play a useful role.

The board of directors of a company, *if* properly constituted and *if* it is discharging its functions properly, can play a positive, constructive role in the prevention of company failure. But we qualified our statement with two 'ifs'. Let us look then at what often happens in practice.

Our first 'if' relates to the constitution of the board. It is an unfortunate fact that 'troublemakers' on a company board usually fail to be re-elected. This means that most company boards are a group of 'yes men', just going along with the management and failing to sound warnings. Our second 'if' related to the proper performance of their functions as directors, whether they are 'yes men' or no. Much caustic comment has been made about directors. It has been said, for instance, that most directors were happy to collect their fees, sip their coffee and enjoy their lunch. It was said that 'the only time they open their mouths is to partake of refreshment'. But what *is* their function? It is to look after the interests of the shareholders and the employees.

Well, what is the answer? A properly constituted board should be able to tell the management through its chief executive how well it expects the company to perform. It just should not be the other way round, with management telling the board what they are doing and propose to do, as is almost invariably the case at present. Once the board assumes its proper role, providing basic direction, it will become really effective. Comparing what is happening with what it was expecting to happen, and seeking the reasons, it will be placing its finger on trouble in store. Seeing danger ahead, it should call for a corporate strategy designed to correct the situation: thus it prods management into action. And we will say it again: prevention is better – far better – than cure. Prevention is cheaper and easier than cure. Taking the 'cure' may or may not be effective: it can so easily be a case of sending good money after bad.

What is good management?

Who are we to tell managements around the world what is good for them? But we make no such claim: we merely examine the facts and point the lessons. We have reverted many times to the importance - the vital importance – of good management. We come back to it once again now because we cannot over-emphasise its value. Good management is crucial, and its absence brings failure sooner or later. We are convinced that good management can, more often that not, avert failure. Even when that is not possible, good management will most certainly minimise its traumatic effects.

But what is good management? Looking around the world, we have seen various styles of management, of which the Japanese seems most successful, having brought that country from poverty to prosperity in some 30 years. But unfortunately you cannot just copy: it is not possible to transplant a management style from one country to another, where the cultural values, history and experience are all so very different. But the essentials can be assessed and the lessons applied. We saw that good management is just plain common sense, honesty and hard work. This lesson was hammered home in a recent *Fortune* survey (6) of the ten most successful plants in the US. These ten turn out products ranging from shoes (E.T. Wright & Co.) to pickup trucks (Nissan Motor Co.), from dishwashers (General Electric) to welding equipment (Lincoln Electric). Each of these companies was at the top of its particular line in terms of productivity or quality, or both. But there the resemblance ends. Their methods, when scrutinised, were seen to be neither American nor Japanese, but just common sense. However, it seems that such sense is not as 'common' as it ought to be. The real point is that each case is so different that no rules can be laid down. These ten factories were vastly different from one another, even when one just walked through them, and the production techniques and management style had to be and had been adapted to suit the specific circumstances.

General Electric's brand new dishwasher fabrication plant looked like a top-class hotel when one walked into it, whereas Lincoln Electric's long established, dimly lit workshops reminded one of a dingy hostel. Yet both had found ways to merge design, manufacturing, quality and automation to produce a product that the market accepted. They were both singularly successful in getting close to both their customers and their workforce. With Nissan it was somewhat different. When building their new facility their top executives doubted whether workers without experience in a similar facility could succeed in producing quality goods. But their Smyrna plant, now producing pickup trucks, has surprised and perhaps humiliated the Japanese. The plant is entirely managed by Americans and 80 per cent of the workforce had no prior experience in building automobiles, yet customer surveys show that the Smyrna trucks are better than those made in Japan. To quote the plant manager:

> The Nissan executives find it a bit hard to take that their children are doing better than their parents.

The moral – and we do hope that you are listening – is that it is *not* the specific management technique, American or Japanese, that brings results, nor sophisticated equipment. What is wanted is common sense, hard work and integrity of purpose.

The voice of experience

We have mentioned the value of seeking independent advice, and the consultant is one person who can be called upon for advice in times of trouble. But it has to be appreciated that to be effective, his is a most intimate role. The consultant, during the period of his assignment, has to be treated as an 'insider'. Whilst a good management consultant comes expensive (upwards of US$1 000 a day plus all expenses) the benefit/cost ratio can be very high indeed. They are seen as a catalyst – which though on the 'inside' does not take part in the reaction. But they will facilitate the reaction and speed it up. Their role can be vital to the growth and success of a business. The preface to a book on the subject identifies the role a consultant should play thus:(7)

> Management consultants often have a talent, knack, skill, flair, call it what you will, of adjusting the pieces of a mental jigsaw into an order which creates a clear picture.

But the consultant cannot guarantee success. That is wholly dependent upon his client. The consultant can only bring about change if his client is willing to listen. In fact, we would go so far as to say that a consultant should not be called in unless the client has already resolved to listen and act upon the advice given. Unfortunately, many of the benefits resulting from the use of a consultant, being confidential, never see the light of day. Even when the press does mention that a consultant has played a role, the name is usually omitted. This is an integral part of the ethics of the profession of consultancy. Yet again, for many a client the wish to engage a consultant is felt to be a confession of failure, and so secrecy is the order of the day. Quite often, as we have found for ourselves, the consultant has to advise his client that he should not proceed with a particular project or plan upon which he has set his heart. This may annoy him intensely, but the advice should be given if it is called for. Pet projects have been the death of many a company and we have presented you with case studies that demonstrate that fact quite clearly. Indeed, the book to which we have just referred quotes a case in point:

> A client (a technical enthusiast) in electrical and electronic engineering ... saw that much of his electrical products were becoming obsolete with the trend for newer electronic technology. Of course, change to electronics ... is a formidable and expensive task. My contribution was to curtail my client's enthusiasm – to point out that there was still several years life in the old products and that he should not get bored with them too soon – particularly as some of his competitors with an equal eye to the future were getting out of the obsolescent market – leaving a greater share of it for my client ...

All consultancy assignments do not have such a happy ending.

The value of figures

We have made some reference to the company accounts and their use. Of course the figures in a profit and loss account or a balance sheet are important, but they should always be treated with reserve. They may not be right and we should not be deceived by their preciseness. Figures can lie – and they often do. Perhaps we should remind ourselves of a few words from the wise:

The facts are wrong	– Einstein
Get your facts first and then you distort them as you please	– Mark Twain
What is it that you want me to prove	– A statistician

Let us never forget that common human tendency to take facts and figures out of context in order to prove what one wants to prove. We are not concerned here with the moral issues involved in such actions, but we simply warn you that such misuse of figures is very prevalent.

In most countries – we would say all, but we have not checked – there is a legal obligation on a public company to publish its annual report within a certain specified time from the end of the accounting period. The statements made in that report give us the state of a company's 'health' in facts and figures. We are shown what has happened during the past year and it is usually accompanied by the chairman's statement, or something similar, summing up past achievements and looking forward to the future prospects for the company. It will include the balance sheet and a profit and loss account, these being the two key documents. The first indicates present status, the second how the company got there during the year. Whilst the balance sheet is a most valuable document, it has some severe limitations inherent not only in the form of presentation of the data, but also in its interpretation. Reading and understanding a balance sheet is an art and several books have been written on that subject alone.

What are these limitations? There are four major subjects dealt with in a balance sheet that are open to misuse and misinterpretation. These are:

Value of assets
This figure equals the initial installed cost of the assets, minus both the installation cost and the accumulated depreciation.(8) This can be grossly misleading, since it represents neither the cash that would be realised if those assets were to be sold, nor their replacement cost, assuming them to be destroyed. Either of these figures has much more relevance when assessing the health of a company than the book value of the assets as normally calculated. To correct this anomaly, the appropriate rules have been framed in certain countries, such as the US, where the *Securities Exchange Commission* introduced a requirement in 1976 to the effect that companies with sales exceeding US$100 million a year *must* provide an estimate of the replacement cost of their assets in the annual accounts.

Intangible assets
Intangible assets never appear in the accounts of a company

despite their critical importance, because they are not 'owned'. Such assets include the inherent knowhow in management and the employees and the staff themselves. These are 'leased' or 'hired', not owned, so they cannot be included as an asset in the accounts of a company. Their importance will depend to some extent on the nature of the business in which the company is involved. A company such as IBM, with a highly trained technical and sales staff, has a tremendous investment in such people and suffers loss when they go elsewhere and have to be replaced – but they cannot quantify them and count them as an asset in the balance sheet. Of course, quantification is not easy, but it is such a significant factor that attempts are being made to assess it and to 'put it in the scales'.

Year-end picture

The balance sheet is a 'snapshot' as it were: a picture of the company at one moment in time: at the year end. But 'snapshot' is not really the right word: it is more a studio portrait. It is in effect a static picture of the company on a single day at the end of the financial year, presented after a lot of preparation. You all know what happens when we are going for a studio portrait. We dress up for the occasion and the photographer does his best to arrange us to advantage, often providing a very artificial background. It is much the same with a balance sheet. Need we say more?

Income

A major constituent of the year-end accounts is the income in the year. Now, whilst the presentation in the balance sheet is static, income is dynamic. It is something that is going on day by day throughout the year, its constituents can change as time passes and it can go up and down. Assets sold contribute to income – but *when* were they sold – at the beginning or the end of the year? That could be crucial, but the information is not revealed in the balance sheet.

The role of the auditor

What is an audit? It is, according to that old friend of ours, the *Concise Oxford Dictionary,* 'an official examination of accounts'. The fact that it is 'official' implies that there are rules laid down that an auditor should see are followed, and that he has a public duty. Yet so many companies on the point of collapse have presented accounts that displayed a very satisfactory position in the US – and we are sure that it is the same worldwide – that it has become a public scandal, prompting congressional probes.(9) One sub-committee, for instance, is focussing its attention on Ernst & Whinney, one of the 'big eight' US accounting firms, for giving an 'unqualified' opinion (that is the best rating) in January 1983 with respect to the United American Bank of Knoxville. Yet within three weeks that bank was declared insolvent, setting off a chain of bank failures that became perhaps the largest commercial banking collapse in American history.

It would seem from all this that we have to assess the auditor as well as the company. Certainly a change from one auditor to another – perhaps because the first one is insisting on keeping to the rules – can well be an indication of financial distress.

What of the future?

Perhaps there is one thing certain when we look into the future: companies will continue to collapse, go bankrupt, be taken into receivership and managers will continue to find life arduous. We have repeatedly warned that forecasting is an impossible task. Nevertheless we think it can be profitable to try and take a 'peek' into the future and assess what is likely to happen in relation to companies and business life in general. Are conditions going to get ever more difficult, worldwide, with the result that an increasing percentage of companies collapse, or will things get easier in the years to come?

Whilst we have just asserted and history demonstrates that forecasting the future is *not* possible, this does not deter the 'futurist' from pursuing his goals. In fact, despite the growing uncertainty and the failure of many established trends, activity in 'futurism' seems to be on the increase, if the volume of material being published is any guide. There are also a continuing succession of seminars on the subject. Let us look for a moment at just one such attempt in a 'best seller' whose approach is based on the premise that 'new trends and ideas' begin in the smaller cities.(10) Naisbitt scanned some 6 000 newspapers every month, mostly from the smaller cities, and analysed over two million local articles about local events. Based on this data, the kind of life to be expected by the year 2000 was depicted and it was asserted that the following trends are likely:

From	*To*
Industrial society	Information society
Institutional help	Self-help
Hierarchies	Net-working
Either/or situations	Multiple options

According to Naisbitt, a glimpse into the business life of the future shows that:

1 As our school system fails us, corporations will become the universities.
2 In the US the guest workers will be the robots.
3 The electronics, information and computer companies will replace the 'General Motors' and 'US Steels' of today.
4 To be really successful, you will have to be tri-lingual: fluent in English, Spanish and the computer.
5 You will tell your boss what to do. He will not tell you.

It is said that the seeds for a future as outlined above have already been sown. As an example, the current robot population in the free world is estimated at around 60 000 and this is expected to increase some three-fold by 1990.(11) Japan is way ahead of any other country in this particular area of development. Most Americans are seen as being engaged in the 'creation, processing and distribution of information', whilst the industrial production centres will have moved to what we now call the 'developing world'. The new leaders of industry are seen as 'facilitators', rather than as 'order givers'. You will remember that when we were discussing the qualities and attributes of the chief executive (Chapter 18) we spoke of him as a 'ferryman', responsible for the transfer of ideas.

Whilst it is interesting to note such trends, we ourselves do not think that the situation will change as radically as is suggested. The basic assumption, which we challenge, is that 'all things continue as they are': that is, current trends will persist. But they do not. That is why it is impossible to forecast the future. An interesting recent example is, of course, the so-called 'oil crisis' of 1973, when some three to six months earlier the forecasts were for a continuation of abundant 'dirt cheap' oil for many years to come. The crisis caused a whole range of graphs that had been going steadily upward to collapse and change direction. The incidence of another 'crisis' – we will not speculate on the nature of the crisis, but merely assert that there will be one – will change it all once again.

Conclusion

It is those companies in the area of innovation that are most vulnerable, as the case studies we have presented demonstrate very clearly. The best means for the prevention of disaster in such a situation is good management. Those innovators who team up with good managers are on the road to success.

Having seen that whatever else the future holds, there will certainly be many companies that fail, go into bankruptcy and need help, we are sure that the techniques we have discussed in this book will have a continuing value. Management matters!

References

1 Altman, E.I., *Corporate Financial Distress. A Complete Guide to Predicting, Avoiding and Dealing with Bankruptcy*, Wiley, New York, 1983.
2 Argenti, J., *Corporate Collapse: the Causes and Symptoms*, McGraw-Hill, 1976.
3 Slatter, S., *Corporate Recovery – Successful Turnaround Strategies and their Implementation*, Penguin, London, 1984.
4 Slatter, S., 'The impact of crisis on managerial behaviour', *Business Horizons*, 7, May/June 1984, pp. 65-8.
5 Taffler, R.J. and Tseung, Meggy, 'The audit going concern qualification in practice – exploding some myths', *The Accountant's Magazine*, July 1984, pp. 263-69.
6 Bylinsky, G., 'America's best-managed factories', *Fortune*, 109, 28 May 1984, pp. 50-8.
7 Tisdall, P., *Agents of change – the development and practice of management consultancy*, Heinemann, 1982.
8 Altman, E.I., Ed., *Financial Handbook*, 5th Edition, Wiley, New York, 1981. (38 chapters with individual paging)
9 Article: 'The SEC turns up the heat on cooked books', *Business Week*, 3 September 1984, pp. 47-8.
10 Naisbitt, J. Megatrends – *Ten New Directions Transforming our Lives*, Warner, New York, 1982.
11 Babani, A., 'Robots – Malthusian Explosion', *Herald Review*, 14 July 1985, pp.42-3.

Index